Cervantes' *Don Quixote*

CERVANTES' DON QUIXOTE

A Reference Guide

Howard Mancing

Greenwood Guides to Multicultural Literature

GREENWOOD PRESS
Westport, Connecticut • London

Library of Congress Cataloging-in-Publication Data

Mancing, Howard, 1941–
   Cervantes' Don Quixote : a reference guide \ by Howard Mancing.
      p. cm.—(Greenwood guides to multicultural literature)
   Includes bibliographical references and index.
   ISBN 0–313–33347–5
   1. Cervantes Saavedra, Miguel de, 1547–1616. Don Quixote I. Title. II. Series.
PQ6352.M24 2006
863′.3—dc22   2005037029

British Library Cataloguing in Publication Data is available.

Library of Congress Catalog Card Number: 2005037029
ISBN: 0–313–33347–5

First published in 2006

Greenwood Press, 88 Post Road West, Westport, CT 06881
An imprint of Greenwood Publishing Group, Inc.
www.greenwood.com

Printed in the United States of America

The paper used in this book complies with the
Permanent Paper Standard issued by the National
Information Standards Organization (Z39.48–1984).

10 9 8 7 6 5 4 3 2 1

For Nancy, again

CONTENTS

Preface   ix

1. Introduction   1

2. Content   21

3. Texts   41

4. Contexts   51

5. Ideas   87

6. Narrative Art   125

7. Reception   151

8. Bibliographical Essay   185

Bibliography   211

Index   213

PREFACE

In 2002, the Norwegian Book Club, affiliated with the Nobel Prize organization, conducted a poll of 100 writers in 35 countries, asking each one to list the 10 works of imaginative literature that he or she thought were the best of all time. Miguel de Cervantes' *Don Quixote* came out as the overwhelming winner, receiving more than 50 percent more votes than the runner-up, Marcel Proust's *Recherche du temps perdu* (1913–28; *Remembrance of Things Past*). How is it that a comic novel first published in 1605 came in so far ahead of any work by Dante, Shakespeare, Milton, Racine, Goethe, Dostoevsky, James Joyce, and dozens of other great writers? Why has *Don Quixote* been

- Translated into more languages and published more often than any book except the Bible?
- Illustrated more than any other book—which helps make the graphic figure of Don Quixote the most recognizable literary character in the world?
- Adapted to the stage more often than any other nondramatic work?
- Adapted to music in the forms of opera, ballet, orchestral music, and popular song more often than any other work of literature?
- The inspiration or source for more films than any other work of literature?
- The source of inspiration for thousands of sequels, continuations, adaptations, and rewritings of *Don Quixote* in fiction—far more than for any other literary work?

How can one explain this eternal and universal appeal of *Don Quixote?*

This book will not answer all these questions; no book, and certainly not one this short, ever could. But this book is an attempt to describe Cervantes' novel, place it in a series of historical and literary contexts, and consider at least some aspects of its appeal. Throughout, I will draw extensively from my own recently published *Cervantes Encyclopedia* (2 vols., 2004). Material borrowed from that much more extensive inquiry into Cervantes and his works (not just *Don Quixote,* but all of his literary production) is adapted to other purposes here, usually rewritten, and always recontextualized. The purpose of that book is to orient readers to as many aspects of Cervantes and his works as possible. It features identifications of many specific matters, often minutia, that may be of interest to specialists but that hold little interest to more general readers. Information is often presented in fragments, as is characteristic of an encyclopedia. There are entries, some of them quite detailed, for hundreds of writers influenced by Cervantes. In other words, the *Cervantes Encyclopedia* is a very different kind of reference work from this book.

The purpose of this reference guide to *Don Quixote* is to concentrate on Cervantes' masterpiece and provide an orientation for general readers, particularly high-school and college students rather than Cervantes scholars, to the novel. Here material is presented in a more narrative form and organized conceptually. This book is a better resource than the *Encyclopedia* for someone who is reading *Don Quixote* for the first time and is interested in a coherent approach to the novel.

This book is written in English, and it is assumed that most of its intended audience has either no knowledge or only limited knowledge of Spanish, the language in which *Don Quixote* was originally written. Not surprisingly, this creates some problems, not the least of which has to do with criticism of the novel. Much of the best theoretical, critical, and interpretive work on *Don Quixote* is written in Spanish and a good bit more is written in other languages. The reader who knows only English and wants to delve further into aspects of the novel will come up against a linguistic barrier at every turn. But all is not lost, by any means. There is a very rich tradition of criticism of *Don Quixote* in English, and throughout this book (and especially in the bibliographical essay in chapter 8) emphasis will be placed on English-language references and sources. But it is not possible to limit everything to English. From time to time, and with some frequency, it will be necessary to cite books and essays written in Spanish (and, very occasionally, in other languages). After all, some who read this book—especially students reading *Don Quixote* in Spanish for the first time, perhaps in a graduate or undergraduate class—will also be able to read Spanish and can therefore profit by a more extensive documentation that includes works in that language.

If an inability to read criticism in Spanish is a problem, a far greater one is the inability to read *Don Quixote* itself in Spanish. The original Spanish text is so much richer than any English version that we are reminded of Don Quixote's comments on literary translation when he visits a bookstore in Barcelona in part 2, chapter 62: "It seems to me that translating from one language to another, as long as it is not from the queens of languages, Greek and Latin, is like looking at Flemish tapestries from the back side, because even though you can see the figures, they are covered by threads that hide them, and you can't see the smooth texture of the front side." (Note: All translations from Cervantes' novel are mine, sometimes done in consultation with published versions, but never following any one exactly. The reader might find it interesting to take note of differences between my version of a given passage and the way that passage is translated in the version being read.) Normally, only the English text will be cited, but sometimes it will be necessary to cite the Spanish text, as in the discussion of style in chapter 6. On these occasions, the text will be taken from the newly revised version of the popular edition of John J. Allen (2005).

The passage on translation cited in the previous paragraph must give all translators of the novel pause to consider the quality of their work, and it should also give all readers pause to consider that when they read not only Cervantes, but also Tolstoy, Mann, Proust, and other novelists in translation, they are always looking at the tapestry from the wrong side and that much, including much that is essential, is simply not visible. Imagine reading Shakespeare in Spanish—or French or Chinese—and not having direct access to his rich cadence, rhythm, imagery, and vocabulary in English. A Spanish reader, for example, who reads Leandro Fernández de Moratín's classic translation of *Hamlet,* may well come away from the experience wondering what is so great about Shakespeare. On the other hand, we should all be grateful to conscientious literary translators, for otherwise much great literature would simply not exist for us. It is better to contemplate the wrong side of the tapestry than never to look at the tapestry at all.

Chapter 1, "Introduction," consists of a brief overview of the life of Miguel de Cervantes, with a very brief assessment of all of his major works—except, of course, *Don Quixote,* which is the subject of the remainder of the book. Chapter 2, "Content," contains a plot summary of the novel, concentrating on the actions of the two main characters, Don Quixote and Sancho Panza. Chapter 3, "Texts," reviews the publishing history of the novel and assesses the major Spanish editions of *Don Quixote,* as well as the major English translations. Chapter 4, "Contexts," places Cervantes in the social and historical contexts of the Spain of the Golden Age, the sixteenth and seventeenth centuries, with emphasis on the literature of the time. Chapter 5, "Ideas," is an examination of some of the major themes and intellectual and aesthetic content of the novel. Chapter 6, "Narrative Art," is an introduction to the style, structure, narrative technique, and presentation of characters in *Don Quixote.* Chapter 7, "Reception," consists of an overview of the reception history of Cervantes' novel with emphasis on its influence on subsequent writers and with some consideration of the pervasive presence and influence of *Don Quixote* in other arts and in popular culture in general. And, finally, chapter 8, "Bibliographical Essay," presents an overview of Cervantes scholarship and suggests how readers might go about further investigation into the critical evaluations of the novel.

The reader might wonder why the name Don Quixote is spelled with an *x* in English but with a *j* in Spanish: Don Quijote. The reason is that sibilants (consonant sounds related to *s*) underwent an interesting transformation in the history of the Spanish language. In Cervantes' times, the *x* was pronounced much like the modern *sh* sound, but later in the seventeenth century the pronunciation of that letter shifted to something more like the way the consonant *h* sounds in English today (remember that the actual letter *h* is silent in modern Spanish and the English *h* sound is best approximated by the *j* in Spanish). Therefore, Cervantes wrote "Quixote" and pronounced it Key-*sho*-tay—which is why the French spelling is *Quichotte* and the Italian is *Chisciotte,* both closer in pronunciation (as is, for that matter, the British *Quixote: Quick-sot*). But in the eighteenth century the Royal Spanish Academy (founded in 1714) was determined to bring consistency and regularity to the national language. For this reason, the academicians decided that all words previously written with an *x* would henceforth be written with a *j.* This is also why many Spaniards today still write Méjico, while the Mexicans, proudly asserting their independence by retaining the original spelling, insist on México, even though the pronunciation is the same. So, today, in Spanish the correct form of the name is "Quijote," pronounced Key-*ho*-tay. In fact, today the name in American English should sound about the same, but it often comes out sounding something like *Key-o-tie* (many British, however, still insist on *Quick-sot*).

The majority of this book is descriptive in a straightforward way. Much of it consists of literary history, basic philological study, and formalist explanation and interpretation. There is no attempt to ground the book in currently fashionable literary theories such as semiotics or poststructuralism or to encumber the text with the sort of jargon that weighs heavily in the discourse(s) of literary theory. But there is one philosopher and literary theorist whose work does indeed inform this book: the Russian Mikhail M. Bakhtin (1895–1975). Bakhtin's work on the theory and history of the novel, together with his concepts of dialogism, heteroglossia, carnival, and great time are all of considerable value in any attempt to understand *Don Quixote,* the novel that Bakhtin most admired and that most influenced his thought on the novel as a genre.

It is necessary to call attention to one more important theoretical assumption that has been employed throughout this book: the elements of literature—authors, characters, and historical and geographical references— are not treated as mere signs or manifestations of language, nor are the writings of Cervantes treated as self-referential, free-floating, decontextualized texts. In other words, Cervantes' works are not dealt with as they would be by most structuralists, semioticians, or poststructuralists. Rather, the assumption is made here that it is legitimate (even necessary) to consider authorial intentions (as best they can be inferred) as being of interest and often helpful, but never absolutely authoritative. Literary texts are treated as though they refer to versions of historical and social reality. Most importantly, literary characters are discussed and treated as imaginative versions of real people rather than as sign systems. An operative theoretical principle throughout this book is what in cognitive psychology is known as *Theory of Mind:* the folk-psychology assumption that all people have minds that function in approximately the same manner; that people (including fictional versions of people) are motivated (they want, hope, remember, need, feel, and so forth) much as any real person would be in most situations; that authors (who have their own intentions and theory of mind) attribute a theory of mind to their characters, and that readers must have such a theory in order to understand characters and plots (see O'Connell, *Mindreading*).

WORKS CITED

Cervantes, Miguel de. *El Ingenioso Hidalgo Don Quijote de la Mancha.* Ed. John J. Allen. 25th ed. 2 vols. Madrid: Cátedra, 2005.

Mancing, Howard. *The Cervantes Encyclopedia.* 2 vols. Westport, CT: Greenwood P, 2004.

O'Connell, Sanjida. *Mindreading: An Investigation into How We Learn to Love and Lie.* New York: Doubleday, 1998.

Chapter 1

INTRODUCTION

Miguel de Cervantes lived and wrote during the most exciting period of Spanish history. His life, somewhat of a legend in itself, is almost as exciting as the fiction he wrote. Cervantes (1547–1616) and Shakespeare (1552–1616) were exact contemporaries, but whereas we know very little about the latter, the life of the former is documented in quite extraordinary detail, although there are some frustrating gaps. The biographical sketch that follows is based largely on the prize-winning biography by Jean Canavaggio (1990), probably the single best account of the life of Cervantes, but it also draws on the biographies by William Byron (1978), Melveena McKendrick (1980), and Donald P. McCrory (2002).

1547–69: YOUNG CERVANTES

Miguel de Cervantes was baptized in the church of Santa María la Mayor, in Alcalá de Henares, on October 9, 1547. There is no record of his birth, but it is generally assumed that he was born on September 29, Saint Michael's Day (Michaelmas), and, following common custom, that he was named Miguel for his saint's day. (In all of Cervantes' works, only two characters mention their birthday: Doña Clara in *Don Quixote* part 1, chapter 43, and Preciosa, protagonist of *La gitanilla.* Both were born on September 29.) His parents, the surgeon Rodrigo de Cervantes (1509–85) and Leonor de Cortinas (1520–93), had married in the early 1540s. They had six children: Andrea (1544–1609), who married twice, had one child—Constanza, Cervantes' favorite niece—and also had affairs with several men; Luisa (1546–ca. 1620), who was a respected Carmelite nun; Miguel; Rodrigo (1550–1600), a career soldier who died in battle; Magdalena (1553–1611), who never married, had no children, and, like her older sister Andrea, was involved in more then one affair; and Juan (ca. 1554–ca. 1593), about whom virtually nothing is known. Many scholars believe that the Cervantes family was of *converso* heritage (i.e., converts, at some point, from Judaism), and therefore somewhat marginalized in society (see chapter 5). No one has ever found proof of Jewish blood in the family, but the professions practiced by most of the men—jurists, surgeons, merchants—were characteristically those dominated by *conversos*. The difficulties Cervantes' parents had in the late 1570s when they attempted to secure a certificate of purity of blood (see chapter 4), together with the lack of successful marriages for the women in the family, strongly suggest that the Cervantes' were *conversos* (see Lokos, "The Politics of Identity").

A surgeon occupied one of the lowest rungs of the medical profession, and Rodrigo seems to have had more vanity than professional skill. Financial difficulties forced the family to move to Valladolid in 1551, back to Alcalá in 1553, then to Córdoba in the same year, and to Seville in 1564. In 1566, when Cervantes was 19, the family moved again, this time to the capital, Madrid, where they remained. Cervantes must have had an uneven education with such frequent moving, but in Madrid he became a student at the Estudio de la Villa, a publicly-funded school founded and endowed by the Catholic Monarchs, Fernando and Isabel, and directed since 1568 by Juan López de Hoyos (?–1583), a distinguished humanist scholar and follower of Erasmus. Apparently, Cervantes was a star student, because when the revered young queen Isabel de Valois (1546–68) died, López de Hoyos was commissioned to prepare a volume of poetry in her honor. Four poems by Cervantes, his earliest known works, are included in the book, and he is referred to as the master's "beloved disciple." Many scholars recognize profound traces of Erasmian thought in Cervantes' works, and it is generally assumed that this reflects the influence of his distinguished school master (see Bataillon, *Erasmo y España,* and Vilanova, *Erasmo y Cervantes*).

Late in 1569, an event took place that has intrigued Cervantes scholars for centuries. He was involved in some sort of altercation, presumably involving a matter of honor, and wounded a man named Antonio de Sigura. Cervantes was to be arrested and brought back to Madrid where he was to have his right hand cut off, and, if he survived this, he was to be banished from the kingdom for 10 years. Later, we will see that when Cervantes returned to Spain, 11 years after this incident, there was apparently no attempt to carry out the sentence. Perhaps the fact that he came back home a war hero helped make it convenient to forget the matter. It has been suggested that the document by which we know of the incident somehow proves Cervantes' homosexuality, but there really is nothing to support such an interpretation. Most recently, dramatist and novelist Fernando Arrabal, in a 1996 biography titled *Un esclavo llamado Cervantes* (*A Slave Named Cervantes*) has vigorously defended the homosexuality theory, but most serious scholars consider his book an imaginative fiction as much as a real biography. Almost immediately after this altercation in 1569, Cervantes is to be found in Rome, in the household service of a young monsignor, soon to be appointed cardinal, named Giulio Acquaviva (1546–74), whom he may have met previously during the priest's visit to Spain in 1568. Also in 1569 Cervantes requested a document from his parents proving his Old Christian status, perhaps needed to get employment (Lokos, "The Politics of Identity"). The document he received was full of ambiguity, equivocation, and hearsay deposition; it was far short of the standards of such official documentation of purity of blood common in the epoch (see chapter 4).

1569–80: SOLDIER AND CAPTIVE

Before long, Cervantes enlisted in the Spanish army based in Italy (large parts of which were Spanish possessions). His timing was good, as he was able to participate in an event that he always considered a landmark in his life, as well as a turning point in history—the naval battle of Lepanto (see chapter 4), where the Spanish-led Christian forces routed the Turkish army. Cervantes and his brother Rodrigo, also a soldier, served in the same regiment, and probably on the same galley. Cervantes was ill and had a high fever at the time of the battle and was granted permission not to participate actively in the fighting. But he chose to place himself at a dangerous location and received three serious wounds during the action. He was shot twice in the chest and his left hand was very seriously injured. Because of his crippling wound, Cervantes received the epithet of the *Manco de Lepanto* (the cripple, or the maimed one, or the one-handed man, of Lepanto). The exact nature of the wound is not known, but it almost certainly did not involve the actual loss of the left hand. More likely, there was some nerve and bone damage and the hand was disfigured (López Alonso, *Cervantes. Manco y bien manco*). Cervantes always took great pride in this visible symbol of his service to his nation and participation in a world-changing event. Because of his valor, he was given precious letters of commendation by Don Juan of Austria (1545–78), half-brother of Spanish king Felipe II and commander of the Christian army and navy at Lepanto, and the Duke of Sessa (?–1578). After his recovery in Naples, Cervantes remained in military service and was promoted to the rank of elite trooper, participating in at least four expeditions in the eastern Mediterranean Sea in 1572 and 1573.

On September 26, 1575, Cervantes and Rodrigo left military service to return home to Spain. But their ship, a galley named *Sol,* was separated from others traveling together in a small fleet and was attacked by mercenary Turkish pirates. The Spanish resisted for some hours but several men were killed and the rest were finally overwhelmed and taken prisoner to Algiers. The economy of this great North-African city was almost entirely based on privateering, slavery, and ransom. A fascinating, multicultural, multilingual city of some 130,000 inhabitants in the late sixteenth century (a population greater than that of any city in Spain), it was the location of some 25,000 Christian captives when Cervantes was there. It is estimated that more than half a million Christian captives spent time in Algiers between the years 1520 and 1660 (Spencer, *Algiers in the Age of the Corsairs*). The captives were held in *baños* (bagnios), which were buildings or prisons consisting of a patio surrounded by small rooms where the prisoners were housed. Common slaves lived in particularly cramped quarters, while those being held for ransom were treated somewhat better. Ransom prices were set according to the perceived value of each prisoner, taking social status and estimates of family wealth into consideration. The slave trade was a brisk business and involved barters and some organized religious groups, particularly the Trinitarians and the Order of Merced, which were constantly raising money from family, friends, and the public to return Christian prisoners to their homes.

Because of his impressive letters of recommendation, Cervantes' ransom was set at a figure considerably higher than the norm, and higher than that of his brother. The Cervantes family was able to raise enough money to ransom Rodrigo in 1577, but Miguel remained in captivity until 1580. During his five years of slavery, Cervantes organized no fewer than four attempts to escape. In every case, something went wrong (usually someone betrayed those making escape preparations) and the efforts all failed. Surprisingly, Cervantes did not receive the usual punishment—death—for such activities, but he did spend long periods of time in chains. Finally, on September 19, 1580, when his master Hassan Pasha (1545–91), the retiring king of Algiers, was preparing to depart for Constantinople, and Cervantes was literally chained to the ship he was about to help row, a Trinitarian friar named Fray Juan Gil arrived with the ransom money and bought Cervantes' freedom. Thus, Cervantes was at last able to return to Spain in October, 1580. By all accounts, Cervantes' conduct during these years was both heroic and exemplary. He was widely admired and respected by his colleagues, a fact we know because of a notarized document describing his activities in some detail (*Información de ... Argel*) and other contemporary written evidence. According to one anecdote, Hassan Pasha was supposed to have said that as long as Cervantes was under lock and key his ships and the city itself were safe. Cervantes constantly recalled his experience in captivity and drew upon it in works written throughout his life (for more on this fascinating period of Cervantes' life, see María Antonia Garcés' prize-winning book *Cervantes in Algiers*).

There is a poem, an epistle, addressed to Mateo Vázquez (1542–91), secretary to King Felipe II, that appears to be a plea from Cervantes for rescue. The poem's authenticity has been questioned, but it is entirely possible that Cervantes wrote it from captivity to convince the Spanish government that Algiers was poorly defended and could easily be taken, thus freeing all the good Christians who were suffering under the yoke of slavery (Fernández de la Torre, "Historia y poesía"). Part of the poem is also placed in the mouth of the character of Saavedra in the play *Los tratos de Argel,* which Cervantes wrote in the early 1580s.

1580–87: BACK IN SPAIN

Cervantes set sail for Spain on October 24, 1580. He landed in Valencia and spent about a month there before continuing on to Madrid. The generous letters of recommendation that documented his valor during the battle of Lepanto had been lost during the years of captivity. Still, Cervantes hoped that, perhaps because of his reputation, he might be rewarded by the crown. In 1581 he went with the king's retinue to Lisbon (Felipe II inherited the Portuguese crown the previous year, and this was his first visit to his new kingdom), where he petitioned for an administrative appointment, but was rewarded only with a brief diplomatic mission (which probably involved some spying) to Orán, a city in Spanish possession in North Africa (and the destination of two of Cervantes' earlier escape attempts). He then settled in Madrid.

His military career over and hopes for a governmental position not panning out, Cervantes turned to a new venture: the theater. At this time, the Spanish stage was just coming into its own as the first permanent *corrales* (the name commonly given to the places where plays were staged) were being constructed. Previously, primitive theatrical performances took place in a variety of locations, often public squares, on which a makeshift stage would be temporarily erected. The Corral de la Cruz, on the Calle de la Cruz, was constructed in 1579, and the Corral del Príncipe, also on the street of that name (today the site is the location of the Teatro Español), was built in 1582 (Allen, *The Reconstruction*). The new concept of theater featured longer, more complex works, and there was abundant opportunity for innovation by creative dramatists. Writing works for the theater became Cervantes' primary (although far from his only) activity during the years 1582–87. Cervantes claimed to have written between 20 and 30 plays during this period of time. None were published and only two remain in manuscript form. One is *Los tratos de Argel (Life in Algiers)*, a heavy-handed four-act drama about love and intrigue among the captives in Algiers. A character named Saavedra is at least a partial reflection of Cervantes himself.

Cervantes' second, little used, surname—Saavedra—is interesting. He should logically have been called Miguel de Cervantes (y) Cortinas, because his mother's name was Leonor de Cortinas, but he never went by this name. The first recorded instance of his use of Saavedra occurs in 1586 in documents relating to his marriage, and later he used the name for his daughter. The name was a distinguished one, as a Saavedra family gained fame for heroism and defense of the faith on the medieval frontier between Christian and Muslim lands. In particular, a certain Juan de Saavedra from Seville became a legendary hero. Cervantes seems to have wanted to associate both his own captivity (he made a reference to himself as "a certain Saavedra" in *Don Quixote* part 1, chapter 40 and that of two of his brave theatrical captives (here and later in *El gallardo español*) with the name (Sánchez Saus, "Los Saavedra").

The second play from this period is *La Numancia,* a four-act partially allegorical representation of the siege and destruction of the Iberian city of Numancia by the Roman general Scipio in 133 BCE. In Cervantes' version, the residents of the besieged city prefer to commit mass suicide rather than surrender, and in the final scene, the last remaining person in the city, a young boy, jumps to his death from a tower rather than be taken prisoner. This is Cervantes' best known theatrical work, the only one to have been performed frequently in modern times. Its value as a symbol of Spanish nationalism and independence led to its use as propaganda in nineteenth-century Spanish civil wars and by both the leftist Republicans and Fascist Nationalists during and after the Spanish Civil War of 1936–39. It is a powerful, although uneven, play that stirs strong feelings whenever it is performed (see Oriel, "Cervantes' *Numancia*," and Schmidt, "The Development of *Hispanitas*").

In 1582, Cervantes attempted to change his fortunes by following the lead of some of his contemporaries and moving to one of the Spanish colonies in America. He applied for an administrative position in New Spain (Mexico), but was turned down, possibly because he was unable to prove adequately that he was an Old Christian, a requirement for such a post.

In 1584, Cervantes had a brief love affair with Ana Franca de Rojas (also known as Ana de Villafranca, 1564–99), wife of a tavern-keeper in Madrid. The result was the birth of Cervantes' only child, a daughter named Isabel (1584–1652), who, after 1599, would play a role in his life. Later in the same year, Cervantes was in the town of Esquivias (on the border of La Mancha) to take care of the legal affairs of the recent widow of a good friend. There he met and married a young woman named Catalina de Palacios (1565–1626), who was barely half his age (he was 37 and she just 19). The marriage produced no offspring and husband and wife lived apart for long periods of time. Because of this, many scholars and historians have assumed that it was an unhappy and unsuccessful union.

The next year, 1585, Cervantes published his first book, a pastoral romance titled *La Galatea*. Such romances—lengthy fictions of refined shepherds who spend much more time lamenting unrequited love, composing verse and song, and shedding copious tears, than they do tending their flocks—were very much in vogue ever since Jorge de Montemayor (ca. 1520–1561) published *La Diana* in 1559 and started the fad. Cervantes' contribution to the genre is quite singular, incorporating an unusual amount of violence and nonpastoral action into the complicated tale of *La Galatea*. Quite popular in its day (there were two editions in the sixteenth century and four more in the seventeenth), praised by a number of writers, and fairly influential in translation (especially in France), *La Galatea* is rarely read today outside of academic contexts (for more on *La Galatea,* see Allen, Rivers, and Sieber, eds., *A Celebration of Cervantes*).

By the latter part of the 1580s a new figure arrived and immediately dominated the Spanish stage: Lope de Vega (1562–1635). Lope's plays were more tightly structured, more lyrical, and better conceived than were those of Cervantes and most other writers. Lope literally took control of theatrical production in Madrid and dominated the scene for nearly half a century, writing perhaps 1,000 plays, earning a considerable amount of money from his works, and enjoying enormous fame and popularity. Cervantes could not compete and, recognizing the fact, withdrew from the scene. Enmity, combined with grudging admiration, characterized the relationship between Cervantes and Lope de Vega throughout Cervantes' life. Cervantes satirized Lope's works in part 1 of *Don Quixote,* and Lope made several disparaging remarks about Cervantes and his novel (Montero Reguera, "Una amistad truncada").

1587–1604: ROYAL COMMISSARY AND TAX COLLECTOR

In 1587 Cervantes took a job as royal commissary and spent the next several years traveling throughout Andalusia (southern Spain) requisitioning grain and oil, much of it to be used by the planned "Invincible" Armada that would soon be sent to conquer England. Twice—in the small towns of Ecija and Castro del Río—he was excommunicated for carrying out his job in opposition to the efforts of local authorities. Most of this time he was separated from his wife (although there were some brief interludes when the couple spent time together in Esquivias), and he spent much time in Seville, the largest city in Spain (it was almost twice as large as the capital, Madrid) and what many considered to be the most exciting city as well.

The Spanish Armada, proudly referred to as the "Invincible," was an overwhelming flotilla designed both to destroy English naval power and, with troops brought over from the Netherlands, take control of the country, stamp out the Protestant heresy, and reestablish Catholicism. But administrative delays, poor equipment, inept leadership, outstanding English generals, and bad weather combined to bring about a resounding defeat (see chapter 4). Cervantes was astounded when the first word of the disaster reached Spain. He composed a heroic ode for the occasion, acknowledging "the confusing sound of the bad news," but stating with confidence that the invincible Christian army would subdue the enemy and that Spain was already singing its victory. Then, when the military rout was confirmed, Cervantes wrote a second ode, this one admitting that the enemy had stepped on the tail of the great lion, but also expressing confidence that the English pirate's day of reckoning would soon come.

In 1590, he again applied for a post in the Spanish colonies. In fact, he petitioned for any one of three open positions in Colombia, Guatemala, and Bolivia. The request was denied with the terse comment, "let him look for a job here." Cervantes' next position, assumed in 1594, was that of tax collector, again in Andalusia. He was jailed at least twice, first, very briefly, in Castro del Río in 1592 and then in Seville in 1597–98, for more than seven months. In 1595 he deposited some tax monies with a businessman in Seville, but the man went bankrupt and absconded with the funds. As a result, Cervantes was served a legal citation and had to exert considerable time and effort to clear his name. During these years and these troubles, he had many of the experiences with *pícaros* and other criminal and marginal types that would later provide him with material for his novels and stories. *Pícaros* referred to a variety of social types: street urchins, usually orphans, who lived by their wits, often in the service of a master, frequently a beggar or petty thief, and not infrequently looking for deceitful ways to make money and move up on the social scale. Meanwhile, Cervantes continued to write, probably working on *Don Quixote* (there are indications that Cervantes wrote much of *Don Quixote* in the final decade of the sixteenth century and that it may have circulated in manuscript for some while before its publication in 1605); some of the short stories that he would publish later; perhaps his last book, the *Persiles*; and, most likely, some poetry. On one occasion in 1592 he signed a contract to write six plays, but apparently he never delivered the works.

In July of 1596 the English, led by Sir Francis Drake staged a daring raid on the city of Cádiz, occupying and sacking it for 24 days. During this time, Spanish military authorities did nothing to defend or rescue the city, waiting until the English forces withdrew before marching into town. Cervantes wrote a devastatingly satiric sonnet about the event, sarcastically praising the bravado of the triumphal arrival by the Spanish troops. Two years later, King Felipe II died after a 42-year reign. A sumptuous catafalque in his honor was constructed in the cathedral of Seville. Funeral ceremonies, however, were delayed by political and religious authorities who squabbled over the details of the event. One day Cervantes walked into the cathedral and proclaimed aloud a sonnet in satiric praise of the structure, claiming that the dead king's soul has left Heaven itself in order to admire it. The poem ends by quoting a braggart soldier that the previous sentiments are true and that anyone who says anything else is a liar; the soldier then puts on his hat with a flourish, rattles his sword, and leaves. News of the scandalous event spread rapidly, and the poem circulated widely throughout the country and was published in several anthologies of poetry. Later in life, in his *Viaje del Parnaso* (ch. 4) Cervantes called this sonnet the "principal honor of my writings." These two satiric sonnets are generally considered the best poems Cervantes ever wrote (Martín, *Cervantes and the Burlesque Sonnet*).

1604–6: THE VALLADOLID INTERLUDE

In 1601, the Spanish royal court was moved from Madrid to Valladolid. Three years later, in 1604, Cervantes moved to the new capital, accompanied by his wife, Catalina, his sisters Andrea and Magdalena, his daughter, Isabel, his niece Constanza, and a serving-woman María de Ceballos. The family lived in a few rooms in a building hastily constructed to accommodate the flood of new residents attracted by the court. During this time, he wrote some short stories and finished writing the first part of *El ingenioso hidalgo don Quijote de la Mancha (The Imaginative Gentleman Don Quixote de la Mancha),* which was published in Madrid in 1605.

We know exactly where the Cervantes family lived on the Calle del Rastro, near the Esgueva River, because on the evening of June 27, 1605, a nobleman named Don Gaspar de Ezpeleta was murdered in the doorway of the building. There was an extensive investigation into the matter, and testimony was taken from all the building's residents but no one was ever arrested (it appears that there was a cover-up by the investigating law enforcement officers). In her testimony, Cervantes' sister Andrea described her brother as "a man who writes, conducts his business, and has many friends." The court records for this case provide a valuable glimpse into Cervantes' personal life (Canavaggio, "Aproximación," 38).

An interesting sidelight of the investigation is that the virtue of Cervantes' sisters, niece, and daughter was called into question; the women were even referred to as *las Cervantas,* the (notorious) Cervantes women. The case of Cervantes' only daughter is interesting. Isabel had lived with her mother until the latter's death in 1599, when Cervantes' sister Magdalena took custody of the teenage girl. In the custody papers she is referred to as Isabel de Saavedra, and Juan de Cervantes is identified as her grandfather. Thus Cervantes indirectly and ambiguously recognized Isabel as his daughter. Isabel married twice and had one daughter who died in infancy. Relations were strained between daughter and her father, and when Cervantes' widow died in 1626 Isabel was not mentioned in the will, although Cervantes' niece Constanza was. When Isabel died in 1652 the Cervantes line was extiguished.

The Ezpeleta murder occurred during the festivities for the important state visit of English admiral and statesman Lord Charles Howard, Earl of Nottingham (1536–1624). After the deaths of King Felipe II of Spain in 1598 and Queen Elizabeth of England in 1603, attempts were made to bring about a political rapprochement between the two bitter enemies. Howard (who had engineered the defeat of the "Invincible" Armada in 1588 and his retinue were received with great pomp and circumstance at the Spanish court in order to ratify a peace treaty. Among the events staged for the visiting diplomat was a parade that included figures representing Don Quixote, Rocinante, and Sancho Panza. This was the first public appearance of Cervantes' characters, just a few short months after the book was published. (Other such festive appearances of Cervantes' characters occurred throughout the seventeenth century in Spain and, beginning in 1607, in the Spanish colonies; see Buezo, *"El triunfo de Don Quijote"*). It is entirely possible that Howard and other visiting Englishmen took back to London news of, and perhaps copies of, Cervantes' novel. It has been speculated that William Shakespeare might have formed part of Howard's retinue, which could then have led to a meeting between Shakespeare and Cervantes. There is, however, no evidence that Shakespeare ever went to Spain or that Cervantes ever heard of him. For a very nice imaginative version of such an encounter, see the story by Anthony Burgess in which Shakespeare and Cervantes do indeed meet and talk ("A Meeting in Valladolid"). A copy of the first edition of *Don Quixote* was imported by Sir Thomas Bodley and placed on the shelves of Oxford's Bodleian Library in 1605, so it is clear that the novel traveled to England almost immediately after publication in Spain. Apparently, Thomas Shelton's translation of *Don Quixote,* which was published in 1612, was complete by about 1608 and circulated in manuscript form. The Lord Howard–*Don Quixote* connection may be impossible to trace in detail, but it was probably important in the early diffusion of the novel abroad.

1606–16: FINAL YEARS IN MADRID

The royal court returned to Madrid in 1606, and Cervantes and his family made the same move in that year. In the wake of the popularity of *Don Quixote,* Cervantes became somewhat of a celebrity, but his financial situation did not improve, as he received little return from the book's publication. He continued writing poetry, theater, and fiction, but published nothing new until 1613, when his *Novelas ejemplares (Exemplary Novels),* a collection of 12 short fictions *(novelas)* appeared. This is arguably the most original and most influential collection of short fictions by a European author before the nineteenth century. The 12 stories, in order, are as follows.

> *La gitanilla (The Little Gypsy Girl),* the longest story in the collection, is the tale of a beautiful and talented young gypsy named Preciosa. Her abilities in song and dance draw the attention of a young nobleman, who is willing to leave home and undergo a probationary period as a gypsy in order to gain the hand of the woman he loves. A series of chance events, however, leads to the revelation that the newborn Preciosa had been stolen from her noble parents, which makes possible an immediate marriage between the two lovers.

El amante liberal (The Generous Lover) is a story of intrigue and romance that takes place in North Africa, Constantinople, Spain, and on the high seas. The lovers Ricardo and Leonisa are frequently separated, threatened, and presumed dead or lost, until, in a dramatic final scene, Ricardo appears, offering all he has to his beloved and giving her over to his rival for her hand. But then Leonisa speaks, asserts her independence, and chooses to marry Ricardo.

Rinconete y Cortadillo (Rinconete and Cortadillo) is the story of two young *pícaros* who meet at a roadside inn, tell each other their life stories, team up, and travel to Seville. There they meet Monipodio, who runs a thieves' guild, a sort of early version of organized crime. After watching the group's activities, and spending some time in the organization, they decide to leave and strike out again on their own. The story reads like the first chapter of what was to be a longer work.

La española inglesa (The English Spanish Girl) begins with the English raid on Cádiz in 1596. A soldier steals a young girl and takes her home to raise as a secret Catholic in Protestant England. The girl, Isabel, becomes popular in Queen Elizabeth's court, and the soldier's son, Ricaredo, falls in love with her. Ricaredo is sent away to gain military experience and soon returns with a captive ship laden with riches. After some serious complications threaten to ruin everything, and following a lengthy separation, the two lovers are united in marriage.

El Licenciado Vidriera (The Glass Graduate) is a satire in which a poor but brilliant university student is poisoned by a woman who loves him. The effect of the poison is to make him believe that he is made entirely of glass. He becomes a wandering street philosopher, making satiric statements of all kinds. When he is finally cured, no one wants to listen to his opinions, so he joins the army, gains fame, and dies in battle.

La fuerza de la sangre (The Power of Blood) opens when Rodolfo abducts and (always hiding his identity) rapes Leocadia, then leaves Spain for Italy. She has a child, Luis, from this encounter, and raises the boy as her nephew. After Luis is almost killed in a chance accident, he is nursed back to health by Rodolfo's parents, who think the young boy looks familiar. Leocadia confirms that this was the house in which she was raped. In the end, Rodolfo is recalled to Spain and a happy marriage is arranged between victim and rapist.

El celoso extremeño (The Jealous Old Man from Extremadura) is the story of an elderly *indiano* (a Spaniard who became rich in America and then returned to Spain) named Carrizales who marries an innocent 13-year old named Leonora. Obsessively jealous, Carrizales turns his home into a fortress, but, of course, it is breached by a young man who spends the night (but does not have sex) with Leonora. The old man recognizes his error, forgives his wife, and dies.

La ilustre fregona (The Illustrious Kitchen-Maid) is about a beautiful young woman, Costanza, raised by an innkeeper. Two young noblemen, off on an adventure, hear of her and come to the inn. Pretending to be peasants, one of them, Tomás, falls in love, while his friend, Diego, has some comic adventures as a water seller. In the end, it is revealed that Costanza is the product of the rape of a noble woman and a series of happy marriages are arranged.

Las dos doncellas (The Two Damsels) tells of how the beautiful Teodosia and her brother search for one Marco Antonio, the man who had taken Teodosia's honor and promised to marry her. They are soon joined by the equally beautiful Leocadia, who is also in search of the man who had promised to marry her—the same Marco Antonio. After a series of adventures and a serious wound to the absent lover, Marco Antonio and Teodosia marry, as do Leocadia and Teodosia's brother.

La señora Cornelia (Lady Cornelia) is about the adventures of two noble Spanish students, Don Antonio and Don Juan, in Bologna, Italy. They become involved in a complicated love affair involving the beautiful Cornelia Bentibolli and the Duke of Ferrara. The two generous and brave Spaniards defend the Duke, take care of Cornelia's illegitimate baby, and help the lovers get back together. In the end, after a comedy of mistaken identity involving two other women named Cornelia, the happy marriage of the two lovers takes place.

El casamiento engañoso (The Deceitful Marriage), shortest of the stories, is about an ensign who tells a friend about a marriage in which he tricked his wife into believing that he was rich and she deceived him by running off with her lover. She also left him with a case of syphilis, and while he was recovering in the hospital one night he heard two dogs talking and wrote down their conversation. His friend reads the manuscript of their conversation, which is the twelfth and final story.

El coloquio de los perros (The Dialogue of the Dogs) opens when two dogs, Berganza and Cipión, discover they have the power of speech. Berganza tells his friend of his various masters and the adventures he has had throughout his life—episodes involving illicit sex between black slaves, life with gypsies, a stint as a sheep dog, fame as a dancing dog, a potentially supernatural episode with a witch, and much more. All the while, Cipión comments on Berganza's story and, in the end promises to tell his life story the next night.

It is certain that Cervantes wrote short fictions throughout his career, as we know that some of these stories were in existence at least a decade before the *Novelas ejemplares* was published in 1613, while it is clear that others were written as late as during the stay in Valladolid. The range of style, technique, and character in the stories is impressive. Five of them follow a romance pattern of the trials and tribulations of a pair of young lovers who are happily reunited in the end. Another five are more novel-like, featuring realistic characters and settings, often with satire. And two are a conscious combination of the two modes (see Mancing, "Prototypes of Genre"). Even if he had never written *Don Quixote,* Cervantes would rank as a major writer on the basis of his short fictions alone (on the *Novelas,* see Sears, *A Marriage of Convenience;* Hart, *Cervantes' Exemplary Fictions;* Ricapito, *Cervantes's "Novelas ejemplares;"* and Clamurro, *Beneath the Fiction*).

The *Novelas ejemplares* was followed in rapid succession by three more books: *El viaje del Parnaso (Voyage to Parnassus)* in 1614, and *Ocho comedias y ocho entremeses, nunca representados (Eight Plays and Eight Interludes, Never Performed)* and part 2 of *Don Quixote* in 1615. The *Parnaso* is a mock-epic in which Cervantes is invited by Apollo to the mythical Mount Parnassus to help defend it from being attacked by bad poets. Along the way a large number of Spanish poets join in, and together they manage to fight off the bad poets and defend good poetry. The majority of the work consists of a long list of poets who are variously praised. The best part is chapter 4 where Cervantes talks about himself in self-deprecating terms. The poem is followed by a prose *Adjunta* (appendix) in which Cervantes returns to Madrid and has a conversation with a fictional dramatist (see Lokos, *The Solitary Journey*).

The *Ocho comedias* contains the scripts of eight plays and eight *entremeses* (short, comic interludes normally performed between acts of full-length plays). It is assumed that at least a few of the eight full-length plays are reworkings of some of Cervantes works from the 1580s. All of them have elements of interest, but none are considered great works (see Friedman, *The Unifying Concept,* and McKendrick, "Writing for the Stage"). In order, they are as follows.

El gallardo español (The Valiant Spaniard) is a tale of valor and romance that takes place during the siege of the Spanish fortress of Orán in 1563.

La casa de los celos y selva de Ardenia (The House of Jealousy and Forest of Ardennes) is a tale of marvelous chivalric deeds, all undermined by absurdities, inconsistencies, and a comic tone that may not be intended.

Los baños de Argel (The Bagnios of Algiers) is an almost documentary treatment of the theme of captivity, quite superior to the earlier *Los tratos de Argel.*

El rufián dichoso (The Fortunate Ruffian) is a play about a handsome *rufián* (pimp, *pícaro*) from Seville who repents, goes to Mexico, and becomes a miracle-working monk.

La Gran Sultana doña Catalina de Oviedo (The Wife of the Great Sultan, Doña Catalina de Oviedo) is a tale of the conflict between religion and love, as a beautiful Christian woman from Spain marries the Sultan of the Ottoman Empire.

El laberinto de amor (The Labyrinth of Love) is an extremely complicated tale of courtly love, involving hidden identities and confusing relationships; very likely a reworking of an earlier, lost play.

La entretenida (The Entertaining Story) is a parody of a cape and sword drama, with hints of incest, multilayered romantic comedy, and an unorthodox ending where no one gets married.

Pedro de Urdemalas is a work in which this folkloric character, here a *pícaro,* becomes a servant, a gypsy, and finally an actor—always existing on the margins of society, living by his ingenuity and wit.

Cervantes' eight interludes are, on the whole, more original and interesting—even brilliant at times—than the long plays; no other writer in this minor genre surpasses his work. Here we see Cervantes' comic genius, keen observation of human psychology, sharp sense of satire, great sense of timing, ability to write lively and realistic dialogue (as he does in *Don Quixote*), and ability to create great characters in a brief space (see Asensio, *Itinerario del entremés,* and Reed, *The Novelist as Playwright*). The eight short works, in order are as follows.

El juez de los divorcios (The Divorce Court Judge) follows the story of a judge as he reviews the cases of several people—comic types such as a harpy, an old man, and a soldier—who want a divorce.

El rufián viudo llamado Trampagos (The Widowed Pimp Named Trampagos) is about the pimp, Trampagos, who interviews candidates to replace his recently deceased prostitute.

La elección de los alcaldes de Daganzo (The Election of Magistrates of Daganzo) presents three ignorant peasants who interview for the position of magistrate.

La guarda cuidadosa (The Vigilant Guard) is about a maid who chooses a sacristan over a soldier who stands vigil outside her house.

El vizcaíno fingido (The Man who Pretended to be from Biscay) is about two men, one pretending to be a Basque, who deceive a woman with a trick involving a fake gold chain.

El retablo de las maravillas (The Marvelous Puppet Show) presents two con artists who convince people in a small town that only those who are of Old Christian stock and legitimate birth can see the figures they pretend to present.

La cueva de Salamanca (The Cave of Salamanca) is about a student who pretends to conjure up (innocent) devils in order to deceive a jealous husband.

El viejo celoso (The Jealous Old Man) is a story about a young wife who, with the help of a neighbor, cuckolds her jealous, old husband before his very eyes.

Of these, the best are probably the last three. The *Retablo,* especially, has been singled out for critical praise. A variant on the theme of the emperor's new clothes, it is a devastating satire on contemporary sexual and religious preoccupations (see Smith, "Cervantes and his Audience").

The appearance in 1614 of an unauthorized sequel to *Don Quixote* probably spurred Cervantes to finish his own continuation more rapidly. The full title of the apocryphal continuation is *Segunda parte del ingenioso hidalgo Don Quijote de la Mancha (Second Part of the Imaginative Gentleman Don Quixote de la Mancha),* by Alonso Fernández de Avellaneda. The author's name is a pseudonym, and the real author has never been identified. It is not a bad novel by any means, but it pales in comparison with Cervantes' superior part 2. In Avellaneda's work, Don Quixote is more like the comic character he was in the earliest chapters of Cervantes' part 1, he is no longer in love with Dulcinea, and his new friends place him in a madhouse at the end. Sancho, meanwhile, is relatively stupid, a coward, and a glutton, especially fond of meatballs. There are, however, some amusing characters and very comic scenes—such as when Don Quixote rushes on stage during a play to save a damsel in distress (see Aylward, *Towards a Revaluation*). The reader who is interested in seeing how another writer deals with Cervantes' characters might want to read Avellaneda's sequel in the English translation of Server and Keller.

Cervantes' *Segunda parte del ingenioso caballero Don Quijote de la Mancha (The Second Part of the Imaginative Knight Don Quixote de la Mancha),* published early in 1615, was an immediate success. It was printed alone three times by 1617, and by the end of the seventeenth century it had been published with part 1 at least 14 more times. (Avellaneda's sequel never had a second printing until 1732.) By this time, Cervantes was quite infirm, suffering from dropsy, perhaps actually diabetes, and was aware that he was dying. He worked, probably quite intensely, on his last book, *Los trabajos de Persiles y Sigismunda (The Trials of Persiles and Sigismunda),* which he most likely began decades earlier.

The *Persiles* is the most enigmatic of Cervantes' works. It is a long story of adventure and romance, in which Persiles, prince of Thule (Iceland),

and Sigismunda, princess of Frisland, travel as brother and sister under the names of Periandro and Auristela, as they make their way to Rome to be married. Along the way, they are frequently separated and reunited, have numerous adventures, and are joined by a constantly changing cast of secondary characters, each of whom has his or her own tale to tell or adventure to undergo. Long considered a mediocre work by a worn-out writer, in the final quarter of the twentieth century the *Persiles* has received a large amount of critical attention and is now regarded as a subtle, complex, and fascinating work. It in no way matches the heights achieved by *Don Quixote,* but it is a truly fascinating fictional tale (see Forcione, *Cervantes' Christian Romance;* Williamsen, *Co(s)mic Chaos;* and Wilson, *Allegories of Love*).

Cervantes finished the *Persiles,* which he hoped would be either the best or the worst book ever written (it is neither, of course), while literally on his deathbed, and the last words he wrote were the prologue and dedication to the novel, on April 19, 1616. He died four days later, on April 23. It is interesting to note that Cervantes and Shakespeare both died on April 23, 1616—but not on the same day. England was at the time still using the old Julian calendar, while Spain had already switched to the revised Gregorian calendar that was to become standard. Thus, Shakespeare died 10 days later than Cervantes. Cervantes' widow, Catalina, saw to the publication of *Persiles* in 1617.

Cervantes was buried in a unmarked grave in the Trinitarian Convent, around the corner from where he lived, on the Calle de Cantarranas (now, ironically, the Calle de Lope de Vega). Cervantes never lived on the street known today as the Calle de Cervantes. At the end of his life he lived in a building on the corner of that street, then called the Calle de los Francos, and the Calle de los Leones, but the entrance was on Leones, not Francos. Lope de Vega, however, did live on Francos and his home, containing several of his personal possessions, is now preserved as a museum in his honor. It is no small irony that Lope lived on the street named for Cervantes and Cervantes is buried on the street named for Lope.

WORKS CITED

Allen, John J. *The Reconstruction of a Spanish Golden-Age Playhouse: El Corral del Príncipe 1583–1744.* Gainesville: U of Florida P, 1983.

———, Elias Rivers, and Harry Sieber, eds. *A Celebration of Cervantes on the Fourth Centenary of "La Galatea," 1585–1985. Selected Papers.* Special issue of *Cervantes* (Winter, 1988).

Arrabal, Fernando. *Un esclavo llamado Cervantes.* Madrid: Espasa Calpe, 1996.

Asensio, Eugenio. *Itinerario del entremés desde Lope de Rueda a Quiñones de Benavente, con cinco entremeses inéditos de D. Francisco de Quevedo.* 2nd rev. ed. Madrid: Gredos, 1971.

Aylward, Edward T. *Towards a Revaluation of Avellaneda's False "Quijote."* Newark, DE: Juan de la Cuesta, 1989.

Bataillon, Marcel. *Erasmo y España. Estudios sobre la historia espiritual de España.* 2nd ed. Mexico City: Fondo de Cultura Económica, 1966.

Buezo, Catalina. "*El triunfo de Don Quijote:* una máscara estudiantil burlesca de 1610 y otras invenciones." *Anales Cervantinos* 28 (1990): 87–98.

Burgess, Anthony. "A Meeting in Valladolid." In *The Devil's Mode.* London: Hutchinson, 1989.

Byron, William. *Cervantes: A Biography.* Garden City: Doubleday, 1978.

Canavaggio, Jean. "Aproximación al Proceso Ezpeleta." *Cervantes* 17.1 (1997): 25–45.

———. *Cervantes.* Trans. J. R. Jones. New York: W. W. Norton, 1990; original French ed., 1986.

Clamurro, William H. *Beneath the Fiction: The Contrary Worlds of Cervantes's "Novelas ejemplares."* New York: Peter Lang, 1997.

Fernández de Avellandea, Alonso. *Don Quixote de la Mancha (Part II): Being the Spurious Continuation of Miguel de Cervantes' Part I.* Trans. and ed. Alberta Wilson Server and John Easten Keller. Newark, DE: Juan de la Cuesta, 1980.

Fernández de la Torre, José Luis. "Historia y poesía: Algunos ejemplos de lírica 'pública' en Cervantes." *Edad de Oro* 6 (1987): 115–31.

Forcione, Alban K. *Cervantes' Christian Romance: A Study of Persiles y Sigismunda.* Princeton: Princeton UP, 1972.

Friedman, Edward H. *The Unifying Concept: Approaches to the Structure of Cervantes' Comedias.* York, SC: Spanish Literature Publications, 1981.

Garcés, María Antonia. *Cervantes in Algiers: A Captive's Tale.* Nashville: Vanderbilt UP, 2002.

Hart, Thomas R. *Cervantes' Exemplary Fictions: A Study of the "Novelas ejemplares."* Lexington: UP of Kentucky, 1994.

Información de Miguel de Cervantes de lo que ha servido a S. M. y de lo que ha hecho estando captivo en Argel … Ed. Pedro Torres Lanzas. Madrid: José Esteban, 1981.

Lokos, Ellen. "The Politics of Identity and the Enigma of Cervantine Genealogy." In *Cervantes and His Postmodern Constituencies.* Ed. Anne J. Cruz and Carroll B. Johnson. New York: Garland, 1999. 116–33.

———. *The Solitary Journey: Cervantes's "Voyage to Parnassus."* New York: Peter Lang, 1991.

López Alonso, Antonio. *Cervantes. Manco y bien manco.* Alcalá de Henares: Universidad de Alcalá, 1997.

Mancing, Howard. "Prototypes of Genre in Cervantes's *Novelas ejemplares.*" *Cervantes* 20.2 (2000): 127–50.

Martín, Adrienne Laskier. *Cervantes and the Burlesque Sonnet.* Berkeley: U of California P, 1991.

McCrory, Donald P. *No Ordinary Man: The Life and Times of Miguel de Cervantes.* London: Peter Owen, 2002.

McKendrick, Melveena. *Cervantes.* Boston: Little, Brown, 1980.

———. "Writing for the Stage." In *The Cambridge Companion to Cervantes.* Ed. Anthony J. Cascardi. Cambridge: Cambridge UP, 2002. 131–59.

Montero Reguera, José. "Una amistad truncada: sobre Lope de Vega y Cervantes (esbozo de una compleja relación)." *Anales del Instituto de Estudios Madrileños* 39 (1999): 313–36.

Oriel, Charles. "Cervantes' *Numancia:* A Speech Act Consideration." *Bulletin of the Comediantes* 47 (1995): 105–19.

Reed, Cory A. *The Novelist as Playwright: Cervantes and the "Entremés nuevo."* New York: Peter Lang, 1993.

Ricapito, Joseph V. *Cervantes's "Novelas ejemplares": Between History and Creativity.* West Lafayette, IN: Purdue UP, 1996.

Sánchez Saus, Rafael. "Los Saavedra y la frontera con el reino de Granada en el siglo XV." In *Estudios sobre Málaga y el reino de Granada en el V centenario de la conquista.* Málaga: Servicio de Publicaciones, Diputación Provincial de Málaga, 1987. 163–82.

Schmidt, Rachel. "The Development of *Hispanitas* in Spanish Sixteenth-Century Versions of the Fall of Numancia." *Renaissance and Reformation* 19.2 (1995): 27–46.

Sears, Theresa Ann. *A Marriage of Convenience: Ideal and Ideology in the "Novelas ejemplares."* New York: Peter Lang, 1993.

Smith, Dawn L. "Cervantes and his Audience: Aspects of Reception Theory in *El retablo de las maravillas.*" In *The Golden Age Comedia: Text, Theory and Performance.* Ed. Charles Ganelin and Howard Mancing. West Lafayette: Purdue UP, 1994. 249–61.

Spencer, William. *Algiers in the Age of the Corsairs.* Norman: U of Oklahoma P, 1976.

Vilanova, Antonio. *Erasmo y Cervantes.* Barcelona: Lumen, 1989.

Williamsen, Amy R. *Co(s)mic Chaos: Exploring "Los trabajos de Persiles y Sigismunda."* Newark: Juan de la Cuesta, 1994.

Wilson, Diana de Armas. *Allegories of Love. Cervantes' "Persiles and Sigismunda."* Princeton: Princeton UP, 1991.

Chapter 2

CONTENT

Don Quixote was published in two parts: part 1 in 1605 with the complete title *El ingenioso hidalgo don Quijote de la Mancha (The Imaginative Gentleman Don Quixote de la Mancha);* and part 2 in 1615 with the complete title *Segunda parte del ingenioso caballero don Quijote de la Mancha (The Second Part of the Imaginative Knight Don Quixote de la Mancha).* In the decade that passed between the two volumes Cervantes' concept of the novel clearly evolved, because part 2 is quite different from part 1. It is equally clear that the intervening publication of the sequel by Avellaneda influenced Cervantes' concept of his work.

The plot of *Don Quixote* is long and complicated and not easy to reduce to a brief summary. In this chapter I summarize the action of the novel primarily in terms of what takes place in the world of the main characters, giving only relatively brief treatment to most metafictional commentary and embedded narratives (see chapter 6). Part 1 is both shorter than part 2 and contains more embedded narratives, so the summary of part 2 is somewhat longer than that of part 1 (for a considerably longer, even more detailed, plot summary, see my *Cervantes Encyclopedia,* part 1, pages 197–240; the subdivisions are the ones I used previously in *The Chivalric World*).

PART 1

Preliminaries

As was customary at the time, the first pages of the book are composed of official government documents (dated late 1604), which give approval to print the book and set the price. Next follows a brief dedication to a patron, the Duke of Béjar. This is followed by a prologue in which the author says that he wishes the book were better than it is, that it was conceived in a jail, and that readers are free to interpret it as they choose. Then Cervantes describes a scene in which he discusses with a friend how to write the prologue. During the discussion it is mentioned repeatedly that the aim of the book is to satirize the romances of chivalry. Last come several burlesque poems written by Cervantes himself.

Chapters 1–6: The First Sally

In a village of La Mancha lives an *hidalgo* (a member of the lower nobility) nearing 50 years of age, who shares his house with a teenage niece and a middle-aged housekeeper. He is so obsessed with the reading of romances of chivalry that he actually decides to become a knight-errant himself. He polishes some old armor, takes the name Don Quixote de La Mancha, renames his old horse Rocinante, and for a lady, chooses a local peasant woman named Aldonza Lorenzo and rechristens her Dulcinea del Toboso (ch. 1). Sallying forth, he comes to an inn (for him, a castle), sees two prostitutes (ladies), and is greeted by the innkeeper (lord of the castle). At the inn, he is served a meager meal (ch. 2). That night he stands guard over his arms, defeating two evildoers who disturb his armor (two mule drivers attempting to get water for their mules), and then is dubbed a knight-errant in a burlesque ceremony (ch. 3). The next day he frees a boy who is being unfairly beaten by his master (the boy has actually stolen some sheep), but the boy is whipped all the harder after Don Quixote departs. Next, a number of merchants refuse to swear that Dulcinea is the most beautiful woman in the world, so Don Quixote charges, but Rocinante falls, and one of the merchants' servants beats him with his own lance (ch. 4). A neighbor named Pedro Alonso helps Don Quixote return home, where his friends the priest, Pero Pérez, and barber, Maese Nicolás, are discussing his madness with the niece and housekeeper. Don Quixote goes to bed and the others decide to destroy the books in his library (ch. 5). While Don Quixote sleeps, they go to his library and examine his books, burning many but keeping several for themselves (ch. 6).

Chapters 7–10: The Second Sally

Don Quixote is told that an enchanter has taken away all his books and made his library disappear (it has been walled up). He identifies the enchanter as the evil Frestón, now his mortal enemy. Don Quixote recruits a local peasant named Sancho Panza to accompany him as his squire, promising him an island to govern for his services (ch. 7). The two set out together and soon see some 30 windmills on a hilltop. Believing they are giants, Don Quixote attacks and is knocked to the ground by one of the windmill's sails. He insists that the enchanter changed the giants into windmills to deny him the glory of victory. Shortly after this, he sees two Benedictine friars and a lady in a coach, each with their retinue, traveling along the road. He routs the friars and then gets into a battle with the lady's squire—but here the manuscript on which the story so far had been based comes to an end (ch. 8). In Toledo the narrator finds a new manuscript of the true history of Don Quixote, written by the Arabic historian Cide Hamete Benengeli. He has it translated into Spanish and this becomes the source for the remainder of Don Quixote's adventures. The battle with the lady's squire continues and, although Don Quixote has half of one ear cut away, he defeats his opponent, and the lady promises to inform Dulcinea about how he rescued her (ch. 9). Sancho is worried about the wounded ear, but Don Quixote says that knights-errant never complain about their wounds and, besides, he will soon prepare a dose of the magic balm of Fierabrás, an elixir that cures all ills. That night they join a group of goat-herds for dinner (ch. 10).

Chapters 11–14: A Pastoral Interlude

After eating, Don Quixote speaks at length about the mythical Golden Age of harmony and plenty. One of the goatherds sings a song to entertain the group and another cures Don Quixote's wounded ear with a mixture of rosemary leaves, saliva, and salt (ch. 11). Then the group hears the news that the famous pseudo-shepherd Grisóstomo has died of grief because his beloved, the cruel Marcela, has rejected him. He is to be buried the next day, and they all decide to attend the funeral (ch. 12). On the way to the funeral the group is joined by other travelers, including a gentleman named Vivaldo who questions Don Quixote about chivalry in a teasing and mocking way. They meet with those accompanying Grisóstomo's bier, and Vivaldo takes a poem titled "Song of Despair" that the dead man had written (ch. 13). He reads the poem, which implies that Grisóstomo's death was a suicide. As the men discuss Marcela's cruelty, she appears high on a cliff overlooking the burial site and delivers a long, rhetorical speech in defense of her integrity, agency, and independence. Then she suddenly disappears and is not seen again (ch. 14).

Chapters 15–22: Chivalric Adventures

After searching in vain for Marcela, Don Quixote and Sancho rest in a pleasant meadow, but Rocinante goes to communicate his erotic needs to a small herd of mares grazing nearby. The mares receive him with their hooves and the herders begin to beat him. When Don Quixote and Sancho come to his rescue, they too are beaten and left lying on the ground. Sancho leads Don Quixote to a nearby inn, which Don Quixote perceives as a castle (ch. 15). The inn is run by a man (named Juan Palomeque, we learn later), his wife and daughter, and a grotesque servant woman named Maritornes. That night Maritornes comes to meet a muleteer (one who drives mules) whose bed is near that of Don Quixote, and the knight believes it is the daughter of the lord of the castle who has come for him. As Don Quixote holds and talks with Maritornes, the muleteer becomes angry and hits Don Quixote, starting a brawl. An officer of the Holy Brotherhood militia, who happens to be staying at the inn, also enters the room, finds Don Quixote unconscious, and attempts to impose order. The innkeeper puts out the light, everyone returns to his or her bed or room, and the law officer leaves to search for a light (ch. 16). Don Quixote tries to explain how an enchanted Muslim interrupted his amorous conversation with the beautiful maiden by striking him. Sancho offers the opinion that there must have been some 400 Muslims who beat him up and that, since he is not a knight-errant, he did not deserve it. Then the officer returns with a candle to see how Don Quixote is, but accidentally insults him, which provokes an insulting response from the ailing knight. The result is that the investigator hits Don Quixote on the head with the candlestick and leaves the room. Don Quixote asks Sancho to bring the ingredients for the balm of Fierabrás (rosemary, salt, wine, and olive oil) and then mixes up the concoction, drinks some, vomits, sleeps a while, and feels better. Sancho also drinks some and is struck with a painful simultaneous attack of vomiting and diarrhea. Don Quixote leaves the inn without paying, and when Sancho tries to do the same some men toss him in a blanket the way they do with dogs at Carnival time. Don Quixote returns but is too sore to help, so he simply watches what is going on (ch. 17). Sancho, in pain and humiliated, wants to return home. But then they see two large clouds of dust and Don Quixote assumes it is two great armies, one Christian and one Muslim, about to engage in battle. He describes the participants and explains to Sancho why they are about to fight, but Sancho can now distinguish that they are merely two herds of sheep. Don Quixote charges one of the armies, spearing several sheep with his lance. The shepherds pelt him with stones and knock out some of his teeth and then take their dead sheep and go off (ch. 18). Darkness closes as Don Quixote and Sancho ride along, and suddenly they see a procession of torches being carried by men in white shirts who are accompanying a dead body. Don Quixote charges and scatters most of the men, stating that he wants to avenge the man's death, but he is told that the man died of natural causes. Sancho dubs his master with a new name: the Knight of the Sad Face (on account of his looks after the beatings and loss of teeth). After Don Quixote is excommunicated for having attacked members of the church, Sancho leads him away. At the end of the day, they stop to rest in a pleasant meadow (ch. 19). That night they hear a loud rhythmic beating sound. Sancho refuses to permit Don Quixote to go and investigate, tying Rocinante's legs so that the horse cannot move. Sancho entertains Don Quixote by telling him a long and silly story. Then, near dawn, Sancho has to do that which no one can do for him, and the foul odor offends Don Quixote. After the sun rises they go to investigate the strange and frightening noise and discover that it has been made by a fulling mill (a machine for beating impurities out of cloth) and they both laugh at the situation (ch. 20). The next day, in a light rain, they see a man riding along with a shining object on his head. Don Quixote is sure it is the magical golden helmet of Mambrino, but in reality the man is simply a local barber who has placed his professional shaving basin on his head for protection from the rain. Nevertheless, Don Quixote attacks, chases the man off and claims the helmet as his own. Don Quixote then summarizes the typical career of a knight-errant, who, after achieving honor and glory, rewards his faithful squire (ch. 21). Next, they see a group of men bound by chains and accompanied by guards—criminals on their way to row in the galleys as punishment. Don Quixote stops the group and questions the men about their crimes. The final prisoner is one Ginés de Pasamonte, a famous criminal who has written his own autobiography. Don Quixote decides the men are being forced against their will and sets them free. When he asks them to go to El Toboso to inform Dulcinea about what he has done for them, they stone him and Sancho, and they flee (ch. 22).

Chapters 23–28: In the Sierra Morena

Sancho leads Don Quixote into the nearby Sierra Morena, where they soon discover a dead mule. In its trappings they find a love poem and a quantity of gold coins. In the distance they see a wild man dressed in animal skins, and they learn from a goatherd that the man is a nobleman (whose name, we learn later, is Cardenio) who recently came to these hills to do penance for love and, ever since, has alternated between lucidity and madness. Nonetheless, the wild man joins them and Don Quixote greets him as a soul brother (ch. 23). Cardenio tells how an unscrupulous former friend, Don Fernando, stole the lovely Luscinda from him after previously deceiving and taking the honor of the beautiful Dorotea, daughter of a rich peasant. A chance mention by Cardenio of the romances of chivalry inspires Don Quixote to interrupt. At this interruption, Cardenio slips into one of his mad intervals and beats Don Quixote, Sancho, and the goatherd before running off (ch. 24). After going further into the mountains, Don Quixote tells Sancho that, in order to impress Dulcinea, he intends to imitate the famous penance Amadís de Gaula did for his beloved Oriana, and also that of Orlando for Angelica. That night the prisoner Ginés de Pasamonte comes across them and steals Sancho's ass. The next day Don Quixote writes a love letter that Sancho is to deliver to Dulcinea and in the act reveals to Sancho who she really is. Sancho is stunned to learn that Dulcinea is not really a princess and exclaims that he knows Aldonza quite well, adding that she is indeed a tough and lusty wench, worthy of a knight's love. Finally, Don Quixote takes off his pants and, before Sancho departs, does a couple of somersaults, which provides Sancho with proof that his master is mad (ch. 25). While Don Quixote makes a rosary out of a piece of his shirt-tail, Sancho goes on his way and arrives at the inn of Juan Palomeque (introduced in ch. 16) where he encounters the priest and the barber from their village who have come in search of Don Quixote. After laughing at Sancho's attempt to recall the letter to Dulcinea (which he has left behind), the two men decide to humor Sancho and Don Quixote with a chivalric trick: the priest will dress as a maiden in distress, with the barber as her squire, and they will lead Don Quixote back home (ch. 26). They borrow some materials from the innkeeper and his wife and dress in their roles, but soon the priest decides that it is not proper for a man of the cloth to take such a disguise, so he proposes that they switch outfits, and only put them on later. Sancho is sent ahead to tell Don Quixote that Dulcinea has summoned him and, while he is gone, the priest and barber have a chance encounter with Cardenio, who tells them more of his story (ch. 27). Then the three men have a further chance encounter with none other than Dorotea, dressed as a man, who tells her version of what had happened and how she has come in search of Don Fernando, hoping that she might convince him to marry her (ch. 28).

Chapters 29–31: Princess Micomicona

Cardenio agrees to help avenge Don Fernando's betrayal of both of them. Sancho returns, and Dorotea offers to help by playing the part of the maiden in distress. The priest introduces her as the Princess Micomicona from the kingdom of Micomicón in Guinea. They meet up with Don Quixote and all head off together (ch. 29). The princess tells her story, saying that she has come to Spain in search of Don Quixote who is to kill the evil giant, restore her throne, and then marry her and inherit the kingdom. At first Don Quixote gloats, but he then realizes that he cannot marry anyone but Dulcinea. Sancho is furious and criticizes Don Quixote, who responds by hitting him. Dorotea, however, manages to reconcile the two. Don Quixote and Sancho then go off alone to discuss the squire's visit to Dulcinea (ch. 30). Sancho describes an invented scene with Dulcinea, based on his concept of the lady as an illiterate peasant. Don Quixote, of course, transforms every detail to conform to his vision of his lady. Then the group encounters Andrés, the boy from part 1, chapter 4, who describes how he was beaten after Don Quixote departed, thus embarrassing and humiliating the knight (ch. 31).

Chapters 32–46: At the Inn

The next day, back at the inn of Juan Palomeque, Don Quixote goes to bed and the others discuss literature and life. The priest decides to read aloud a manuscript in the innkeeper's possession: *El curioso impertinente* (ch. 32). The story is set in Florence and involves two close friends named Anselmo and Lotario. Anselmo marries the beautiful Camila but becomes obsessed with her fidelity. He convinces Lotario to attempt to seduce her. At first he only pretends to do so, but Anselmo catches him in the lie, and so the seduction plan begins in earnest (ch. 33). Eventually Camila gives in and the two lovers conspire to deceive the husband. But Camila's maid ruins the scheme by introducing her own lover into the house. An elaborate scenario is staged in which Camila stabs herself, inflicting a superficial wound, in order to convince Anselmo of her faithfulness (34). Don Quixote, dreaming that he is fighting the evil giant who has usurped Micomicona's throne, punctures some wineskins with his sword, spilling red wine on the floor. Once he is put back to bed, the priest finishes reading the story, which ends when the affair is discovered and the lovers run off. Anselmo absolves his wife of all guilt and dies; soon afterward, Lotario and Camila also die (ch. 35). Some new travelers arrive at the inn: Don Fernando and his retinue, with Luscinda. After a complicated and confusing series of recognitions, Dorotea convinces Don Fernando to accept her as his wife. Cardenio and Luscinda are also reunited (ch. 36). Then two more people arrive: a Spanish soldier and a beautiful Muslim woman.

They have recently escaped from Algiers and the woman, named Zoraida (but she prefers to be called María), plans to be baptized so that they can be married. After dinner, Don Quixote delivers a speech on the theme of arms and letters (ch. 37). Don Quixote finishes his speech and the soldier agrees to tell his story (ch. 38). His name is Ruy Pérez de Viedma (although this is not actually mentioned until part 1, ch. 42), oldest of three brothers, who has been a career soldier. He served in a series of historic battles, including Lepanto, and then was captured and taken prisoner to Algiers (ch. 39). One day, he receives a note from a beautiful young Muslim women providing him with money, informing him that she is a secret Christian, and offering to marry him if he takes her away. Elaborate plans for escape are made (ch. 40). They manage to get away but have to abandon Zoraida's father, Agi Morato, who tearfully begs his beloved daughter to return. After several adventures, they finally reach Spain where they hope to marry and live happily (ch. 41). Soon more people arrive at the inn, this time a judge and his beautiful young daughter, a 16-year-old girl named Doña Clara. The judge is none other than the younger brother of the captive soldier. The two brothers are happily reconciled. That evening, Don Quixote volunteers to stand guard outside the castle (ch. 42). Doña Clara has been followed by a neighbor, a wealthy young nobleman named Don Luis, who is in love with her. Meanwhile, as Don Quixote stands guard, Maritornes and the innkeeper's daughter trick him into standing on his horse and reaching his hand up to a window, where they tie it so that he cannot get down. He spends the night this way. At dawn, several more horsemen arrive and Rocinante goes to sniff at one of their horses, moving out from under his master, leaving Don Quixote dangling from his tied hand (ch. 43). Maritornes cuts Don Quixote down and he is ignored as the newcomers, who have been sent by Don Luis' father, search for the boy. As the Luis-Clara situation is further discussed, yet another man arrives at the inn—the barber from whom Don Quixote had taken Mambrino's helmet (i.e., the shaving basin). The barber and Sancho get into a fight over ownership of the saddle trappings Sancho had taken as spoils, and the question of the basin also arises. Sancho goes for it and returns with what he calls a *baciyelmo* (a basin-helmet) (ch. 44). After much discussion, a vote is taken and the majority opinion is that it is indeed the magic helmet. Those not in on the joke protest the vote and a fight breaks out and there are blows, cries, blood, and general confusion everywhere. Finally, Don Quixote calls a halt to things and calm reigns. But soon an officer of the Holy Brotherhood, who happens to be at the inn, recognizes Don Quixote as the criminal who set the condemned prisoners free, and another fight breaks out (ch. 45). Calm is again restored and Don

Fernando pays for all damages and the lodgings. Dorotea wants to get on with her life with Don Fernando, and therefore no longer wants to carry on as Princess Micomicona, so the priest and the others come up with a new idea. Dressed in disguise that night, they enter Don Quixote's room, and inform him that he is enchanted but predict that he (the Manchegan lion) will eventually be united with Dulcinea (the Tobosan dove). Don Quixote is to be taken away in a cage hauled on a cart drawn by two oxen (ch. 46).

Chapters 47–52: The Return Home

The next day the procession with the oxcart heads home. Soon they are joined by another traveler, a canon (staff priest) from Toledo and his retinue. Pero Pérez and Maese Nicolás explain that Don Quixote is enchanted, but Sancho accuses the priest and barber of having lied to Don Quixote and staged this phony enchantment out of envy. The village priest takes the canon aside and fills him in on Don Quixote's madness. In a long discourse, the canon then criticizes the romances of chivalry (ch. 47). The canon and the priest continue their discussion of literature, both fiction and the theater. Meanwhile, Sancho asks Don Quixote if he has to relieve himself, and the knight says that indeed he does (ch. 48). Sancho convinces the others to let Don Quixote out of his cage as they stop to take some food, and they agree. Don Quixote gets into a discussion with the canon about the historicity of the romances of chivalry (ch. 49). To prove how wonderful the romances of chivalry are, Don Quixote tells the story of the Knight of the Lake, who descends into a dark lake and has a marvelous adventure in a fabulous castle. Just then a goat comes by, followed by a goatherd. The man is invited to join them for something to eat (ch. 50). The goatherd, Eugenio, tells the story of how the beautiful Leandra was seduced and abducted by a young dandy and braggart soldier named Vicente de la Rosa who stole her money and jewels—but, she says, not her honor (ch. 51). Eugenio insults Don Quixote and a fight breaks out between them. Sancho tries to help his master, but the others prevent him from doing so, while the entire company laughs uproariously and jumps with joy. At this moment a procession of hooded penitents carrying a figure of the Virgin Mary comes by. Don Quixote intervenes to rescue the damsel in distress but is knocked to the ground. They proceed on their way and soon arrive back at the village of La Mancha, and Don Quixote goes straight to bed. Sancho, meanwhile, talks with his wife, defending the time he spent with Don Quixote (ch. 52).

PART 2

Preliminaries

After the obligatory pages of permissions and approvals, Cervantes' prologue is largely a satiric reply to Avellaneda's sequel to part 1 that had appeared the year before. The prologue ends with two anecdotes about dogs and books. The dedication to the Count of Lemos includes a clever fiction about the emperor of China. There are no prefatory verses.

Chapters 1–7: The Third Sally

Cide Hamete Benengeli recounts that after Don Quixote has rested comfortably at home for a month, he is visited by the priest and barber, and the talk turns to matters of chivalry. The barber tells the story of a madman of Seville who was supposedly cured in an asylum, but turned out to be as mad as ever. Don Quixote insults the barber and once again defends the legitimacy of knight-errantry (ch. 1). Sancho comes to visit and tells Don Quixote that a local resident, Sansón Carrasco, has just returned from his studies at the University of Salamanca and has said that a book, written by a Muslim, has been published titled *El ingenioso hidalgo Don Quijote de la Mancha* (ch. 2). Sansón arrives and they discuss the book, its reception, and what people are saying about Don Quixote. Sancho goes home for dinner, and the bachelor dines with Don Quixote (ch. 3). Sancho returns and, in response to Sansón's question, explains just how it was that Ginés de Pasamonte was able to steal his ass as he slept. Don Quixote asks if the author plans to publish a continuation and Sansón assures him that he does. Sancho approves, and Don Quixote decides to sally forth again, this time going to Zaragoza where some chivalric jousts are held. Sancho speaks about his hopes of gaining fame as a squire (ch. 4). Sancho goes back home and talks with his wife, Teresa, about leaving again, his possible governorship, and the marriage prospects for their daughter, Sanchica. Teresa reluctantly grants approval for her husband's departure (ch. 5). Meanwhile, Don Quixote has a brief conversation with his niece and housekeeper about knight-errantry, lines of descent, and arms and letters (ch. 6). Sansón offers to serve as Don Quixote's squire, but Don Quixote prefers to keep Sancho, and a few days later, at nightfall, the knight and squire set out on another sally, headed for El Toboso (ch. 7).

Chapters 8–29: Pseudoadventures

Don Quixote and Sancho ride out, discussing chivalry and related matters, and soon arrive at El Toboso, where they wait for nightfall to enter the town (ch. 8). In the darkness they search for Dulcinea's palace, but come across the church. Sancho suggests that they leave town so that the next day he can return and arrange a meeting with Dulcinea, a suggestion Don Quixote gladly accepts (ch. 9). The next morning Sancho goes off alone and decides that he will try to make Don Quixote believe that the first woman who passes by is Dulcinea—enchanted. Just as he returns, he sees three peasant women from the town, and he tells Don Quixote that they are Dulcinea and two of her ladies riding lovely horses, but Don Quixote sees only three peasants on donkeys. Eventually, Don Quixote accepts that they must be what Sancho says. Dejected, Don Quixote decides to go on and he and Sancho head off for Zaragoza (ch. 10). Shortly after this, they come across a cart belonging to an acting troupe with the actors still dressed in costume. Don Quixote calmly accepts their explanation of who they are, but then a clown causes Rocinante to buck Don Quixote off and the clown then steals Sancho's ass. Don Quixote wants to take revenge, but Sancho convinces him to leave them alone, and they continue on their way (ch. 11). That night as they rest, Don Quixote and Sancho hear another voice, apparently that of a knight-errant lamenting his love for the beautiful Casildea de Vandalia. Don Quixote introduces himself and the two knights begin to talk, and the two squires go off on their own (ch. 12). Sancho and the other squire spend the night sipping wine and talking. The squire of the Knight of the Forest suggests four times that they leave their masters and return home to their families, but Sancho insists that he will follow his master, at least until he sees what happens in Zaragoza (ch. 13). The Knight of the Forest and Don Quixote agree that early the next day they will engage in combat to determine whose lady is the most beautiful. The Knight of the Mirrors, now so called for the armor he wears, is defeated by Don Quixote— and when his visor is lifted the face of Sansón Carrasco is revealed. Don Quixote makes his adversary admit that Dulcinea is more beautiful than Casildea and also confess that he is not really Sansón (ch. 14). It is explained that Sansón had consulted with the priest and barber and then decided to use the trick of pretending to be a knight-errant in order to defeat Don Quixote and make him return home, but the plan has failed. He vows to encounter Don Quixote again, but this time motivated by revenge (ch. 15). As Don Quixote and Sancho ride on they are joined by another traveler, Don Diego de Miranda. He and Don Quixote get into a long conversation about children and poetry. Sancho, meanwhile, wanders off to buy some curds and whey from a nearby group of shepherds. Suddenly, a cart adorned with royal banners approaches and Don Quixote assumes that it must be a new adventure (ch. 16). His master calls, and Sancho hurriedly places his purchase in Don Quixote's helmet. When Don Quixote puts the helmet on, the whey runs down his face—and Sancho suggests that enchanters are to blame. The cart contains two African lions, and Don Quixote makes the lion-keeper open the cage. But the lion refuses to come out, and it is agreed, after the lion-keeper is given two gold coins, that Don Quixote has won a victory. Don Quixote now christens himself the Knight of the Lions. Don Diego invites the knight and squire to his home (ch. 17). Don Quixote and Sancho spend four days visiting at the comfortable home, spending some time reading and discussing poetry with Don Diego's son, Don Lorenzo. Then they leave to head for the Cave of Montesinos (ch. 18). On the way, Don Quixote and Sancho join a group of travelers who tell them of the upcoming wedding of the rich peasant Camacho and the beautiful Quiteria, much to the dismay of the poor but talented man named Basilio. Two of the travelers get into an argument over which of two fencing styles is better and have a duel right then and there. The one who employs the scientific method easily defeats the other who simply attacks with strength and emotion (ch. 19). They arrive at the site of the wedding, and Sancho is pleased to see the abundance of food available, while Don Quixote is more interested in an elaborate, allegorical dance that is being staged (ch. 20). The ceremony begins, but Basilio interrupts, declares his love for Quiteria, and runs himself through with a sword. With his dying breath, he asks that Quiteria marry him so that he can die happy and then she, a widow and a virgin, can then marry Camacho. Quiteria agrees, the two are married, and then Basilio jumps up and reveals that it was all a trick done with a hollow tube filled with blood. The angry Camacho is convinced to accept the fact that Quiteria is now the legal wife of Basilio and continue the feast. The newlyweds, however, depart, accompanied only by Don Quixote and Sancho (ch. 21). After spending three days with the newly married couple, Don Quixote and Sancho depart for the Cave of Montesinos, accompanied by a cousin of one of the swordsman, a humanist scholar who discusses the books he is writing. At the cave, Don Quixote ties a rope around his waist so that he can be lowered into the cavern. The rope goes slack, and after an hour passes Sancho and the cousin pull Don Quixote, apparently asleep, out of the cave (ch. 22). Don Quixote describes how, after taking a short nap, he found himself in a beautiful setting featuring a palace of transparent crystal. There he met and talked with Montesinos and his dead cousin Durandarte. Montesinos explained that Merlin had enchanted them and how the nearby Lagoons of Ruidera and the Guadiana River were formed. Then Don Quixote saw two groups of women, in one was Durandarte's beloved Belerma and in the other was the enchanted Dulcinea. Sancho believes nothing of what Don Quixote has described, but Don Quixote insists that it is all the truth (ch. 23). They continue on their way and the cousin notes that nearby is a hermitage occupied by a hermit who has a pious reputation, and they decide to visit, but when they get there, they learn from a female assistant that the hermit is not there. Back on the road, they meet a man about to join a troupe of soldiers and Don Quixote talks briefly about the soldiers' life. They arrive at an inn (which Don Quixote does not see as a castle) (ch. 24). At the inn, they learn about two alderman who, while searching for a lost ass, repeatedly mistook each other's braying for the real thing. This led to a rivalry between the two villages, the inhabitants of which are to meet in combat. At this time, the puppeteer Maese Pedro, accompanied by a young boy and a talking ape, arrive at the inn. The ape informs his master who Don Quixote and Sancho are and answers a question about the Cave of Montesinos in an equivocal way. The puppet show is prepared (ch. 25). The show begins: it is the story of how legendary French hero Don Gaiferos rescues his wife, Melisendra, who is being held captive by the Muslims in Spain. Suddenly, Don Quixote jumps up, takes out his sword, and comes to the defense of Melisendra, attacking the puppets and wrecking the scene, and then Don Quixote pays for the damage. The next morning all the guests go on their way (ch. 26). It is explained that Maese Pedro is actually the galley slave Ginés de Pasamonte from part 1, chapter 22, who uses a trained ape for his deceits. Three days later, Don Quixote and Sancho see a group of men with banners depicting braying donkeys. Don Quixote advises them not to take up arms for trivial purposes. Sancho then decides to demonstrate how well he, too, can bray, but this is taken as an insult, and one of the townspeople knocks Sancho to the ground. Don Quixote, seeing so many well-armed enemies, turns and flees, holding his breath in hopes that he is not shot in the back (ch. 27). Sancho joins Don Quixote and suggests that perhaps it is time for him to return home to his family. Don Quixote offers to pay Sancho for his good efforts as a squire, but as they begin to negotiate the price, Don Quixote becomes angry and calls Sancho an ass (ch. 28). Two days later they reach the Ebro River and see a small boat tied to the shore. Don Quixote believes that an enchanter has left it for him to be transported magically to an adventure. They enter into the boat and soon see a large watermill in the river, and Don Quixote says that although it looks like a watermill it could be a fortress where someone is held prisoner. The boat capsizes and the millers help them out of the water, and Don Quixote concludes that there have been two rival enchanters at work. He has Sancho pay the fishermen for their boat, and they return to their beasts (ch. 29).

Chapters 30–57: With the Duke and Duchess

Sancho quietly decides that he should return home, but the next day something unexpected happens. They meet a beautiful duchess and her husband, the duke, who invite them to visit their nearby country house (ch. 30). Don Quixote is received great with great ceremony, and it is suggested that this was the first time he felt himself to be a real knight-errant and not a pretend one. At dinner they meet the house priest, who sternly advises Don Quixote to go home to his family, mind his own business, and stop making a fool of himself (ch. 31). Don Quixote responds with respect and moderation, defending his life as a knight-errant. Then the duke offers to make Sancho the governor of a spare island that he has. Four maidens enter to lather and wash Don Quixote's beard, leaving the soap to dry on his face as they go for more water, and Sancho goes off to have his beard washed by servants. As the duchess and Don Quixote talk about Dulcinea, Sancho bursts into the room saying some servants had tried to wash his beard with dirty dish cloths. Don Quixote retires for a siesta, and the duchess invites Sancho to talk with her and her attendants (ch. 32). Sancho tells the duchess how he tricked Don Quixote by presenting three peasant woman as Dulcinea and her ladies, and he believed that they were enchanted. But the duchess turns the tables on him by saying that she has it on good authority that it really was Dulcinea and that the enchanted one is Sancho himself (ch. 33). Six days later, after a wild boar hunt, at nightfall, horns announce an arrival: a devil, who says that they are about to learn how Dulcinea can be disenchanted. A procession of enchanters begins (ch. 34). A large cart arrives bearing the figures of Dulcinea and the enchanter Merlin. In verse, Merlin explains that the spell placed on Dulcinea can only be lifted if Sancho whips himself 3,300 times, to which Sancho only consents if he can do it when and where he chooses (ch. 35). Sancho has a letter written to his wife informing her that he is about to become a governor. The duchess reads the letter. Just then, a group arrives led by a man named Trifadín of the White Beard, squire to Countess Trifaldi, a woman in distress who has come from the kingdom of Candaya in search of Don Quixote (ch. 36). The arrival of the countess is announced (ch. 37). Trifaldi enters and tells a tale about a princess named Antonomasia who had a love affair with a man named Don Clavijo (ch. 38). The evil enchanter Malambruno turned the young couple into metal statues. Don Quixote is the only one who can disenchant them, along with the countess and her accompanying *dueñas,* who, at this point, remove their veils and reveal that all their faces are covered by beards of various colors (ch. 39).

Malambruno has sent a wooden horse named Clavileño the Swift who can be guided by a wooden peg in its forehead and will magically transport Don Quixote and Sancho to Candaya (ch. 40). The horse is brought in and, reluctantly, Sancho agrees to mount it, as he and Don Quixote are blindfolded for the ride. After a fake flight, the horse crashes amidst fireworks, and a parchment states that Don Quixote has completed the mission simply by undertaking it. Sancho makes up a story about what he saw in heaven during the ride. Don Quixote doubts what Sancho says, but makes him a deal: he will believe Sancho's story if Sancho agrees to believe what Don Quixote says he saw in the Cave of Montesinos (ch. 41). Don Quixote takes Sancho aside to give him advice for his governorship: first, fear God, for in fearing Him is all wisdom, and second, know yourself, which is the most difficult kind of knowledge there is. There follows a series of other matters of advice (ch. 42). The advice continues, covering a wide variety of subjects, and at the end, Sancho offers to renounce his command if Don Quixote thinks he should. For Don Quixote, this offer alone proves that Sancho is worthy of the job (ch. 43). The next day, Sancho leaves for his island while Don Quixote sits alone in his room, missing his friend, and contemplating a number of holes in one of his stockings. Then he hears voices outside his window and listens as a woman named Altisidora sings a long love song to him (ch. 44). Sancho arrives at his island and is placed on a throne and required to adjudicate three cases (one involving an alleged rape), all of which he judges wisely and correctly, amazing everyone with his natural intelligence (ch. 45). The next day Don Quixote prepares to reply to Altisidora's song with one of his own. That night, accompanying himself on a kind of guitar, he sings his reply. As he finishes his song, a bag containing cats with bells tied to their tails is lowered in front of his window, frightening him with the noise they make. Some cats escape and enter the room, and one of them scratches him very badly on the nose. The duke and duchess are sorry their cat trick ended badly (ch. 46). Sancho is taken to a banquet hall where a sumptuous meal is placed before him, but a pompous doctor named Pedro Recio de Agüero refuses to let him eat what he calls unhealthy dishes. Sancho orders the doctor out, under pain of death. A messenger arrives with word that some enemies are preparing to attack the island. Another messenger announces the presence of a man who requests a dowry so that his son can marry the supposedly beautiful Clara Perlerina, but who is described grotesquely as missing one eye, being hunchbacked, and so forth. Sancho has the man thrown out (ch. 47). As Don Quixote recovers from the wound inflicted by the cat, the venerable Doña Rodríguez comes to explain that the son of a local wealthy man, who lends money to the duke, has taken her daughter's honor, but the duke will do nothing about it. She also tells him that Altisidora is not attractive and that even the duchess has two open sores on her thighs where the evil humor in her body is drained off. At that moment, some people break into the room, the light goes out, and Doña Rodríguez is beaten while Don Quixote is repeatedly pinched (ch. 48). The next day Sancho has a good meal and then discusses his philosophy of government, which involves favoring peasants, respecting *hidalgos,* rewarding the virtuous, and honoring religion. After dinner that evening, Sancho and his staff make their rounds of the island. They encounter several interesting people, especially a young woman and her brother from a local family who have escaped their carefully guarded house. Sancho thinks the young man might make a good husband for his daughter (ch. 49). It was the duchess and Altisidora who followed Doña Rodríguez to Don Quixote's room and then broke in when she revealed the secret of the duchess's sores. The duke enjoys hearing about the joke. The duchess sends a page with a letter to Teresa Panza, who is stunned to learn that her husband is a governor. Teresa immediately plans on dressing like a lady and buying a carriage, and she gets a young acolyte to write a letter in response for her (ch. 50). The next day Sancho judges another case, this one a variant of the liar's paradox. He and Don Quixote exchange letters updating each other on what is happening. Then Sancho promulgates several excellent laws for the island which, to this day, are respected as *The Constitutions of the Great Governor Sancho Panza* (ch. 51). Doña Rodríguez and her daughter interrupt Don Quixote and the duke at dinner and ask again for the knight to right the wrong done to the girl. Don Quixote decides to challenge the offender, and the duke accepts in his name, promising to arrange a combat between the two of them. Two letters from Teresa Panza arrive, one for the duchess and one for Sancho (ch. 52). On the seventh night of his governorship, the expected attack on the island takes place. Sancho is tied between two large shields, knocked down, and trampled repeatedly during the mock battle. Soon, victory is declared, but Sancho wants no more of political rule. He goes to the stable, embraces his beloved ass, resigns his governorship, and departs, taking with him only a bit of bread and cheese (ch. 53). The duke substitutes a lackey named Tosilos for the youth who wronged Doña Rodríguez's daughter, instructing him to defeat Don Quixote without hurting him. Meanwhile, Sancho encounters a group of pilgrims, among whom is an old *morisco* (converted Muslim) friend named Ricote, and they discuss how the edict to expel the *moriscos* has affected his family. Ricote has spent time in France, Italy, and Germany, where, he says, religious freedom is practiced. His wife and daughter, Ricota, however, had departed for Algiers. He offers Sancho some 200 *escudos* (gold coins) to help him retrieve a treasure he has hidden, but Sancho refuses (ch. 54). That night in the darkness Sancho and his ass fall into a deep pit and cannot climb out. The next day, Don Quixote comes across him, identifies him when he brays like an ass, and goes for help to get Sancho out of the pit (ch. 55). The following day, Don Quixote prepares to meet Tosilos in combat, but when the lackey sees the beautiful young woman he is supposedly refusing to marry, he admits defeat and asks for her hand. Doña Rodríguez and her daughter are offended at first, but decide to accept Tosilos' offer of marriage. The duke, however, decides to postpone the marriage two weeks (ch. 56). As Don Quixote and Sancho prepare to leave the castle, the duke's majordomo gives Sancho 200 gold *escudos*. But Altisidora accuses Sancho of stealing some things and the duke challenges Don Quixote to combat, which Don Quixote refuses. Then Altisidora admits there was no theft, so Don Quixote and Sancho depart for Zaragoza (ch. 57).

Chapters 58–73: To Barcelona and Back

Don Quixote's first comment after leaving the duke's palace is that freedom is one of man's most precious gifts. They then encounter some men who are transporting four carved figures of Christian saints (George, Martin, James, and Paul). Don Quixote comments on each of them in terms of chivalry. Shortly afterward, they come across a clearing where some people have set up a scene in which to recite pastoral poetry. Don Quixote goes out to guard the nearby road. Soon, a group of men herding some bulls comes along, and Don Quixote and Sancho are trampled by the bulls (ch. 58). Don Quixote, dejected, suggests that this might be a good time for Sancho to lash himself and disenchant Dulcinea, but Sancho refuses. The next day they come to an inn (which Don Quixote does not see as a castle) and, inside, they hear two men talking about the newly published sequel to Cide Hamete's *Don Quixote,* written by someone named Avellaneda. Don Quixote joins them and they discuss the book. When he learns that it is written that he went to Zaragoza, Don Quixote decides to change course and head for Barcelona in order to expose the book's lies (ch. 59). They travel for six uneventful days, and then, one night Don Quixote decides to whip Sancho himself, but Sancho trips Don Quixote and pins him down, saying that he is his own master. Then they are taken prisoner by a group of some 40 Catalonian bandits whose leader, Roque Guinart, insists that Don Quixote be treated with respect. A young woman named Claudia Jerónimo arrives and tells Roque how she has just shot her unfaithful lover. Investigation shows it was a misunderstanding, and so Claudia decides to enter a convent. Roque sends word to friends in Barcelona that Don Quixote and Sancho will soon be arriving (ch. 60). After three days with the bandits, Don Quixote and Sancho go on to Barcelona, where they see the sea for the first time in their lives. They are met and guided to the home of a wealthy noble-man (ch. 61). Don Quixote's host is Don Antonio Moreno, who parades his guests through the city with signs on their backs identifying who they are. One man approaches Don Quixote and criticizes him, telling him to stop being a fool and go home. Then Don Quixote is entertained at a dance and, the next day, questions a supposedly magic bronze talk-ing head about the Cave of Montesinos, and the head responds equivo-cally. On a walk through the city, they visit a bookstore/print shop, where Don Quixote comments on literary translation in general and some books being printed there (ch. 62). The next day they all visit a ship in the harbor and unexpectedly get involved in a skirmish with a Turkish ship, which is taken captive. The ship is commanded by a woman in disguise, and she is none other than Ricota (here called Ana Félix), daughter of Sancho's friend Ricote, who also turns out to be on the scene. Everyone is pardoned and a plan is devised to rescue Ana's lover, Don Gaspar Gregorio, who has remained behind in Algiers, dressed as a woman (for his own pro-tection) (ch. 63). One day Don Quixote rides out on the beach dressed in full armor and is approached by another knight-errant who identifies himself as the Knight of the White Moon. This new knight challenges Don Quixote to admit that his lady is more beautiful than Dulcinea. They meet in combat and Don Quixote is quickly defeated. He asks his oppo-nent to kill him, maintaining to the end that Dulcinea is the most beautiful woman in the world. The other knight refuses to press home his lance, stating only that Don Quixote must return home for a period of one year (ch. 64). Before departing, the knight explains to Don Antonio and some others who he is—Sansón Carrasco—and says that, moved by pity for a friend, he has come to make Don Quixote return to sanity. Don Quixote remains in bed for six days while the matter involving Ana Félix (Ricota) and Don Gregorio is happily resolved. Two days afterward, Don Quixote and Sancho depart for home (ch. 65). Upon leaving Barcelona, Don Quixote remarks that his fortune has fallen, never to rise again, noting that things do not happen by sheer chance but by divine providence and that we all make our own fortune. That night they have a chance encounter with Tosilos, the duke's lackey, who informs them that the duke gave him

100 lashes and prevented him from marrying Doña Rodríguez's daughter, who has entered a convent, while her mother has left the duke's employ and returned to Castile (ch. 66). Don Quixote decides to spend his mandatory year at home by taking on the identity of shepherds. He will take the name Quijotiz and Sancho can be Pancino, and even their friends can join them (ch. 67). That night, they hear a strange noise and before they can react, they are trampled by a herd of some 600 pigs. The next day a group of men accosts them and leads them back to the duke's castle (ch. 68). At the castle there is a staged scene in which Altisidora is presented as having died of love for Don Quixote. She can be restored to life only if Sancho is smacked, pinched, and jabbed with pins. He is forced to accept and Altisidora suddenly comes alive (ch. 69). Altisodora explains that while she was dead and in hell she saw two devils playing tennis, but using a book they describe as being so bad that they could not make it worse themselves—Avellaneda's *Don Quixote*—in place of a ball. When Don Quixote reiterates his undying love for Dulcinea, Altisidora becomes angry, tells him that everything was a big joke, and says that she could never love a man like him. The next day Don Quixote and Sancho leave the castle and head home (ch. 70). Desperate for Sancho to disenchant Dulcinea, Don Quixote promises to pay him for every lash he administers to himself. After negotiating a price, Sancho begins his task, but gets Don Quixote to double the price and then lashes not himself but the nearby trees (ch. 71). At an inn, Don Quixote meets Alvaro Tarfe, a major character in Avellaneda's book, and has him sign an affidavit confirming that Don Quixote and Sancho are the real people by that name, and not the ones with whom he spent time previously. After Sancho completes the disenchantment of Dulcinea they finish the journey home to the village of La Mancha (ch. 72). When they arrive, Sancho is greeted by his wife, who asks if he brings money, but Sancho responds that he brings things of greater value than that, presumably thinking of the value of his experiences, his increased knowledge about the world in general, and his new sense of self-worth. Meanwhile, Don Quixote goes home and, not feeling well, goes to bed (ch. 73).

Chapter 74: The Death of Alonso Quijano el Bueno

One day, after a good sleep, Don Quixote awakens and announces that he has recovered his sanity and now despises the romances of chivalry. His friends try to cheer him up, but to no avail. The priest hears his confession and then he makes his will, leaving money to Sancho and his niece,

Antonia Quijana. Finally, the end arrives, and Don Quixote dies. Sansón Carrasco composes a comic epitaph for him. Cide Hamete hangs up his pen, with a warning that no one else should try to write a sequel to the story of Don Quixote (ch. 74).

WORKS CITED

Mancing, Howard. *The Cervantes Encyclopedia.* 2 vols. Westport, CT: Greenwood P, 2004.

———. *The Chivalric World of "Don Quijote": Style, Structure and Narrative Technique.* Columbia: U of Missouri P, 1982.

Chapter 3

TEXTS

GENESIS OF *DON QUIXOTE*

There has been much speculation about how *Don Quixote* came to be written. In the prologue to part 1, Cervantes claims that the book was conceived in a prison. Since Cervantes was jailed briefly in Castro del Río in 1592 and then spent some seven months in the infamous Seville jail in 1597–98, it is entirely possible that he conceived, and maybe even started to write, the book at one of these times. Local legend in the small Manchegan town of Argamasilla del Alba has it that Cervantes conceived and began to write his novel when he was supposedly jailed there in 1601–3 in what is known as the Cueva de Medrano (Medrano's Dungeon). In 1863, the Romantic dramatist Juan Eugenio Hartzenbusch (1806–80) quixotically moved the entire printing apparatus of the prestigious Rivadeneyra publishing house to Argamasilla in order to print a luxury (but textually not very good) four-volume edition of *Don Quixote* in the jail. The trouble with the legend is that Cervantes was in fact never jailed in Argamasilla.

There are, however, other possibilities. One is that perhaps he conceived the basic idea for the novel during his five years of captivity in Algiers in 1575–80. Because he makes what otherwise might be an unorthodox and surprising move by making the fictional "original" author of most of the text a Muslim historian, Cide Hamete Benengeli, it could be speculated that he had ample opportunity to hear performances by Arabic and Turkish storytellers at that time and somehow conceived the basic approach to the story within that context. But then perhaps all this is nothing more than scholarly (or just romantic) wishful thinking, an invention of a fiction to explain what we cannot know for sure. (For a brilliant fictional rendition of Cervantes' indebtedness to Arabic *ráwi,* or storytellers, see the biographical/historical novel by Stephen Marlowe, *The Death and Life of Miguel de Cervantes.*) Such a tale, attractive as it is, is by no means the only way to explain the genesis of *Don Quixote.*

It is also possible that there was a literary model that inspired the original idea for the novel. There was an anonymous theatrical farce, dating probably from the late-sixteenth or early-seventeenth century, titled *Entremés de los romances (Interlude of the Ballads),* in which a peasant named Bartolo loses his mind from reading traditional ballads about chivalric heroes, sallies forth in search of adventure, reciting lines from a number of these poems (including some that Don Quixote also cites), and in the end is beaten for his efforts. It is easy to see the work as being related to *Don Quixote,* but the question is whether Cervantes read and used it as a model for some of the events of the early chapters of part 1 of *Don Quixote,* or whether the anonymous author adapted the early chapters of the novel for the short farce, or whether Cervantes himself is also the author of the interlude (Stagg, "*Don Quijote* and the 'Entremés de los romances' ").

But, in the end, there certainly is no reason why Cervantes could not have come up with the idea of a parody and satire on romances of chivalry entirely on his own, given his obvious interests in these books and his apparently ambivalent attitude toward them (see chapter 5). Perhaps this is both the simplest and the most likely scenario.

DATE OF COMPOSITION OF PART 1

Approval to print *Don Quixote* was given in the final months of 1604, while Cervantes was living in Valladolid, and the novel appeared early in 1605. Presumably, the final chapters were written shortly before publication, but the obvious question is: When was the novel begun? During Cervantes' imprisonment in Algiers in the late-1570s? Sometime during the 1580s, perhaps when he first went to Esquivias? During his brief imprisonment in Castro del Río in 1592 or his longer stay in the Seville jail in 1597–98? There is no way to know.

An intriguing possibility is that he wrote the majority, perhaps nearly all, of the novel in the late-1580s or early-to-mid 1590s. The evidence for this thesis is circumstantial, but reasonable. Perhaps the most interesting suggestion of an early composition is found in the revealing scrutiny of the books in Don Quixote's library. It has been noted that the latest published work mentioned is Bernardo de la Vega's *El pastor de Iberia (The Shepherd from Iberia),* published in 1591, some 14 years before Cervantes' novel appeared. Two other books published in the late-1580s are referred to by the narrator in part 1, chapter 9 as "modern." Evidence from the narrative of the escaped captain in part 1, chapters 39–41, and the poem sung in part 1, chapter 43 also give credence to the thesis that the majority of part 1 of the novel was written in the 1590s.

It is possible that Cervantes wrote the first section of the novel, consisting of the first five or six chapters, as a short fiction and circulated it in manuscript form or read it at some sort of *tertulia,* or literary academy. Perhaps inspired by encouraging comments, he then divided it into chapters and continued the story, introducing Sancho Panza and greatly expanding the scope of the story. Sharing of works in progress in informal oral settings and encounters among writers was a common feature of the era, and there is ample evidence of a number of works (Francisco de Quevedo's *Buscón* foremost among them) gaining fame well before publication (Rodríguez Moñino, *Construcción crítica*). The speculation is attractive, but not conclusive. All we can say is that it seems most likely that part 1 of *Don Quixote* was written between about 1590 and late-1604.

DATE OF COMPOSITION OF PART 2

Evidently, part 2 of the novel was written between 1605 and 1615, when it was approved to be published. We have no precise idea how soon after 1605 Cervantes took up his pen to begin his sequel nor at what pace he wrote, but we do have a few indications of Cervantes at work. The appearance of Avellaneda's continuation in 1614 (see chapter 1) seems to have spurred Cervantes to finish his own sequel, which appeared less than a year before his death in April, 1616. The first mention of the anonymous rival's book occurs in part 2, chapter 59, about four-fifths of the way through the novel. If, as many assume (or at least suspect), Cervantes immediately incorporated references to Avellaneda's *Don Quixote* as soon as he heard of it, then Cervantes was well on the way to finishing his own novel, but the unauthorized sequel may have provided extra incentive for Cervantes to finish the novel. Certainly, there is ample satiric reference to Avellaneda's work throughout the rest of Cervantes' novel (see scenes in chapters 61, 62, 70, 72, and 74, as well as the prologue), and it is not unreasonable to assume that Cervantes was anxious to finish his book and outshine his rival. In part 2, chapter 36, Sancho writes a letter to his wife and dates it June 20, 1614. This has led many readers to assume that Cervantes was writing this chapter on that date.

TEXTUAL PROBLEMS

The first printing of the 1605 *Don Quixote* contained some inconsistencies and errors, and there were attempts to correct them in later printings, beginning with the second Madrid printing, also of 1605. Throughout the years, the text of *Don Quixote* has presented scholars with a series of fascinating and difficult—perhaps insurmountable—problems. After centuries of speculation and conjecture about Cervantes' carelessness, missing passages, misplaced chapter titles, printing errors, and the like, a series of scholarly investigations in the latter part of the twentieth century has made it possible for us to approximate the establishment of a reliable text of *Don Quixote*. First came the surprising but convincing proposal by Geoffrey Stagg that Cervantes must have relocated certain segments of the book from their original place—especially chapters 11–14, which must originally have been part of the episodes in Sierra Morena, chapters 23–29 (Stagg, "Sobre el plan primitivo"). Next in its impact came the groundbreaking work of R. M. Flores, who painstakingly collated early printings of the novel and studied the minutia of the printing process (Flores, *The Compositors* and "The Compositors"). The precision and clarity with which he demonstrated the role of the compositors in determining specifics of the language of the first printings of the first edition of *Don Quixote* is exemplary.

Subsequent studies have made it possible to resolve the proper location of the passage of the theft of Sancho's ass by Ginés de Pasamonte (in part 1, ch. 25), which had been omitted from the first printing of the novel and badly placed (in part 1, ch. 23) in the second printing (this passage, as well as that of the recovery of the ass in part 1, chapter 30, are almost unanimously assumed to be authored by Cervantes, as they seem to be very consistent with his style; without actual manuscript pages, however, the possibility is open that these passages are in fact by someone else), and the proper placement of the beginning of part 1, chapter 43 (see Flores, "El caso del epígrafe"). Other textual problems considered over the years include the division of the work into chapters, the composition and placement of chapter titles, some apparently incorrect chapter titles, and various types of textual inconsistencies (see Martín Morán, *El "Quijote" en ciernes*). In addition to further correction of printing errors and inconsistencies, there are some textual variants in later editions where the Inquisition took exception to a few (relative minor and inconsequential) statements and ordered brief passages deleted (see Castro, "Cervantes y la Inquisición," and López Navío, "Sobre la frase de la duquesa").

DON QUIXOTE IN SPANISH

Francisco de Robles (?–1623), who inherited the title of *librero del rey* (King's publisher) from his father, Blas de Robles (?–1592), published both the 1605 and 1615 first editions of *Don Quixote,* which were printed in the shop of Juan de la Cuesta. The 1605 edition sold out very quickly, and Robles prepared a second printing in that year, this time securing a new governmental privilege extending his original grant, which was only for Castile, to Portugal and Aragon. The primary reason for this was the publication of two pirated editions in Lisbon in 1605. There were a total of 10 printings of the novel in the 10 years before part 2 appeared. Overall, the novel was published 28 times in the seventeenth century in Spain and 14 times more in Spanish in other parts of Europe controlled by Spain (mostly in Lisbon, Brussels, and Antwerp). We must note, however, that even this extraordinary record of popularity only puts part 1 of *Don Quixote* in second place among contemporary bestsellers. The first part of *Guzmán de Alfarache* (1599), by Mateo Alemán (1547–ca. 1616), was published no fewer than 23 times in the five-year span of 1599–1604.

The first fine edition of *Don Quixote* is one sponsored by Lord Carteret and published in London in 1738, featuring engravings by John Vanderbank; and the first scholarly edition of the novel that of John Bowle in 1781 (see chapter 7). The first pretentious Spanish edition, inferior to the English ones, was the four-volume work published in 1780 by the Royal Spanish Academy and edited by Vicente de los Ríos (it also includes illustrations by six different artists). This was followed in 1797–98 by the five-volume edition, also with Royal Academy sponsorship, by Juan Pellicer. Without doubt, Diego Clemencín's monumental edition of *Don Quixote* (1833–39) is the greatest of the nineteenth century. It remains unsurpassed to this day for its documentation of the relationship between Cervantes' novel and the romances of chivalry and other earlier works (see the excellent modern edition published in 1966).

The twentieth century was a Golden Age for editions of Cervantes' novel. There were hundreds of editions in Spanish—an accurate count is probably impossible—ranging from cheap reproductions of the text, to lavish and expensive books illustrated by famous artists, and including both handy and useful annotated editions for students and editions with a scrupulous text and massive scholarly annotations. No attempt here will be made to survey them all, but some important ones will be mentioned. Landmark editions are the four-volume edition by Rudolfo Schevill and Adolfo Bonilla (1928–41), as a part of their authoritative *Obras completas* of Cervantes;

the 10-volume edition by Francisco Rodríguez Marín (1947–49); and the 3-volume edition by Vicente Gaos (1987). Good, reliable, affordable editions, most of them published in popular and readily available series of literary texts, are also available. Some of the best are those by Martín de Riquer, John J. Allen, Luis Murillo, Juan Bautista Avalle-Arce, and Florencio Sevilla Arroyo and Antonio Rey Hazas, to name but a few. There are also two very good recent editions in Spanish edited specifically for English language natives, one by Tom Lathrop and another by Salvador Jiménez-Fajardo and James A. Parr.

At the end of the century there appeared an edition that some have called definitive, and it is certainly the best possible text available to readers today. This is the massive collaborative project headed by the distinguished scholar Francisco Rico and involving contributions by more than 50 Cervantes scholars worldwide that was published in 1998. Volume 1 consists of the text of both parts of the novel, while Volume 2 complements it with several fundamental overview essays by major scholars, other types of documentary material, extensive commentary and notes on each chapter, and a superb bibliography. The set is accompanied by a CD-ROM of the text of the novel for Windows (for typical critical opinion, see the reviews by Allen and Eisenberg). A second, corrected (even though there was little to correct) and updated edition appeared early in 2004. The anniversary year of 2005 has also seen the publication of many editions of the novel, some new and some old editions reprinted, some expensive and lavishly illustrated and some inexpensive and unadorned editions. Of these, one that deserves particular mention is the excellent and inexpensive edition of the Rico text, with some good introductory and critical material, by the Real Academia Española.

DON QUIXOTE IN ENGLISH

The first translation of Don Quixote into any language was Thomas Shelton's *The History of the Valorous and Wittie Knight-Errant, Don Quixote of the Mancha* in 1612, which he followed with *The Second Part of . . .* in 1620. Shelton's version, being the closest to Cervantes himself, is lively and colloquial, although, as to be expected, quite uneven. Other important early translations include those by Peter Motteux (1700), Charles Jarvis (1742), Tobias Smollett (1755), and John Ormsby (1885).

In the twentieth century there was a steady stream of quality translations. Three from mid-century are particularly noteworthy: those of Samuel Putnam (1949), J. M. Cohen (1950), and Walter Starkie (1957). More recently there are four others of note: the first is the excellent revision and modernizing of the classic Ormsby translation by Joseph R. Jones and Kenneth Douglas (1981), prepared for the respected Norton Critical Edition series by Jones, with the sort of judiciously selected background material and scholarly criticism always included in that series. This immediately became established as the standard classroom text for reading and teaching *Don Quixote* in English translation. Burton Raffel's lively version for contemporary American readers came out in 1995, and has since been edited by Diana de Armas Wilson and published (1999) as a replacement for the Ormsby-Jones-Douglas Norton Critical Edition. This has proven to be a controversial move, as some scholars and teachers feel that it is less accurate and less faithful than the Ormsby et al. version, while others applaud its vibrant style (for two very different views, see Raffel's "Translating Cervantes," and the review by Moore); the new critical apparatus is also excellent. More recently, a new translation by John Rutherford (2000) has been published in the Penguin Books series, replacing the Cohen translation.

The newest translation is that of Edith Grossman (2003), the first woman to translate *Don Quixote* into English. The book has quite consistently received excellent reviews, some of which are downright ecstatic (although some Cervantes scholars are less generous in their assessment). It achieved bestseller status on the *New York Times* list and ranked high on the Amazon.com list of books sold, and Grossman (previously best known as translator of the works of Colombian novelist Gabriel García Márquez) has achieved some degree of celebrity status (at least for a translator!), with frequent interviews and appearances on talk programs. The text reads very smoothly, as Grossman has been quite successful in creating a consistent and convincing tone throughout the course of the novel. Overall, she clearly achieves her goal of translating Cervantes' "astonishingly fine writing into contemporary English" (xx). On the whole, this is the version of *Don Quixote* that most contemporary American readers should turn to. The Ormsby-Douglas-Jones version may be more accurate and may better capture a classic Cervantine tone in certain aspects, and some British readers might prefer the recent Rutherford version.

WORKS CITED

Allen, John J. "A *Don Quijote* for the New Millennium." *Cervantes* 19.2 (1999): 204–14.

Castro, Américo. "Cervantes y la Inquisición." In *Hacia Cervantes*. Madrid: Taurus, 1957. 159–66.

Cervantes, Miguel de. *The Adventures of Don Quixote.* Trans. J. M. Cohen. Harmondsworth: Penguin Books, 1950.

———. *Don Quijote.* Trans. Burton Raffel. Ed. Diana de Armas Wilson. New York: W. W. Norton, 1999.

———. *Don Quijote de la Mancha* Ed. Francisco Rico *et al.* 2 vols. + CD-ROM. Barcelona: Instituto Cervantes, Crítica, 1998.

———. *Don Quijote de la Mancha* Ed. Francisco Rico *et al.* 2 vols. + CD-ROM. Barcelona: Galaxia Gutenberg/Círculo de Lectores/Centro para la Edición de los Clásicos Españoles, 2004.

———. *Don Quijote de la Mancha.* Ed. Juan Bautista Avalle-Arce. 2 vols. Madrid: Alhambra, 1979.

———. *Don Quijote de la Mancha.* Ed. Martín de Riquer. Barcelona: Planeta, 1975.

———. *Don Quijote de la Mancha.* Madrid: Real Academia Española, 2005.

———. *Don Quixote.* Trans. Edith Grossman. Intro. Harold Bloom. New York: Ecco, 2003.

———. *Don Quixote.* Trans. John Ormsby. Rev., ed. Joseph R. Jones and Kenneth Douglas. New York: W. W. Norton, 1981.

———. *Don Quixote of La Mancha.* Trans. Walter Starkie. New York: New American Library, 1964.

———. *El ingenioso hidalgo Don Quijote de la Mancha.* Ed. Diego Clemencín. Madrid: Castilla, 1966.

———. *El ingenioso hidalgo don Quijote de la Mancha.* Ed. Rudolfo Schevill and Adolfo Bonilla. 4 vols. Madrid: Gráficas Reunidas, 1928–41.

———. *El ingenioso hidalgo don Quijote de la Mancha.* Ed. Francisco Rodríguez Marín. 10 vols. Madrid: Ediciones Atlas, 1947–49.

———. *El ingenioso hidalgo don Quijote de la Mancha.* Ed Vicente Gaos. 3 vols. Madrid: Gredos, 1987.

———. *El Ingenioso Hidalgo Don Quijote de la Mancha.* Ed. John J. Allen. 2 vols. 25th ed. Madrid: Cátedra, 2005.

———. *El Ingenioso Hidalgo Don Quijote de la Mancha.* Ed. Luis Andrés Murillo. 2 vols.. Madrid: Castalia, 1978.

———. *El ingenioso hidalgo Don Quijote de la Mancha.* Ed. Florencio Sevilla Arroyo and Antonio Rey Hazas. Rev. ed.. Alcalá de Henares: Centro de Estudios Cervantinos, 1994.

———. *El Ingenioso Hidalgo Don Quijote de la Mancha.* Ed. Tom Lathrop. 4th printing rev. Newark, DE: Juan de la Cuesta, 2001.

———. *El ingenioso hidalgo Don Quijote de la Mancha.* Ed. Salvador Jiménez-Fajardo and James A. Parr. Asheville, NC: Pegasus P, 1998.

———. *The Ingenious Gentleman Don Quixote de la Mancha.* Trans. Samuel Putnam. New York: Modern Library, 1949.

———. *The Ingenious Hidalgo Don Quixote de la Mancha,* Trans. John Rutherford. Intro. Roberto González Echevarría. London: Penguin, 2000.

Eisenberg, Daniel. "Artículo-Reseña: Rico por Cervantes." *Hispanic Review* 69 (2001): 84–88.

Flores, R. M. "El caso del epígrafe desaparecido: el capítulo 43 de la edición príncipe de la Primera Parte del *Quijote.*" *Nueva Revista de Filología Hispánica* 28 (1980): 352–59.

———. *The Compositors of the First and Second Madrid Editions of "Don Quijote," Part I.* London: The Modern Humanities Research Association, 1975.

———. "The Compositors of the First Edition of *Don Quixote,* Part II." *Journal of Hispanic Philology* 6 (1981): 3–44.

López Navío, José. "Sobre la frase de la duquesa: 'Las obras de caridad hechas floja y tíbiamente' (*Don Quijote,* 2, 36)." *Anales Cervantinos* 9 (1961–62): 97–112.

Marlowe, Stephen. *The Death and Life of Miguel de Cervantes: A Novel.* New York: Arcane Publishing, 1991.

Martín Morán, José Manuel. *El "Quijote" en ciernes. Los descuidos de Cervantes y las fases de elaboración textual.* Torino: Dell-Orso, 1990.

Moore, Roger Gerald. "A Dog Is a Dog Is a Dog!: A Neo-Postmodernist Reading (Cum Grano Salis) of Burton Raffel's New Translation of *Don Quijote.*" *International Fiction Review* 25 (1998): 12–28.

Raffel, Burton. "Translating Cervantes: *Una vez más.*" *Cervantes* 13.1 (1993): 5–30.

Rodríguez Moñino, Antonio R. *Construcción crítica y realidad histórica en la poesía española de los sigloss XVI y XVII.* Prol. Marcel Bataillon. 2nd ed. Madrid: Castalia, 1968.

Stagg, Geoffrey L. "*Don Quijote* and the 'Entremés de los romances': A Retrospective." *Cervantes* 22.2 (2002): 129–50.

———. "Sobre el plan primitivo del *Quijote.*" In *Actas del Primer Congreso Internacional de Hispanistas.* Ed. Frank Pierce and Cyril A. Jones. Oxford: Dolphin, 1964. 463–71.

Chapter 4

CONTEXTS

The story of Spain's meteoric rise from a loose coalition of Christian king-doms in the Iberian Peninsula in the mid-fifteenth century to a position of world dominance by the mid-sixteenth century is unique in European—or even world—history. Its decline from its greatest heights to what was in effect a European backwater by the middle of the seventeenth century was equally rapid. Miguel de Cervantes was born in 1547, when the nation was at the pinnacle of its power. By the time he died in 1616, the decline was well underway. This chapter outlines aspects of the historical and cul-tural circumstances in which Cervantes lived and wrote.

SPAIN: FROM MUSLIM CONQUEST TO THE CATHOLIC MONARCHS

In 711 Visigothic King Rodrigo, the last of his line, abducted and raped a young woman named Florinda, the daughter of the noble Count Julián. Furious, and in an act of revenge, Julián called in Muslims from North Africa, who immediately defeated Rodrigo. The Muslims proceeded to overrun nearly all of the peninsula, and thus began the seven-century Islamic presence in Spain and Portugal. At least, that is the legendary story behind the Muslim invasion and occupation of this major part of Europe.

The only area of the peninsula never conquered by the Muslims was a small section of the mountainous region of Asturias in the north. Here, around 718, in the small mountain town of Covadonga, the Christian forces led by King Don Pelayo confronted and defeated the Muslims for the first time. This was the beginning of what became known as the Reconquest. Arabic Spain had always been strongest in the south, in Andalusia, where by the eleventh century the city of Córdoba had become the largest city in Europe, a glorious multicultural center of learning and the arts. The great mosque of Córdoba was the most important shrine in the Islamic world outside the Middle East. Spain under Muslim rule was, on the whole, the most tolerant and advanced culture in Europe. Muslims, Jews, and Christians lived and worked in relative harmony and with a high degree of mutual respect. This era in history is often referred to as the Spain of the three cultures.

But, beginning from their outpost in the north, the Christians slowly began to win back areas of the country. Spanish medieval life was one of constant skirmish and warfare; there was always a moving frontier or border between areas occupied by Christians and Muslims. Spanish-held areas divided themselves up into kingdoms loosely allied in their common goal of expelling the Muslims from the peninsula. The two most powerful of these kingdoms were Castile and Aragon. As the Muslim-dominated area continued to shrink, eventually becoming limited to the kingdom of Granada, the two major Christian kingdoms were definitively linked with the marriage of Isabel of Castile (1451–1504) to Fernando of Aragon (1452–1516) in 1469. The connection became complete when Fernando ascended to the throne of Aragon and Isabel claimed the throne of Castile, both in 1474. After consolidating their power, completing the reconquest was their major goal. This goal was achieved early in 1492 when Granada fell and Spain, more or less in its modern configuration, came into being (before that time it was common to refer not to a single Spain but to *las Españas,* the multiple kingdoms that constituted the Christian lands of the Iberian Peninsula). In 1496 Pope Alexander VI gave the royal couple the name of the *Reyes Católicos* (Catholic Monarchs) in recognition of their achievements as staunch defenders of the faith.

HAPSBURG SPAIN

In 1517, barely a year after Fernando's death, the Spanish crown was assumed by the 17-year-old Hapsburg prince Carlos (1500–1558), thus beginning the Hapsburg reign in Spain that lasted until 1700. Carlos had been raised and educated in the Netherlands, had never set foot in Spain, and barely spoke Spanish when he became king. Increasingly Hispanized however, Carlos I became the most beloved and the most capable of all

Spanish kings. An extraordinary administrator and statesman, he soon was named head of the Holy Roman Empire, the fifth Charles of that institution and thus known as Carlos V. His empire consisted of Spain, Flanders (i.e., basically the modern Belgium, Luxembourg, and parts of the Netherlands), much of Italy, and the vast Spanish possessions in the New World; it was the most extensive empire history had ever seen.

Carlos V resigned the crown and withdrew to a monastery in 1556. He was succeeded by his son Felipe II (1527–98), who ruled Spain during the majority of Cervantes' life. Less bold and imaginative than his father, Felipe was the supreme bureaucrat king, more a civil servant and a book-keeper than a leader, attending to every detail of his vast empire.

His son, Felipe III (1578–1621), was a weak and frivolous man more interested in entertainment than in matters of state. He turned the reins of government over to his *privado* (favorite), the corrupt Duke of Lerma (1553–1625). Upon his death, he was succeeded by Felipe IV (1605–65), whose reign continued Spain's downward spiral. The final Hapsburg king was Carlos II (1661–1700), called *el hechizado* (the bewitched), a pathetic, inept, and impotent creature whose rule was in the hands of his regents and other politicians. When Carlos II died childless, the Spanish crown went to the French Bourbons and has remained with that family ever since.

THE SPANISH EMPIRE

Fernando and Isabel finally expelled the Muslims from Granada in January of 1492. By March of that year, they took a second major step toward unifying the nation of Spain and issued a decree requiring all Jews either to leave the country or convert to Christianity. (Muslims throughout Spain suffered the same fate a decade later in 1502.) This major policy decision may have contributed to religious and cultural unity, but in the long run it was a fatal diluting of intellectual, commercial, and artistic talent. In the fall of 1492, the Catholic Monarchs agreed to finance a crazy voyage to the ends of the earth proposed by a Genoese navigator (perhaps from a Catalonian family), Cristoforo Colombo, known as Cristóbal Colón in Spanish and Christopher Columbus in English (ca. 1451–1506). Little did anyone know how enormous the implications of this decision would turn out to be.

Thus it was that in the space of just a few years, Spaniards turned their attention directly from the seven-century reconquest of the Iberian Peninsula to the conquest and settlement of the New World, even as they dreamed of the conquest of the Muslims and Turks in Africa and the Middle East and the Protestants in England and Northern Europe. In the time between the marriage of Fernando and Isabel and the beginning of Carlos V's reign, less than half a century, Spain transformed from a loose coalition of minor kingdoms into a great, cohesive empire. It had barely come into existence as a country when suddenly it ruled much of the world. No other nation has ever experienced such a rags-to-riches scenario.

The brilliant and rapid—if bloody and cruel—conquest of the Aztec and Inca empires led to the establishment of a series of colonies, which were exploited to provide what at first seemed like an endless supply of gold and silver. These unexpected riches were used to finance the nation-building project in Spain and the colonies, as well as the royal court and extensive military activities. The Spaniards considered their colonies to be an integral part of their nation, far more so than other European colonizers, and therefore the domination and exploitation of native Americans was accompanied by the creation of a vast civic structure. Former Spanish colonies throughout the world still feature churches, government buildings, and parks of great beauty and grandeur from the age of Spain's control—municipal structures that have few counterparts in the former English, French, or Dutch colonies. From their small home base, and with a rudimentary technology, the Spanish monarchs maintained sovereignty over their far-flung—but surprisingly coherent—collection of colonies for nearly three centuries.

Spaniards such as Hernán Cortés (1485–1547) and Francisco Pizarro (ca. 1475–1541) rose from modest means to achieve fame in *las Indias* (the Indies), as the American colonies were generally called. Many Spaniards went to the Indies in hopes of returning home wealthy and respected (recall Cervantes' applications for administrative posts in the New World), and those who did were called *indianos*. Great flotillas of ships arrived in Seville twice a year laden with gold and silver, as well as spices, tobacco, and other exotic plants and animals. These ships also brought news of fabulous tales of conquest, native American empires, and encounters with English and other pirates, and news from the New World spread rapidly throughout the country. Spain's American holdings were a constant source of interest and excitement. But by the late sixteenth century the supply of riches from abroad began to decline seriously and Spanish military setbacks became more common. By the early seventeenth century the royal court became more decadent, and a sense of national purpose was lost. France and England soon replaced Spain as the most powerful countries in Europe.

THE SPANISH MILITARY ENTERPRISE

One of the major military leaders in the age of the Catholic Monarchs was Gonzalo Hernández de Córdoba (1453–1515), known as the *Gran capitán* (Great General). The Spanish army was honed into a superb fighting force, largely under his leadership, during the wars of Granada and in Italy. It remained undefeated on land for a century and a half until the battle of Rocroi in 1643. Cervantes considered his military service (1569–75, or until 1580 if the years of captivity in Algiers are included) to be a high point in his life, and he was always proud of his mutilated left hand, a symbol of valor and victory.

Early in his career, Carlos V's greatest rival was Francis I (1494–1547) of France. In the battle of Pavia, Italy, in 1525, an entire French army of some 30,000 troops was killed, wounded, or taken prisoner, and Francis himself was captured. He was taken to Madrid and imprisoned for nearly a year while terms of surrender and concession were negotiated. After his release and return to France, however, Francis failed to honor the terms of the treaty. The Spanish army again routed the French at the battle of San Quintín in France on August 10, 1557. In order to commemorate this victory, Felipe II ordered the construction of a great palace-monastery in the village of San Lorenzo de El Escorial in the Guadarrama Mountains just west of Madrid. The site was chosen for its proximity to the capital and because it provided a pleasant respite from the intense summer heat, but also because of the town's name. The victory had been won on the day of Saint Lawrence (San Lorenzo), and so the name of the town made it particularly appropriate. The construction of the enormous structure, now known simply as the Escorial, took a mere 21 years under the direction of the famed architect Juan de Herrera (1530–97).

All the while, there were constant skirmishes with the Turks throughout the Mediterranean Sea and along North Africa. Algiers was taken by the Turks in 1529 and remained in their possession throughout Cervantes' lifetime. In 1541 an expedition sent by Carlos V failed to retake the city, primarily because a terrible storm off the North African coast sank about 150 ships and cost the lives of some 12,000 men. The disaster was a major setback for Spain, and it left the western Mediterranean largely in control of the Turks until the battle of Lepanto in 1571.

Lepanto is the name of a bay in the Gulf of Corinth, near Greece, where the decisive battle took place on October 7, 1571, between the Turkish forces led by Ali Pasha and the combined allied forces of the Holy League (i.e., Spain, Venice, and the Papacy) led by Don Juan of Austria, illegitimate half-brother of Felipe II. The three-hour encounter ended in the complete rout of the Turkish army and navy, including the nearly complete destruction of the more than 200 Turkish ships that participated. More than 20,000 Turkish soldiers were killed or wounded, and thousands more were taken prisoner. Christian losses were also high (over 8,000 casualties), but the battle marked the end of Turkish domination in the Mediterranean and eliminated the possibility of an Islamic advance on Europe in general. Arguably, however, the greatest benefits from the battle had more to do with public relations and propaganda. The Turkish reputation of invincibility was shattered. Spanish confidence in the nation's international and religious enterprise increased notably. Throughout the rest of Europe, the myth of Spanish invincibility both impressed political and religious rivals and made Spain more imposing (see Hess, "The Battle of Lepanto," and Guilmartin, *Gunpowder and Galleys*).

By the middle of the sixteenth century, many Spaniards became convinced that they had inherited the mantle of God's chosen people. After all, they owned large parts of Europe, controlled fabulous new continents that provided (it seemed) inexhaustible riches, had an unbeatable army and navy, and both exemplified and defended Christianity better than anyone else. Spain saw itself as the logical successor to ancient Greece and Rome and believed that it was literally destined to rule the world. In order to achieve world domination, it would be necessary to force the demonic Protestants to return to the fold, conquer the Islamic infidels in Africa and the Middle East, and convert native Americans and other heathens to Christianity. Not to be outdone in the glorious task of extending Christianity throughout the world, young king Sebastião of Portugal (1554–78), who ascended to the throne in 1577, decided to undertake the conquest of Africa himself. He personally and rashly led an army of 800 ships and 18,000 troops to Africa. The expedition met with disastrous defeat, and Sebastião was killed, along with the majority of his troops, at the battle of Alcazarquivir. His death led to Spain's annexation of Portugal in 1580, which completed the Spanish throne's control of the Iberian Peninsula and added new colonial possessions to its empire. Portugal eventually regained independence in 1640, when Spain was too weak to maintain its control.

Almost unbelievably, Spain actually thought it could remake the world in its own image. The 1571 victory over the Turks was a major step in the right direction, and the "civilizing" process in the colonies was well underway. Next on the agenda was the Protestant problem, and the solution was simple: send the world's largest and strongest naval flotilla to the English Channel to destroy the English navy, and transport a seasoned army of 24,000 Spanish troops already stationed in the Netherlands under the able command of Alejandro Farnesio, Duke of Parma (1545–92), to take control of the country, stamp out Protestantism, and reintroduce Christianity (in Spain, Protestants were not considered Christians). The original plan was for Alvaro de Bazán, Marqués of Santa Cruz (1526–88), Spain's most experienced and capable naval officer at the time, to command the fleet. But Bazán's death in January, 1588, made it necessary to find a replacement. Unfortunately, Felipe II chose the young, inexperienced, and mediocre Alonso Pérez de Guzmán, Duke of Medina Sidonia (1550–1615), to head the expedition. The Armada sailed from Lisbon, where it had been assembled, in May 1588, but had to put into port at La Coruña, on the northwest corner of Spain, for refitting. The great fleet finally departed in mid-July, and the battle itself took place late in July 1588.

The Armada consisted of some 200 fighting ships, over 350 supply vessels, and about 20,000 soldiers. In Spain, confidence was high and credit for the forthcoming victory was already accorded to the Virgin, who would guarantee success, just as she had done in the battle of Lepanto. But instead of a great victory, the Spanish suffered a humiliating defeat, brought about by a fatal combination of several factors: long delays in preparation, bad weather, superior English leadership (by Lord Howard and Sir Francis Drake), smaller and more mobile English ships, the inability of Parma's troops to mobilize and move on time, and poor leadership by Medina Sidonia. A probable victory was turned into a complete rout. Most of the ships and 9,000 soldiers were lost either in battle or in bad weather along the Scottish and Irish coasts during the desperate attempt to return home by circling north around the British Isles. More than any other single event, the defeat of the Invincible Armada marked the end of unchallenged Spanish hegemony and the beginning of Spain's decline toward mediocrity.

After the defeat of the Armada and the loss of the reputation for invincibility, setbacks started to come more frequently for Spain. With weak leadership and a greatly diminished supply of riches from the New World, Spain dramatically cut back its military operations. Peace treaties became more common, starting with the treaty with England in 1604 (see chapter 1). The Spanish army was resoundingly defeated in the battle of Rocroi in 1643, the first time in over a century that such a thing had happened. In 1659, the Peace of the Pyrenees was negotiated between Spain and France, with Spain making major concessions of a sort that would never have happened during the reigns of Carlos V and Felipe II. Spain was no longer the most powerful country in Europe; its military glory and cultural supremacy were long gone.

RELIGIOUS TOLERANCE AND INTOLERANCE

It is impossible to understand Cervantes' Spain without being acutely aware of a series of concepts related to the main religious tensions of the time. As indicated previously, the Muslim occupation of much of the Iberian Peninsula from the early eighth century until the late fourteenth century had a profound effect on the life of the people who lived there. During this time, Christianity was basically unchallenged in the rest of Europe and was able to consolidate its power. In many parts of Europe the Jews were the primary non-Christian presence and, as a result, often suffered persecution, pogroms, and expulsion. This did not happen in Muslim Spain, where Jews from elsewhere often found a safe harbor, and there was a relative harmony and mutual acceptance among Muslims, Jews, and Christians. There was a long tradition in Islam of considering Judaism and Christianity the two other "peoples of the Book," and revering figures such as Abraham and Jesus. Spain during this era in history was often described as the Spain of the three religions. To some degree, it was this religious tolerance that made Muslim Spain so successful and one of the most advanced civilizations in Europe at the time.

At first, a similar tolerance reigned in areas retaken by Christian forces. The city of Toledo, for example, was a great Islamic center of the arts and learning when it was reconquered by the Christians in 1085. There was no massacre, expulsion, or other type of repression of non-Christians, and the city continued to function as one of the great intellectual centers of Europe. Trilingual teams of scholars systematically translated from Arabic scholarly treatises in philosophy, mathematics, astronomy, medicine, and other sciences. Slowly, however, this changed as the Christians gained ascendancy in large parts of the peninsula, and the concept of religious tolerance was lost. By the middle of the thirteenth century, major Christian advances had taken place and important cities, such as Córdoba and Seville, fell. By the fourteenth century, the situation of Jews, especially, became difficult in Christian lands.

The Jews tended to live in Jewish quarters called *juderías,* often more by coercion than by choice. Their long tradition of superior education and mercantile success, together with their administrative skills and experience in professions such as medicine, made them targets of envy and suspicion by the largely illiterate Christians. The same forces that had resulted in the expulsion of the Jews from England in the thirteenth century and from France and Germany in the early part of the fourteenth century came to the fore in Christian areas of the Iberian Peninsula in the latter part of the fourteenth century. There were relatively minor incidents of religious intolerance in a number of places, but in 1391 there was a major riot in Seville, when a crowd was incited against the Jews, the Jewish quarter was attacked, and over 4,000 Jews were massacred. Many others were forced to convert to Christianity. Such anti-Semitic violence became increasingly common throughout the peninsula and, more and more frequently, many Jews were forced to convert.

These acts of forced conversion (and, occasionally, some sincere conversions) slowly created an important and growing subculture within Christianity: the *conversos,* or *cristianos nuevos*—New (i.e., converted) Christians (another term, more vicious and degrading, applied to Jewish converts was *marranos*—swine; this term, intended to mock Jewish prohibition of eating pork, is derived from the Arabic phrase *maran atha,* in the sense of an anathema, something unspeakable; ironically, however, the words actually mean "the Lord has come"). Old Christians *(cristianos viejos)* became increasingly suspicious of *conversos,* convinced that they were still secretly carrying out Jewish practices. The old mistrust and hatred of Jews became increasingly directed at these converts. Prejudice and hatred—racial, ethnic, religious—thrives, especially among an illiterate or badly educated populace, as the examples of segregation, ethnic cleansing, and fundamentalist religious hatred and terrorism in our own time illustrate only too well. *Conversos* were often forbidden to hold certain governmental positions or even, sometimes, to join religious orders. As time passed, it was not merely those who actually converted from Judaism who were suspect, but so too were their descendants. In order to apply for many official positions, it became necessary to document one's religious heritage, and thus the idea of *limpieza de sangre* (purity of blood) became important. To hold a certificate of proof that you were an Old Christian, descendant of Old Christians for generations, was both a badge of honor and the ticket to success. So it was that many of the most educated and refined inhabitants of Christian territories in Spain were excluded from government and church, were suspected and harassed, and became marginalized in nearly every way, while many ignorant peasants and petty nobles proudly and ostentatiously flaunted their Old Christian status. The ultimate badge of religious legitimacy was to have proof that you descended directly from the pre-invasion Goths (or Visigoths). It was a matter of pride to call yourself, or to be called by others, a *godo* (Goth), in spite of the implications of ignorance and relative barbarity of those people.

By the middle of the fifteenth century, statutes making *limpieza de sangre* official policy were promulgated. Anti-*converso* riots became increasingly common as New Christians were sometimes accused of crimes such as ritual sacrifice and witchcraft. Occasionally, under torture, the accused admitted to these and other crimes and were punished, sometimes executed. Not long after the 1469 marriage of the Catholic Monarchs, Fernando (who, ironically, inherited Jewish blood from his mother's side of the family, and, technically, therefore, was a *converso* himself) and Isabel received permission from the pope to establish the Holy Roman and Universal Inquisition (also called the Holy Office) in 1478.

THE INQUISITION

The Inquisition—not a Spanish creation, but an institution that had existed, in much milder versions, in France and Italy since the thirteenth century—was probably the most famous official institution of religious and political suppression in European history. The structure was governed by the Supreme Council of the Inquisition, a board whose chair held the title of Inquisitor General (or Grand Inquisitor). The Inquisition, like other royal councils, was a governmental and secular, rather than an ecclesiastical, institution, though its officials were priests. The first Inquisitor General was the infamous Tomás de Torquemada (1420–98), who, like King Fernando, was also a *converso.* In fact, although the name of Torquemada has become synonymous with fanaticism, torture, and repression, he was overall no worse than others in comparable positions in other countries.

More than anything else, the Inquisition was zealous in investigating the suspected secret Jewish activities of *conversos.* In pursuit of this goal, anyone accused of crypto-Judaism was investigated, interrogated, often tortured, and usually punished. Meticulous records were kept throughout, and the dedication of the investigators actually to determine the truth, evident in the lengths that were often taken to verify certain accusations, was, in some perverse way, admirable. Most other religious tribunals of the time were far less scrupulous. Still, in trials in which anonymous testimony and torture (which was justified by the assumption that it encouraged victims to reveal God's truth) were common practices, few suspects were found completely innocent of the charges brought against them.

At first, it was almost exclusively the new or recent converts from Judaism who were most persecuted, but eventually, as the Inquisition grew in power, *moriscos* (converts from Islam, the Muslim equivalent of *conversos*), anyone suspected of participation in Protestant, Erasmian, or other heterodox activity, and even supposed witches and warlocks, came under its purview. One of the most frequent and serious penalties the Inquisition prescribed was the wearing of a *sambenito* (a large yellow robe adorned with a red cross visible at a distance as a warning that its wearer was a heretic) for a period of time, or for one's natural life (after which it was hung in the parish church as a damnation of the wearer's descendants). When the crimes were deemed to be most serious, the penalty was an *auto de fe* (usually written *auto-da-fe* in English, an "act of faith"), a public ceremony of humiliation, punishment or execution, normally by burning at the stake (which, contrary to general opinion, was not the usual or normal result). The purpose of such public displays was often meant to inspire fear among those who witnessed it as well as to punish the guilty.

Religious intolerance was the norm throughout Europe at the time. Although the Inquisition is the most obvious official symbol of this fact in the late Middle Ages and Renaissance, and in spite of its legendary reputation for secrecy, fanaticism, and cruelty, it was by contemporary standards no worse than other European tribunals, both official and unofficial. Across the continent, heretics of all kinds were murdered on a grand scale in the name of God. In fact, there were probably no more religious executions—and there may have been fewer—in Spain than in some other countries during the same period. With the passing of time, the Inquisition became an ever less important factor in Spanish life, although the institution was not formally abolished until 1843.

One of the important activities of the Inquisition was to censor and control the publication of books, which led to the creation of the *Index of Forbidden Books*. The Inquisition issued such lists—which included works by Erasmus, the Valdés brothers, and Fray Luis de Granada, as well as *Lazarillo de Tormes*—in 1545, 1551, 1558 (which also included a ban on all books imported from other countries), and 1559. Further, by the late-sixteenth century a complicated governmental machinery was put in place to regulate publication of new material. Censorship must have had the effect of making writers of the time wary of official intervention and reluctant to deal with certain topics, but the age that produced the greatest poetry, drama, and prose fiction of all times in the Spanish language can hardly be characterized as one severely inhibited by (at least the threat of) censorship. But another effect of censorship was to force writers to "write between the lines" (Strauss, *Persecution and the Art of Writing*), a skill that was developed by writers such as Fernando de Rojas, the anonymous author of *Lazarillo de Tormes*, and Francisco Delicado long before Cervantes (see Costa Fontes, *The Art of Subversion*).

Cervantes seems never to have had any direct difficulty with the Inquisition, but there are clear references to it in *Don Quixote*. The most interesting is the scene of the burning of the books in part 1, chapter 6. It is the women of his household, his niece and the housekeeper, who, in part 1, chapter 5, propose burning the books. The niece specifically says to the priest that they should "burn all these evil books, for he has many of them, and they deserve to be burned, as if they were heretics." In part II, chapter 62, during Don Quixote's visit to Barcelona, his host Don Antonio Moreno puts on display a marvelous bronze head that can answer questions—and then the narrator assures the reader about how the apparently magic trick works and, to cover his bases, adds that Don Antonio had previously informed the Inquisition of the device and how it worked. But, even with this, shortly afterward he is ordered to dismantle it in order not to deceive people with apparent magic.

NOBILITY

Spanish Renaissance society was divided into (what was intended to be) clearly distinguished hierarchical sectors: royalty, nobility, clergy, and peasants. The royal family, of course, was in a class by itself, with all the usual luxury, privilege, deference, and power associated with the crown. Nearly 10 percent of the Spanish population held some title of nobility, a percentage higher than that of any other contemporary European nation. Noble status, which assumed purity of blood, carried certain official recognition, especially the exemption from personal taxes. But nobility also symbolized a hierarchical social superiority—nobles were assumed to possess honor and virtue, and it was taken for granted that they were born leaders.

The highest rank was that of *grande* (grandee), explicit acknowledgment as the head of one of the great families of the land. This category was invented by Carlos V in 1520 in recognition of men of special merit, wealth, possessions, political and social power, and prestige; a grandee also normally carried a title. The rank carried certain unique privileges, the most symbolically important of which was that a grandee had the right to wear his hat in the presence of the king. At first there were exactly 35 families granted this rank, but by the end of the sixteenth century, about 100 were so designated. After the *grandes,* came the *títulos* (titled nobles), men with titles such as *duque* (duke), *marqués* (marquis), *conde* (count), or *vizconde* (viscount).

In part 1 of *Don Quixote,* Don Fernando, prominent in the complicated love story that unfolds in several of the chapters between 23 and 47, is the second son of a grandee. In part 2 of the novel—in chapters 31–57 and again in 69–70—Don Quixote and Sancho are hosted at the castle, or lavish country estate, of an unnamed duke and duchess. These are the highest-ranking and most powerful people the knight and squire meet during their travels. They are also the people who are least sensitive to Don Quixote's and Sancho's humanity and who expend the most effort to entertain themselves at their expense (see chapter 5).

The next noble rank was that of *caballero* (gentleman; literally, a horseman). Unlike the grandee—a recent honorific created to gain support of the most powerful nobles of the land—*caballero* was a medieval term, originally created to recognize men of merit and religious standing in the ongoing civil war against the Muslims. Normally a *caballero* held at least fairly sizeable holdings of material goods, including, by definition, a horse. Often a distinction was made between *caballeros* who were members of one of the military orders and those who were not. Sometimes, titles (including lesser titles such as *señor* [lord]) were accorded to *caballeros* as a form of recognition and distinction.

An important facet of nobility was the existence of some military/ religious orders made up exclusively of *caballeros* or men of higher rank. Three great military orders—Calatrava (founded in 1158), Santiago (1170), and Alcántara (1176)—were established during the long war of reconquest. They were comparable to the Knights Templar, the Order of Malta (or Saint John), and other orders established to win back the Holy Land from the Muslims. Once the reconquest was complete, the orders became more a matter of social status than active military service for God and country. Members of these orders ostentatiously wore the insignia of their order on their garb in order to be recognized by everyone. There are several *caballeros* in *Don Quixote,* perhaps the most prominent being Grisóstomo, who dies of unrequited love (part 1, chs. 12–14); the frustrated lover Cardenio (part 1, chs. 23–47); the love-sick youth Don Luis (part 1, chs. 43–45); and Don Antonio Moreno in Barcelona (part 2, chs. 62–65). Almost without exception they have little to do but worry about love affairs and amuse themselves at Don Quixote's expense.

The lowest level of nobility was that of *hidalgo* (from *hijo de algo,* the son of something or someone), a title created by Fernando and Isabel in the late fifteenth century to acknowledge service and standing in the reconquest. It was a rank below a *caballero* and higher only than the *labrador* or *vulgo* (peasantry or common folk). In general, an *hidalgo cortesano* (courtesan) was more highly esteemed than an *hidalgo rural* (like Don Quixote). But by the late sixteenth century the title was often a hollow honor, in spite of the pretentious *ejecutoria* (letter officially recognizing nobility) carefully guarded by many *hidalgos*. Probably the most treasured benefit not extended to *hidalgos* was the right to place the honorific title of *Don* before their first names. Parenthetically, it should be noted here that a common but erroneous practice among English and American literary scholars (and other writers not familiar with Spanish language and culture) is to refer to Don Quixote as "the Don." *Don* (*Doña*, feminine) is an honorific title that goes with the first name of a Spanish nobleman holding the rank of *caballero* or above or lady of equivalent status; its use by Don Quixote is explicitly ironic and satiric. The word should not ever be used as a noun. There is undoubtedly some confusion here with the English noun *don*, in the sense of a head or tutor—the etymology of both words is the same: the Latin *dominus*—at Oxford or Cambridge; or, nowadays perhaps, with a Mafia boss. Referring to someone as "the Don" is approximately the equivalent of calling someone "the Sir."

The *hidalgo* was in some ways an anachronism in Renaissance society. *Hidalgos* often had little money or property but, because they were noble, they were above any kind of labor or commercial activity. The proud but impoverished *hidalgo* became a common stereotype, as can be seen in this figure's frequent appearances in literature. The two most famous examples are the ostentatiously proud and starving *hidalgo* from the anonymous picaresque novel *Lazarillo de Tormes* (1554) and the resident of a small village in La Mancha who becomes Don Quixote. The other interesting *hidalgo* in *Don Quixote* is Don Diego de Miranda who meets Don Quixote on the road and then invites him to his very comfortable home to meet his wife and son (part 2, chs. 16–18). Recall that the honorific "Don" is supposedly denied to *hidalgos,* yet the narrator comfortably uses it with reference to the affluent Don Diego. This is an illustration of how in actual practice the supposedly clear-cut boundaries break down.

Spain was proud to consider itself the most Christian (i.e., Catholic) of nations. Rome may have been the site of the Vatican and the heart of the Church, but that venerable old city was also viewed as a den of iniquity, corruption, and vice. Spain, on the other hand, exemplified (for the Spaniards) what a real Christian nation should be like: free of heretics, loyal to the Virgin, spreading God's word throughout the world, defending the faith against all manner of infidels, and favored by God in its military and colonizing missions. The presence and influence of the Church was universally manifest—in the great cathedrals, churches, convents, and monasteries that were constructed; in the glorious institution of the Inquisition; and in the priests and nuns who seemed to be everywhere. Actually, the clergy only constituted about two or three percent of the entire population, but even this was a figure greater than anywhere else in Europe at the time.

There are, of course, several clergymen in *Don Quixote*. The most important is Pero Pérez, the parish priest of the village where Don Quixote lives and one of his closest friends. He is a significant figure in part 1 of the novel, particularly important in the burning of his friend's library in part 1, chapter 6, and then takes on major importance when he leaves the village in order to find Don Quixote and make him return home (part 1, ch. 26). He is one of the most active and influential figures in the affairs of Cardenio, Dorotea, and that group of lovers (chs. 27–31 and at the inn) and again in the many events that take place in the inn of Juan Palomeque (chs. 32–47) and on the return trip home (chs. 47–52). He puts in brief appearances in part 2, but his role is much reduced. Until he takes the confession of the dying Alonso Quijano in the final chapter, his activities seem to be much more secular than sacred (Weiger, "Cervantes' Curious Curate"). Other religious figures are the friars of the order of Saint Benedict whom Don Quixote vilifies and attacks in part 1, chapter 4; the priests he attacks as they escort a dead body at night in part 1, chapter 19; the canon of Toledo who briefly accompanies the procession returning to the village and discusses literary matters with Pero Pérez and Don Quixote (part 1, chs. 47–52); and the pretentious house priest who admonishes Don Quixote at the home of the duke and duchess in part 2, chapter 31. It is possible to see some degree of satire and criticism of the clergy in nearly every one of these figures.

The great mass of the population, over 80 percent, was made up of peasants, that is, everyone who was not of the nobility or clergy. A number of terms were employed to refer to this large and varied population. The most common were *labrador* (farmer; a general term for those who worked the land), *villano* (villager), and *vulgo* (common people, with a connotation of ignorance and vulgarity). In the city there was the *hampa* (vagabonds; the underworld) and *pícaros,* as well as the *mercaderes* (merchants and shopkeepers) and the *artesanos* (tradesmen).

Powerful conservative forces attempted to make the social and economic lines clear-cut and obvious to everyone, but in fact the boundaries between categories were often blurred. A journeyman farm worker, for example, occupied the same category as—but stood at the opposite end of the spectrum from—a small but important group of wealthy *labradores,* whose economic condition was often far better than that of the lowest rank of the nobility, the *hidalgos,* even if their social status was inferior. This group of well-to-do, often fairly well educated, peasants clearly held a certain fascination for writers and others of the time. Good examples of such social types can be seen in first-rate plays such Lope de Vega's *Peribáñez* and Calderón de la Barca's *El alcalde de Zalamea,* works in which relationships between nobles and the daughters of well-to-do and politically influential *labradores* form the central action. In *Don Quixote* there are also a number of such figures: Juan Haldudo the Rich in part 1, chapter 4; Dorotea's father in part 1, chapter 28; Leandra's father in part 1, chapter 51; Camacho the Rich in part 2, chapters 20–21; and the unnamed wealthy peasant who lends money to the duke in part 2, chapter 48.

There are many other common folk throughout *Don Quixote,* too many to list in detail, but including a wide variety of innkeepers, servants, lackeys, maids, pages, merchants, mule drivers, mule boys, cattlemen, swineherds, goatherds, shepherds, farmers, soldiers, barbers, students, *pícaros,* prostitutes, criminals, bandits, and the inhabitants of Sancho's island. Although some of these characters display cruelty toward Don Quixote and Sancho or derive laughs at his expense, many of them are kind, gentle people, who come across as more decent than many of the frivolous nobles (see chapter 5).

It seems that Spaniards were constantly on the move throughout the country; supplies and material goods of all kinds were transported from one area to another. Much of the travel was basically north-south, especially between Madrid, the capital, and Seville, the commercial center, in southern Spain. Because there was a constant movement of soldiers, nobles, churchmen, merchants, muleteers (the truck-drivers of the day; recall that the transport union in modern America is called the "Teamsters," from the early mule teams such drivers used), rogues, and *pícaros,* from one place to another, a network of overnight stopping places was essential. The roads were dotted with wayside *ventas* (inns, the truck-stops and motels of the day), that provided welcome respite from the heat, dust, and inclement weather. Occasionally these inns were fairly comfortable places to take meals and spend the night, but more often they were spare, minimally-furnished, and noisy places, enlivened at night by the drinking, carousing, and gambling of the muleteers and other low-life types. It was normally expected that the travelers themselves would provide bed clothing and food, but exceptions could always be made for guests wealthy enough to pay for these extra services (see Madrazo, "Los caminos"). Good examples of life and customs in these inns can be seen in *Don Quixote* part 1, chapters 2–3, the inn where Don Quixote is dubbed a knight-errant; the inn of Juan Palomeque in part 1, chapters 16–17, 26, and 32–46, overall the most sustained and best example; the inn where Maese Pedro presents his puppet show, part 2, chapters 25–26; the inn in which Don Quixote learns of the publication of the book by Avellaneda, part 2, chapter 59; and the inn in which Don Quixote meets Alvaro Tarfe, part 2, chapters 71–72.

HONOR

One of the most important aspects of Spanish culture in the time of Cervantes was the noble obsession with honor *(honor, honra)*. A distinction was often, but not always, made between *honor* and *honra*. Most of the time the two terms were used interchangeably, but at times *honor* was employed to suggest the abstract quality itself, while *honra* tended to refer to the "honorable" opinion (i.e., *fama* or reputation) one was accorded by others. The exaggerated code of honor that played such an important part in Spanish life and literature can be traced back at least as far as the legal treatise of Alfonso X called the *Siete Partidas* (1256; *Seven Divisions*), where it was stated that a defamed man, even if innocent, was considered dishonored. A man's honor could be sullied by a mere rumor, and it was his duty to defend his reputation as a good Christian, a nobleman, a man above any sort of menial labor, a man of his word, a faithful husband, a protective father, and—above all—the proud possessor of a recognized virtuous wife and virginal daughter. A stain on one's honor often led to a sword fight and bloodshed. There was a spectacular (if rare) case of honor and revenge in Seville in 1555, in which a man proved his wife's adultery in court and received permission to punish both her and her lover. In a public act, he stabbed them to death and then removed his hat to show to all in attendance that he had no horns (the metaphorical symbol of cuckoldry, the state of having an adulterous wife). Although a woman's honor was sometimes referred to, women were seen primarily as the (naturally weak) vessel of their husbands' (or fathers') honor.

The embedded tale titled *Curioso impertinente* in part 1 of *Don Quixote* (chs. 33–35) provides a good illustration of how the matter of honor was perceived and discussed. In this story, Anselmo reveals to his close friend Lotario that he is obsessed with the idea of the faithfulness of his wife, Camila, and he asks Lotario to attempt to seduce her in order to prove her loyalty. His concern, in a nutshell, is his feeling "that a woman is virtuous only to the degree to which she is or is not solicited, and that the only woman who can be called virtuous is one who does not give in to promises, to gifts, to the tears, and to the continual advances of attentive lovers. After all, how can you be thankful and say that a woman is good, if no one is tempting her to be bad?" (part 1, ch. 33). Lotario argues at length against the proposition and warns his friend, "Because if I try to take away your honor, it is clear that I am also taking away your life, for the man without honor is worse off than one who is dead." He continues, saying that if Camila merely thinks Lotario is attempting to seduce her, she will consider that she has somehow given the impression that she can be tempted and this alone will make her consider herself dishonored, and therefore Anselmo will be dishonored:

> And this is why it is so often said that the husband of an adulterous woman—even though he does not know about it nor has he given her any reason to do anything improper, nor has it been in his power to do anything about it, for he has neither been careless nor negligent—is still referred to by a vile and reproachful name [i.e., cuckold]. And to some degree those who know of his wife's evil ways look at him with contempt, rather than with pity, seeing that on no account of his own but because of his evil companion's lust, he has had such misfortune. (part 1, ch. 33)

This passage perfectly illustrates the idea that honor (in the sense of *honra*) is not an inherent characteristic of a person but depends entirely on what others think of that individual: appearance is more important than reality itself. Furthermore, Lotario continues, the nature of the holy sacrament of matrimony reinforces this idea. For in marriage, although husband and wife

> have two souls, they have only one will. And it follows from this that, since the flesh of the wife is one with that of her husband, the stains that fall upon her, or the defects that appear in her, redound to the flesh of the husband, even if he has done nothing, as I have said, to bring such damage upon himself. For in the same way that a pain in the foot or any other member of the human body is felt throughout that body, since it is all one flesh, and the head feels the pain in the ankle even though it has not caused it, so the husband is a participant in the dishonor of his wife, because he is one flesh with her. And since all honor and dishonor in this world is born of flesh and blood, and the sins of the evil woman are of this sort, it is necessary that the husband share in them, and be held dishonored even though he doesn't know it. (part 1, ch. 33)

It should not pass without note here that all the discussion is about how a woman makes her husband dishonored. The misogyny behind the thinking displayed here is obvious, and it is reinforced throughout this tale (as it was throughout Spanish society in general). The unquestioned assumption was that a woman is a weak and imperfect animal, a fragile vessel easily broken. There were two simultaneous challenges to men in this context. First, a father or a husband had to do everything possible to guarantee his wife's fidelity and his daughter's virginity. But, second, there was the challenge of seducing someone's daughter or wife. Such a seduction would prove a man's successful masculine sexuality, his virility, and, at the same time, show that he can deceive and get the better of other men. This male rivalry was, at heart, little more than a simplistic macho competition. There is a reason why Don Juan Tenorio is called the *burlador* (trickster) and not the *seductor* (seducer) of Seville: deceiving the father or husband is as important as—if not even more important than—enjoying the sexual favors of the woman.

In a society where men are so preoccupied with reputation and lack concern for women as human beings, the role of women is a precarious one. Note that at no point in the discussion quoted previously is it even hinted that adultery on the part of a husband sullies the honor or reputation of his wife. The husband of an unfaithful wife might kill her in order to preserve his honor and make it known that he has valued his honor over his wife's life, but the wife of an unfaithful husband had no such recourse. If anything, the philandering husband was more esteemed by other men for his successful conquests, a mark of his virility.

As the story of the *Curioso impertinente* unfolds, the inevitable takes place: Lotario and Camila do indeed become lovers and, when they believe they are about to be found out, flee. In the end, Anselmo finds himself completely alone: "He reflected on how in an instant he found himself without his wife, without his friend, and without his servants, abandoned, it seemed, by the heaven above him, and, *worst of all, without his honor,* because he saw his perdition in Camila's absence" (part 1, ch. 35; emphasis added). It is one thing for a man to lose his wife, jewels, lifelong best friend, and servants, but the thing that matters most to him is his loss of honor.

What is astonishing, however, and what sets Cervantes apart from virtually every other writer who deals with the theme of an adulterous wife, is that Anselmo begins to write a letter absolving his wife of all blame: "A foolish and impertinent desire has cost me my life. If the news of my death should reach Camila's ears, let her know that I forgive her, because she was not obliged to perform miracles, nor should I have expected them of her; and since I am the architect of my own dishonor, there is no reason why . . . " (part 1, ch. 35). He dies before completing the letter, thus confirming Lotario's threat that taking away his honor is equivalent to taking away his life. But in recognizing that the fault is his, he is quite unique in the literature of the era (we should note, however, that in Cervantes' short story *El celoso extremeño,* the elderly husband again forgives what he believes to be his young wife's adultery in spite of his earlier attempts to keep her from having any contact with the world). A final note: Lotario and Camila also pay for their sin, as he dies in battle and she takes the veil and then also passes away. In many ways, the theme of honor, especially when emphasis is on *honra,* is a quintessential example of the reality-appearance theme discussed in the next chapter.

RENAISSANCE SPAIN: THE BLACK LEGEND

The great German scholar Jakob Burkhardt stated famously that Spain never had a Renaissance. Ever since that time, it has been assumed by many—tacitly or explicitly—that Spain was a backward country so dominated by ignorance, superstition, intolerance, and the Inquisition, that a "reawakening" of interest in the classics, humanism, and scientific thought was impossible. It is not uncommon in books on the European Renaissance even today to see virtually no mention of Spain. Such ignorance can be understood as a remnant of the infamous Black Legend, the widespread and exaggerated European myth of Spanish excess, cruelty, and stupidity, promoted from the sixteenth century through the eighteenth century, primarily by the English, French, and Dutch. Like most versions of the "Evil Empire" or Axis of Evil" approach to diplomacy, the aim of the propaganda campaign was to deprecate and demean the enemy in order to make one's own policies and history look enlightened by comparison.

As noted previously, in the sixteenth century Spain was the most powerful and most feared nation in Europe. Rising almost overnight from relative isolation and obscurity, Spain suddenly headed the most extensive empire in European history. The Spanish attempted to spread their hegemony literally throughout the world, and they were arguably the most successful colonizer of all time. In retaliation, her enemies fomented exaggerated (or even invented) tales of Spanish arrogance (by far the most frequent complaint, and it certainly was not without foundation), pride, presumption, fanaticism, intolerance, cruelty, and excess. The Spanish, it was said, had humiliated the refined Italians and viciously crushed Dutch nationalism during the periods of occupation of these countries. With the bloody instrument of the Inquisition, they had supposedly murdered countless thousands of innocent Protestants and

Jews. In their American colonies, they slaughtered the natives and forced them into slavery. (It is worth noting, however, that in Spanish America today there is a far greater percentage of native Americans in the general population than there is in the United States—which suggests that these peoples were not exterminated as efficiently as they were in the English American colonies—and there has never existed any concept of a "reservation" where they should be confined.) The fact that the Spanish had indeed been haughty, fanatical, excessive, cruel, and genocidal to some degree gave the necessary degree of truth that informed the legend. *But*—and this is a big *but*—neither the English, nor the French, nor the Dutch, nor the Portuguese were any better, a fact never mentioned by the perpetrators of the legend. No part of Europe at the time was particularly enlightened with respect to their enemies or magnanimous in their colonial enterprises. At the heart of the Black Legend was the idea that the Spanish were a primitive people whose typical activities were the cruel bullfight, the simple guitar, and the frenzied dancing of ignorant gypsies. Over the years, it became an article of faith that Spain failed as a political power because of inherent weaknesses in the Spanish character. To at least some degree this is a racist attitude, because Spain was the only nation in Europe with a substantial Muslim "racial" component.

To no small extent, the Spanish had themselves to blame for part of the growth of the Black Legend. The single most important indictment of Spanish practices in the New World colonies was that of Fray Bartolomé de Las Casas (1474–1566) in his book *Brevísima relación de la destrucción de las Indias* (1552; *Very Brief Relation of the Destruction of the Indies*; translated as *The Tears of the Indians*). Las Casas, a true humanitarian in the best sense of the word, documented (and exaggerated) the extermination, enslavement, and general mistreatment of the natives by the Spanish conquerors and colonists. This was picked up by Spain's enemies and disseminated far and wide as the absolute truth. The enormous popularity of Las Casas' book, which had more than 50 editions in at least 6 languages by the eighteenth century, helped "prove" that the Spanish were the worst of all possible religious fanatics and imperialists. Sadly, no writer in any other European nation criticized his own country with the enlightened concern for the welfare of native Americans as did Las Casas, and it is more than slightly ironic that the overall effect of his book, at least outside of Spain itself, was exactly the opposite of what he hoped to achieve.

By the eighteenth century, Spain was less a powerful enemy than a pathetic backwater, but the Black Legend continued, now with increased emphasis on the elements of stupidity and cultural barrenness. When Nicholas Masson de

Morvilliers wrote the article on Spain for the great French *Encyclopédie* (1751–65), under the general editorship of Denis Diderot (1713–84), he asked what sort of contribution Spain had ever made to the world. Then he answered his own question: None at all. The Spanish response to this attack on national pride inevitably featured Cervantes and *Don Quixote*. Bathed in emotional and rhetorical excess, these books, essays, and newspaper articles regularly trotted out the idealistic knight, along with his practical squire, skinny nag, and idealized lady, as one of mankind's greatest achievements. It was not an argument that convinced many people outside of Spain.

RENAISSANCE SPAIN: THE GOLDEN AGE

Arguably, the Spanish Renaissance may have been second only to that of Italy itself in splendor and accomplishment. One of the characteristics of the Renaissance is the rise of humanism, a profound interest in things human, as opposed to things divine. In Europe during the Middle Ages, emphasis was generally centered on the spirit and the afterlife more than on the body and the here-and-now. Thinking during this period was dominated by vertical imagery and metaphors; in Dante, for example, and in the pre-Renaissance period in general, the world was arranged along a vertical axis, with all movement either up toward heaven or down toward hell. But all this changed in the Renaissance, and imagery and metaphor shifted "to the horizontal lines, to the movement forward in real space and in historic time" (Bakhtin, *Rabelais and his World* 403). There was a gradual increase in concern with the history, nobility, dignity, and potential of humankind itself. Although it is often asserted that Roman Catholic dogmatism prevented any "rebirth" of the secular human spirit in Spain, that is simply not the case. The Renaissance first flourished and was more glorious and illustrious in Italy than anywhere else on the continent. Certain central aspects of humanist thought, such as scientific inquiry and religious renovation, were under consideration in other countries more prominently than they were in Spain. The Council of Trent (1545–64) further isolated Spain from more liberal intellectual currents. This congress of the heads of the Catholic Church was a (somewhat belated) response to the Lutheran Reformation. At this prolonged assemblage, dominated by Spanish Jesuit theologians, traditional Church dogma was reaffirmed in the face of the Protestant heresy, and a new stern, conservative, even reactionary, tone—the Counter Reformation *(Contrarreforma)*—was set for the Spanish Church as the official champion of orthodoxy in Europe.

But none of this necessarily leads to the conclusion that there was no such thing as a Renaissance in Spain.

Spanish humanism flourished to an extent greater than is often recognized. It was only natural that new ideas and new challenges to tradition should find particularly enthusiastic reception in heterodox quarters, which meant that the *converso* community was often the locus of humanistic activity in Spain. By the same note, it was the *converso* subgroup that was most suspect as a fertile ground for ideas and activities most objectionable to the reigning ideology. Censorship and repression led to the forced or voluntary exile and prolonged foreign residence of some of the finest original humanist scholars of the period: Juan de Valdés (ca. 1490–1541) and his brother Alfonso (ca. 1500–32), Benito Arias Montano (1527–98), and Luis Vives (1492–1540). Yet it is undeniable that a new spirit and a new attitude characterized the Spain in which Cervantes was born and lived.

Humanism was distinguished by an intense interest in history, classical erudition, and intellectual and literary scholarship. Important works of foreign humanists—especially the Italians Pietro Bembo (1470–1547), Baldassar Castiglione (1478–1529), Lorenzo Valla (1405–57); the Portuguese-Spanish-Italian León Hebreo [Leone Ebreo] (1460–1521); and the Dutch Erasmus of Rotterdam (1465–1536)—were translated into Spanish and received much admiration, attention, and imitation, particularly during the first half of the sixteenth century. The study of the Greek and Latin languages; the reading, translating, and commentary on classical authors; and the renewed interest in Platonism and Aristotelianism, all flourished to a notable degree. The great universities at Salamanca and Alcalá de Henares, among the finest in Europe, were major centers of humanist thought. Spain welcomed all intellectual, cultural, and artistic imports from Italy, to such an extent that Italy was the only European nation to have a significant, direct impact on Spanish thought. In addition to the humanists cited above, the following Italian writers were widely read, admired, and imitated in Spain: Pietro Aretino, Ludovico Ariosto, Matteo Bandello, Matteo Maria Boiardo, Giovanni Boccaccio, Giambattista Giraldi Cinthio, Dante Alighieri, Giovanni Della Casa, Marsilio Ficino, Giambattista Guarini, Niccolò Machiavelli, Pedro Mártir, Andrea Navaggiero, Francesco Petrarca, Jacopo Sannazaro, and Torquato Tasso.

Some of the most significant examples of genuine humanism in Spain are to be found in the works of Antonio de Nebrija (1442–1522) in classical philology and grammar; Juan de Mal Lara (1523–71) in proverbs; Juan de Valdés (ca. 1490–1541) in linguistics; Pero Mexía (1497–1551) in classical rhetoric; Alonso de López Pinciano (ca. 1547–ca. 1627) in aesthetics; Juan Huarte de San Juan (ca. 1530–ca. 1588) and Bartolomé de Las Casas (1474–1566) in medicine; and Fernán Pérez de Oliva (ca. 1494–1533) in philosophy. Humanist thought thoroughly informed the poetry of Spanish authors Garcilaso de la Vega (1501–36), Fray Luis de León (1527–91), Fernando de Hererra (1534–97), and others.

Cervantes' formal education was limited at best, but his early teacher and mentor was the humanist/Erasmian Juan López de Hoyos. Furthermore, Cervantes traveled and lived abroad, especially in Italy, and may well have gained much of his familiarity with humanist thought by reading some works directly in Italian. Clearly he had the sort of natural intellectual curiosity that aligned him sympathetically with humanism and humanistic concerns, as reflected in characters such as the protagonist of *El licenciado Vidriera*. In addition, Cervantes had a considerable knowledge of Greek, Roman, Italian, and Spanish literature, history, and culture in general. But at the same time he could be skeptical and critical. The portrait of the unnamed pedantic humanist scholar who accompanies Don Quixote and Sancho to the Cave of Montesinos in part 2, chapter 22, is typical. While we might not actually classify Cervantes as a humanist himself, the writer we know would not have been possible without the humanism of the Spanish Renaissance.

Art and science flourished in Spain to such an extent that it became known as the Golden Age. The Golden Age of Spanish culture and history in general, and literature in particular, is an ill-defined period of nearly two centuries including most of the sixteenth and seventeenth centuries. The beginning of the Golden Age might be designated by the landmark year of 1492, and it extended continuously until the year 1681, when Pedro Calderón de la Barca died (1600–81), the last great writer of the period. In the sixteenth century, under the reigns of Carlos V and Felipe II, Spain—with its estimated 10 million inhabitants—dominated European politics, warfare, the economy, and the arts as had no other country before it.

During the sixteenth and seventeenth centuries, Spanish art, intellectual inquiry, and literature flourished as it never had before and never would again. For example, in the late sixteenth century the center of painting gradually shifted from Italy to Spain, particularly in the work of El Greco (1541–1614) and Diego de Velázquez (1599–1660), but also including the notable achievements of José de Ribera (1591–1652), Francisco Zurbarán (1598–1664), Bartolomé Esteban Murillo (1617–82), and others. Velázquez is arguably the single most original and influential European painter before the twentieth century. His best-known and most-admired canvas is *Las meninas* (1656; *The Maids in Waiting*), a work whose technique has often been compared with that of Cervantes. In it, Velázquez himself is seen, standing before a canvas with palate and brush in hand, staring out at the viewer. In the distant background there is a mirror in which we can see reflected the faces of the king (Felipe IV) and queen, as though they were the subject of the canvas the artist is painting, standing where the viewer is located. Occupying the majority of the canvas, however, is the infanta Margarita and her maids-in-waiting, standing as though they, too, were looking out of the canvas at the royal couple (and the viewer). The painting is, in effect, a metapainting, foregrounding the act of its being painting. In this it cannot help but recall *Don Quixote,* a metafiction that foregrounds the act of its being written. There is no indication of any personal contact between Cervantes and Velázquez or of the latter's having read anything by the former, although Cervantes gained fame as a writer during Velázquez's teenage years, and it is probable that Velázquez knew Cervantes' works. But, whether or not the relationship is direct, the parallels are striking. Velázquez is to modern self-conscious painting what Cervantes is to modern self-conscious fiction.

SPANISH LITERATURE OF THE GOLDEN AGE

In many ways, the most significant evidence of the success of Renaissance thought in Spain can be found in literature. And the new spirit of the times was expressed first in lyric poetry. Courtier poet Juan Boscán (ca. 1487–1542) was encouraged in 1526 by the Venetian ambassador to the Spanish court to study and write poetry with the sort of meter used successfully by Italian poets. Whereas the metrical norm throughout the late Middle Ages in Spain had been the short octosyllabic (8-syllable) line that was the standard form for the ever-popular *romances* (ballads), the Italinate meter featured longer lines and more complex internal line structures. There were two major features of the new poetry, one metrical and one stylistic. The metrical innovation was the hendecasyllabic (11-syllable) line with a system of internal accents that provided the writer with more flexibility and permitted patterns of imagery and emphasis that the short lines could not accommodate. The sonnet form depends on this sort of line, and it is the sonnet that became the single most important type of poem to be written throughout the next two centuries.

The stylistic innovation was the adaptation of the conventions of imagery and metaphor perfected by Francesco Petrarca (1304–74) in his amorous sonnets to Laura, the most influential poetry of the Eruopean

Renaissance. Specifically, Petrarca (Petrarch in English) is famous for the series of metaphors he employed to describe the beauty of his beloved: hair of gold, eyes that glow like the sun, lips of coral, teeth of pearls, and so forth. Cervantes uses such imagery from time to time, usually in a parodic or satiric context sense (as in Don Quixote's description of Dulcinea in part 1, ch. 13). Boscán shared with his friend Garcilaso de la Vega the concepts involved in the new poetic meter, and Garcilaso took to it immediately.

Boscán was a good poet, but Garcilaso was a great one. His small body of work consists of about three dozen sonnets, five *canciones* (songs), three eclogues, and a handful of other poems. When Boscán's widow published *Las obras de Boscán y algunas de Garcilaso* (1543; *The Works of Boscán and Some by Garcilaso*), the book became an immediate best seller: within 10 years it was published over a dozen times in Spain and throughout the Spanish-speaking world in Europe. Garcilaso's poetry was immediately recognized as truly innovative and profound. The poet's early death in battle cut short what might have become an even greater career, but what he had done in a few short years was sufficient to secure his place in literature. By the latter part of the sixteenth century Garcilaso's work was published alone, and there were even two scholarly, annotated editions of his complete works, elevating him to the status of a contemporary classic. Garcilaso was by far the most revered and imitated poet of the Golden Age; he was undoubtedly Cervantes' most beloved poet and is cited and praised by him more often than is any other poet.

When the Italianate poetic meter was adopted in France (later than in Spain), it completely replaced traditional, indigenous forms. But such was not the case in Spain. For the next two centuries, new and old poetic forms coexisted, and most writers practiced both of them. The result was a varied and wide ranging corpus of poetic works, as poetry was read, recited, listened to, memorized, and quoted by members of all levels of society in the Golden Age. Especially popular was the traditional ballad or *romance,* and collections, known as *Romanceros,* of both traditional, anonymous ballads and newly-written ones by contemporary poets, including Cervantes (who had a reputation as one of a very few Spanish poets with a recognizable ballad style), were frequently published throughout the period.

Garcilaso was the first in a series of great Golden Age poets, of whom only five will be mentioned briefly here. The first is the *converso* poet, theologian, humanist, essayist, and professor at the University of Salamanca, Fray Luis de León. His odes on religious themes, particularly in praise of solitude and contemplation, are profoundly beautiful. San Juan de la Cruz

(1542–91) is another *converso* religious poet. Influenced by Santa Teresa de Jesús (1515–82), Juan de la Cruz wrote beautiful mystic poetry of the union of the soul with God, employing the metaphoric language of sexual union. There is no indication that Cervantes knew either Fray Luis or San Juan personally, but he was well connected with many of the poets of his generation (recall his laudatory list of poets in his *Viaje del Parnaso* and a similar list in *La Galatea*).

Cordoban priest Luis de Góngora (1561–1627) is often considered the greatest of all Spanish poets. His cultured, cultivated, artificial style (often called *culteranismo* or *gongorismo*) was both praised (as it was, lavishly, by Cervantes) and damned and satirized by his contemporaries (especially by Quevedo). He wrote hundreds of short, simple lyric poems and ballads in traditional Spanish meters, about 200 sonnets, and two long poems that are extremely difficult and complicated. Cervantes' disliked but admired rival Lope de Vega (1562–1635) may have gained fame primarily as a dramatist, but he was also a superb and prolific poet, writing both traditional lyrics and Italianate verse, and several long epic poems. Finally, the titled nobleman Don Francisco de Quevedo (1580–1645), with whom Cervantes always maintained good personal relations, was a courtier and multifaceted writer, excelling in both prose and poetry. He produced a large corpus of poetic works with contemplative, philosophical, amorous, scatological, political, and satiric themes.

Just as Spanish poetry flourished throughout the Golden Age, the theater came of age in the latter part of the sixteenth century and was the most public and most discussed of literary genres. As discussed briefly in chapter 1, drama in Spain evolved from primitive public performances to more highly-structured full-length plays presented in permanent semi-indoor structures known as *corrales* by the 1580s, and Cervantes was an important dramatic writer at that time. But Lope de Vega further refined the work of his predecessors and became the dominant figure in Spanish theater; overall, he was by far the most famous and most popular Spanish writer of his time. In fact, Lope was probably the most famous person in Spain, perhaps only after the king himself. He was so well known that there was a popular saying to praise something: *es de Lope* (it's by Lope). When he died, his nine-day funeral was the occasion for over 100 orations in remembrance, and his funeral procession was witnessed by thousands. His first biographer claimed that he had written some 1,800 plays, surely an exaggeration, as the figure of perhaps 1,000 (of which only half still survive) is more realistic. His formula of a work in three acts in polymetric verse, about 3,000 lines long in total, became standard. His themes and subject matter were wide-ranging: religious, mythological, pastoral, historical, novelistic, customs and manners (see Hayes, *Lope de Vega,* and McKendrick, *Playing the King*).

Lope de Vega inspired a long and rich theatrical tradition that had no equal in Europe—at least as far as quantity was concerned. In England, Shakespeare wrote a few dozen plays; in France, Corneille, Molière, and Racine wrote a few dozen among them; their contemporaries in England and France among them wrote, at best, hundreds. Lope alone wrote several hundreds, and so did several of his contemporaries. Thousands of original plays were performed in Golden Age Spain, where the theater was the most popular of arts.

Among Lope's dozens of contemporary dramatists, two particularly stand out. The first is Tirso de Molina (ca. 1580–1648), pseudonym of the Mercedarian priest Gabriel Téllez, who wrote about 400 dramatic works. He is best-known as the (probable) author of *El burlador de Sevilla (The Trickster of Seville),* a play featuring the legendary Don Juan Tenorio, the irresistible lover who seduces hundreds of women, a character whose fame rivals that of Don Quixote. Cervantes most likely knew the young Tirso and alludes to him in his *Viaje del Parnaso.* Tirso, on the other hand, admired Cervantes' short fictions and once referred to him as "our Spanish Boccaccio" (Tirso de Molina 236; translation mine).

Pedro Calderón de la Barca, author of over 100 plays himself, was the last of the great writers of the Golden Age, and the year of his death is often considered the end point for that era. Calderón's philosophical masterpiece, *La vida es sueño* (1636; *Life Is a Dream*), bloody honor plays, extravagant court operatic productions, and *autos sacramentales* (one-act allegorical plays on the theme of the sacrament of communion) are superb theatrical pieces. He was too young to have had any meaningful contact with Cervantes, but he was clearly an admirer of elderly novelist's work. In 1637 he staged a play in the royal palace with the title of *Don Quijote de la Mancha* (also cited as *Los disparates de don Quijote—Don Quixote's Nonsense*), but unfortunately this work has been lost. Several other of Calderón's works either feature Quixote-like characters or make specific mention of Cervantes' novel and characters.

If anything, it is in the area of prose fiction that the literary achievement of Golden Age Spain is most original. Spanish works were the models for subsequent chivalric, sentimental, pastoral, and adventure romance throughout Europe. Similarly the novel in dialogue and the picaresque novel, together with *Don Quixote,* laid down the foundations for the German, French, and English novel which would develop later. Only in the area of short fiction did Spain follow the lead set by another country: the earlier Renaissance Italian tradition best exemplified by Giovanni Boccaccio (1313–75), Mateo Bandello (ca. 1485–ca. 1561), and Giambattista Giraldi Cinzio (1504–73).

Chivalric romance was not as well developed in the Spanish Middle Ages as it was in England, France, and Germany. The best-known indigenous romance of chivalry in Spain was the anonymous fourteenth-century *Amadís de Gaula,* only a small fragment of which survives. But in the final decade of the fifteenth century Garci Rodríguez de Montalvo (ca. 1440–ca. 1505) took the primitive *Amadís* and revised and modernized it as *Los cuatro libros del virtuoso caballero Amadís de Gaula (The Four Books of the Virtuous Knight Amadís de Gaula).* He published this book in about the mid-1490s, but no copy of that edition remains; the earliest known edition is that of 1508. The book was a huge success, becoming probably the single most read fiction of the sixteenth century, both at home and abroad. Translated into French (1541–43), Italian (1546), German, (1569–71), English (1590–91 partial; 1619 complete), and Dutch (1598 partial; 1619 complete), *Amadís* was read and admired throughout the continent and even became a sort of manual of the perfect courtier in seventeenth-century France (see Pierce, *Amadís de Gaula,* and O'Connor, *"Amadis de Gaule"*). Montalvo's *Amadís* underwent at least 19 printings in sixteenth-century Spain, where it was read by an extraordinarily high percentage of the literate public and where it inspired both a series of sequels (eventually there were 12 volumes in the *Amadís* series) and numerous other chivalric romances. Among the latter, noteworthy are the four romances that comprise the *Palmerín* cycle, of which the second, *Palmerín de Inglaterra* (1547), by Francisco de Moraes, is the best; and individual romances such as *Belianís de Grecia* (1547) by Jerónimo Fernández and *Espejo de príncpes y caballeros* (1555; *Mirror of Princes and Knights*) by Diego de Ordóñez de Calahorra. Romances of chivalric adventure were the most popular reading in Spain in the first half of the sixteenth century, and these books were published or reprinted at the rate of about one per year for the whole century (see Eisenberg, *Romances of Chivalry*).

It is interesting to note also the importance these books played in the conquest of the New World. Bernal Díaz del Castillo (1492–1582), in his *Verdadera historia de la conquista de la Nueva España* (not published until 1632; *The True History of the Conquest of New Spain*), refers to the Aztec capital of Tenochtitlán as resembling an enchanted city straight out of the pages of a chivalric romance. The region of Patagonia was named after a tribe of monsters in Francisco de Enciso Zárate's *Primaleón*

(1533), and California was named after a kingdom of Amazons led by Queen Califa in Montalvo's own sequel to *Amadís,* titled *Las sergas de Esplandián* (1510; *The Deeds of Esplandián* [son of Amadís]). It was the reading of these chivalric romances that drove Don Quixote mad and thus provide the point of departure for Cervantes' novel (see the next chapter for more on the profound influence this genre had on Cervantes). In addition to Cervantes, the Catholic Monarchs, Carlos V, Teresa de Avila, and Ignacio de Loyola were among the famous fans of the genre.

Late in the fifteenth century, Diego de San Pedro published two sentimental romances, of which the most popular was *Cárcel de Amor* (1492; *Prison of Love*). This romance became the prototype of the genre (and may be considered the first epistolary novel in European literature, preceding those of Samuel Richardson by some two and a half centuries), and it enjoyed enormous popularity both in Spain and throughout Europe, especially in France and Italy. It was published over a dozen times in France as a bilingual text and was often used in the study of the Spanish language (Whinnom, *Diego de San Pedro*). The tragic story of love and sacrifice is told primarily in an exchange of letters, and, interestingly, the author makes himself a major character in this early experiment with metafiction. Cervantes never mentions San Pedro's works but was almost certainly familiar with them.

Inspired in part by the pastoral love poetry of Garcilaso de la Vega and by the 1549 translation of *La Arcadia* by Jacopo Sannazaro (1458–1530), the Portuguese Jorge de Montemayor wrote in Spanish the pastoral romance that was to become the prototype of the genre: *La Diana* (1559), a work that is perhaps the finest expression of the pastoral in fictional prose in European Renaissance letters. Numerous sequels and imitations soon followed, and these stylized tales of unrequited love among tearful shepherds soon replaced chivalric romances as the most popular reading material in Spain in the second half of the sixteenth century. Cervantes' first published book was *La Galatea* (1585), a pastoral romance, and pastoral themes are found throughout his work, including *Don Quixote.*

Greek romances of adventure (sometimes called Byzantine romances) featuring young lovers who overcome hardships, separation, and near scrapes with death, but who are eventually united in marriage, were translated into Spanish and other European languages during the sixteenth century. The best known of them was the *History of Theogenes and Chariclea* (better known simply as *The Ethiopian History*) of Heliodorus (third century CE), which appeared in 1554 in a translation based on a French version of the romance. Cervantes knew either the 1581 reprint of this work or the 1587 original translation of Fernando de Mena, and in the prologue to his own *Trabajos de Pesiles y Sigismunda* (1617) he states that his book "dares to compete with Helodorus" (translation mine). Cervantes' novel was then influential on a few later writers such as Lope de Vega in his *Peregrino en su patria* (1618; *The Pilgrim in His Own Land*).

These chivalric, sentimental, pastoral, and adventure fictions are all more romances than novels. The romance-novel distinction is made most often and most clearly in English, as all the major continental languages have a single term that covers both types of fiction: Spanish *novela* (although in Cervantes' day this term, from the Italian *novella,* meaning something new or novel, was used only for shorter fictions; recall Cervantes' *Novelas ejemplares;* long fictions tended to be called *historias,* or just *libros*), French *roman,* Italian *romanzo,* and German *Roman.* Note that the Spanish could not use the term *romance* for prose fictions, as that word was used for poetic ballads. Romance and novel are not by any means two clear-cut, easily defined, binary opposites; rather, it is a matter of emphasis. Almost all romance consists to a greater or lesser degree of novelistic elements, while almost all novels include romance elements. That said, however, it is still possible and advantageous to distinguish between two prototypes of prose fiction (see Mancing, "Prototypes of Genre"). The first, romance, with its roots in antiquity, consists of stories about noble and beautiful young characters who fall in love, suffer difficulties and separations, have marvelous adventures, and eventually are reunited and marry. Later medieval and Renaissance variants preserve large elements of the ancient romance while adapting the love story to specific situations, such as the world of chivalry or the pastoral setting.

The novel, on the other hand, is harder to define—essentially a novel is all that which romance is not. A novel tends to be more realistic, more comical, more self-conscious, more dialogic, more protean (see Bakhtin's extraordinary discussion of the "two stylistic lines," basically romance and novel, in the final section of his most famous essay, "Discourse in the Novel," titled "The Two Stylistic Lines of Development in the European Novel" in his *Dialogic Imagination,* 366–422). Like *Don Quixote,* it is often written specifically in opposition to (and as a satire or parody of) romance; its characters tend to be individuals rather than types. Romances tend to be relatively easy to categorize generically: adventure, chivalric, sentimental, pastoral, and so forth. Novels are harder to categorize and the categories tend to be larger, less well defined, more ambiguous, more amorphous, more generally associated with broad literary movements through the centuries: comic, romantic, realist, naturalist, psychological, modernist, postmodern, and so forth. *Amadís* is romance while *Don Quixote* is a novel, and it is impossible to conceive of them as being the same type of fiction. Cervantes could not have written *Don Quixote* unless he had a clear sense of a difference between novel and romance (Riley, "Cervantes: A Question of Genre," and *Don Quixote*).

It is important to keep the novel-romance distinction in mind as we consider types of early novels written in Golden Age Spain. The first is the dialogued novel, of which the prototype is *La Celestina* (1499) by Fernando de Rojas (ca. 1474–1541). Often considered the greatest work of Spanish literature after *Don Quixote,* its full original title was *Comedia de Calisto y Melibea (Comedy of Calisto and Melibea),* but from the beginning it was popularly known by the name of the most original and powerful character in the work, the old bawd Celestina. The first version consisted of 16 acts in prose, clearly preserving the form of theater, but the work was never intended to be acted on stage. Many scholars prefer to understand *La Celestina* as drama, rather than as novel; it is, after all, written in dialogue form. The problem with this is that as written it is far too long to actually be performed in a theater. In fact, it has never been performed on stage in its original form, only in abridged or condensed adaptations—exactly like what is done with novels when they are adapted to the theater. By 1502, the text had been expanded to 21 acts and the title was revised to *Tragicomedia de Calisto y Melibea (Tragicomedy of Calisto and Melibea).* The work takes place on two levels, that of the upper-class noble lovers named in the title, and that of Calisto's lower-class servants, together with Celestina and her stable of prostitutes. *Celestina* is clearly not in any way a romance, as the work's individualized characters, realistic dialogue, urban setting, and contemporary tone are all much more novelistic. There were multiple sequels to *Celestina* and several other dialogued fictions (including Cervantes' *Coloquio de los perros*) were written in Golden Age Spain. This generic hybrid was developed more in Spain than in other countries. Like everyone else, Cervantes appears to have revered Rojas' work, referring to it in the prefatory poems to part 1 of *Don Quixote* as "a book, in my opinion, that is divi[ne] / even if it includes more the hum[an]" (see Dunn, *Fernando de Rojas;* Corfis and Snow, *Fernando de Rojas and "Celestina";* and the journal *Celestinesca*).

Celestina aside, probably the greatest fictional innovation in Renaissance Spain was the picaresque novel. The first work in the genre is the anonymous short novel *La vida de Lazarillo de Tormes y de sus fortunas y adversidades (The Life of Lazarillo de Tormes and of his Misfortunes and Adversities),* which was published in four separate cities in 1554, suggesting that there was an earlier edition that has been lost. *Lazarillo* is the story of an orphan who serves a series of masters, lives by his wits, struggles against hunger, and winds up married to the mistress of an archpriest. A satire on many elements in society, this artfully constructed tale is also the first novel to have the key word *vida* (life) in its title and the first to begin with the first-person pronoun *yo* (I). Immediately popular, the figure of the boy who guides a blind beggar became a generic noun: such a guide is a *lazarillo*. The novel was placed on the 1559 *Index of Prohibited Books* and in 1574 was published in a sanitized version as *Lazarillo castigado (Lazarillo Chastised)*.

After a half-century with no significant continuation or imitation (in 1555 there appeared a silly anonymous sequel in which Lazarillo leaves home, is in a shipwreck, and becomes a tuna fish). Later, in 1620, in Paris, exiled Protestant Spaniard Juan de Luna published the *Segunda parte de la vida de Lazarillo de Tormes* (1620; *Second Part of the Life of Lazarillo de Tormes*), both a continuation of the original *Lazarillo* and a criticism of the 1555 sequel; it is a sometimes brilliant, mordant religious satire. Before this, however, there appeared in 1599 the second picaresque novel and what was probably the most popular fiction of the period: *Primera parte del Pícaro Guzmán de Alfarache (First Part of the Pícaro Guzmán de Alfarache)* by Mateo Alemán. Several times longer than *Lazarillo, Guzmán* is the auto-biography of a criminal who writes from the galleys. The text consists of a blend of first-person narrative and didactic, digressive commentary, spiced with illustrative anecdotes and some long embedded narratives (Mancing, "Embedded Narration"). The book was so frequently read and talked about that it was known simply as *El Pícaro*. It was *Guzmán* that sparked the vogue of picaresque fictions that were the most popular fictional genre in the first half of the seventeenth century. After the appearance of a poor sequel by a rival in 1602, Alemán published part 2 of his novel, with the subtitle of *Atalaya de la vida humana (Watchtower of Human Life)*, in 1604. *Guzmán* was translated into all major European languages, beginning with James Mabbe's translation into English (1622–23), and it inspired a number of versions, sequels, and imitations in English, French, Dutch, and German (for more on the diffusion of *Guzmán* and other Spanish picaresque novels in Europe, see Bjornson, *The Picaresque Hero*). Cervantes only cites and discusses *Guzmán* on one occasion, in the story *La ilustre fregona*. How-ever, in *Don Quixote* part 1, chapter 22, there is a character named Ginés de Pasamonte—clearly modeled on Guzmán—a criminal condemned to the galleys who has written an autobiography that he says is better than *Lazarillo de Tormes* or any other work in that genre.

Of the 20 or so picaresque novels that followed, the most famous is the *Vida del Buscón llamado don Pablos* (written by about 1605, published in 1626; *Life of the Swindler Named Don Pablos*) by Francisco de Quevedo. Usually considered the third canonical picaresque novel, the *Buscón* features the author's spectacular prose style, brutal and explicit reality, and cynicism about lower class aspirations to rise in society. The last great exemplar of the genre, and one of the best of all, is *Vida y hechos de Estebanillo González, hombre de buen humor* (1646; *Life and Deeds of Estebanillo González, Man of Good Humor*), the semi-historical, perhaps (at least partially) legitimately autobiographical, story of a dwarf and court jester. Overall, the picaresque novel is the first novelistic type that consistently tells a life of an individual, rather than recounting someone's adventures, and that displays a generic self-consciousness. It is also the first sustained genre of first-person autobiographical narrative and thus a major predecessor of (and influence on) the genre of (nonfictional) autobiography that flourished beginning in the eighteenth century (Mancing, "The Protean Picaresque"). Like *Celestina,* the picaresque fictions are novels and not romances. The genre was extraordinarily popular both in Spain and throughout Europe. Cervantes never wrote a full-fledged picaresque novel (he never wrote a novel with a first-person narrator), but four of his short fictions are about *pícaros* and explicitly relate themselves to the genre.

Adaptations, sequels, and imitations of the Spanish picaresque novels are to be found at the headwaters of nearly every European national tradition of the novel. Among the major works directly inspired by the *Lazarillo, Guzmán* and others, are Johann Jakob Christoffel von Grimmelshausen's *Simplicissimus* (1669), Alain-René Lesage's *Gil Blas* (1715, 1924, 1735), and Daniel Defoe's *Moll Flanders* (1722), all fundamental early fictions in their national literature. In more modern times, works like Mark Twain's *Huckleberry Finn* (1885), Saul Bellow's *The Adventures of Augie March* (1953), and Thomas Mann's *Adventures of Felix Krull, Confidence Man* (1954) are all clearly related to the picaresque. There is no way to exaggerate the importance of the Spanish picaresque tradition in the formation, history, and practice of the novel (see Maiorino, *The Picaresque,* and Dunn, *Spanish Picaresque Fiction*).

Spain was the major source of new fiction throughout Europe for at least the first two centuries following the invention and diffusion of the printing press (the first known printing press in Spain was that of Lambert Palmart in Valencia in 1474, two years before William Caxton established the first English printing press in Westminster; by the end of the fifteenth century there were at least 25 presses in Spain and over 700 books had been printed—about half that many were printed in England during the same period). Works like San Pedro's *Cárcel de Amor,* Montalvo's *Amadís,* Rojas's *Celestina,* the anonymous *Lazarillo,* Alemán's *Guzmán,* Montemayor's *Diana,* and Cervantes' major fictions—*Don Quixote, Novelas ejemplares,* and *Persiles*—were translated into other European languages, frequently had multiple printings, and were much admired and imitated. Meanwhile, virtually nothing from other European literatures, except Italian, was translated into Spanish.

Many of the romances and novels discussed above were international bestsellers on a scale that dwarfs the later and more limited success of eighteenth-century works like Samuel Richardson's *Pamela* (1740). From the early sixteenth century to near the end of the seventeenth, most of the original fiction read in Europe came from Spain. *Don Quixote* was the single most published, translated, read, praised, and imitated work of literature in all of Europe in the seventeenth and eighteenth centuries.

It may appear that much of this section has been overstated in superlatives, but Spain's was the single most brilliant national literature of Europe in the sixteenth and seventeenth centuries. It is, after all, for good reason that this was called the Golden Age. It had no parallel in other literatures or in later Spanish literature.

WORKS CITED

Bakhtin, M. M. *The Dialogic Imagination: Four Essays.* Ed. Michael Holquist. Trans. Caryl Emerson and Michael Holquist. Austin: U of Texas P, 1981.

———. *Rabelais and His World.* Trans. Hélène Iswolsky. Bloomington: Indiana UP, 1984.

Bjornson, Richard. *The Picaresque Hero in European Fiction.* Madison: U of Wisconsin P, 1977.

Corfis Ivy A., and Joseph Thomas Snow, eds. *Fernando de Rojas and "Celestina": Approaching the Fifth Centenary: Proceedings of an International Conference in Commemoration of the 450th Anniversary of the Death of Fernando de Rojas, Purdue University, West Lafayette, Indiana, 21–24 November 1991.* Madison: Hispanic Seminary of Medieval Studies, 1993.

Costa Fontes, Manuel da. *The Art of Subversion in Inquisitorial Spain: Rojas and Delicado.* West Lafayette, IN: Purdue UP, 2005.

Dunn, Peter N. *Fernando de Rojas.* Boston: Twayne, 1975.

———. *Spanish Picaresque Fiction: A New Literary History.* Ithaca: Cornell UP, 1993.

Eisenberg, Daniel. *Romances of Chivalry in the Spanish Golden Age.* Newark: Juan de la Cuesta, 1982.

Guilmartin, John Francis. *Gunpowder and Galleys: Changing Technology and Mediterranean Warfare at Sea in the Sixteenth Century.* Cambridge: Cambridge UP, 1974.

Hayes, Francis C. *Lope de Vega.* New York: Twayne, 1967.

Hess, Andrew. "The Battle of Lepanto and Its Place in Mediterranean History." *Past and Present* 57 (1962): 55–73.

Madrazo, Santos. "Los caminos en el tiempo de *El Quijote.*" In *La ciencia y El "Quijote."* Ed. José Manuel Sánchez Ron. Barcelona: Crítica, 2005. 69–95.

Maiorino, Giancarlo, ed. *The Picaresque: Tradition and Displacement.* Minneapolis: U of Minnesota P, 1996.

Mancing, Howard. "Embedded Narration in *Guzmán de Alfarache.*" In *"Ingeniosa Invención": Essays on Golden Age Spanish Literature for Geoffrey L. Stagg in Honor of His Eightieth Birthday.* Ed. Ellen M. Anderson and Amy R. Williamsen. Newark, DE: Juan de la Cuesta, 1999. 69–99.

———. "The Protean Picaresque." In *The Picaresque: Tradition and Displacement.* Ed. Giancarlo Maiorino. Minneapolis: U of Minnesota P, 1996. 273–91.

———. "Prototypes of Genre in Cervantes' *Novelas ejemplares.*" *Cervantes* 20.2 (2000): 127–50.

McKendrick, Melveena. *Playing the King: Lope de Vega and the Limits of Conformity.* London: Tamesis, 2001.

O'Connor, John H. *"Amadis de Gaule" and Its Influence in Elizabethan Literature.* New Brunswick: Rutgers UP, 1970.

Pierce, Frank. *Amadís de Gaula.* Boston: Twayne, 1976.

Riley, E. C. "Cervantes: A Question of Genre." In *Medieval and Renaissance Studies on Spain and Portugal in Honour of P. E. Russell.* Ed. F. W. Hodcroft et al. Oxford: Society for the Study of Mediaeval Languages and Literatures, 1981. 69–85.

———. *Don Quixote.* London: Allen and Unwin, 1986.

Strauss, Leo. *Persecution and the Art of Writing.* Glencoe, IL: Free P, 1952.

Tirso de Molina. *Cigarrales de Toledo.* Ed. Luis Vázquez Fernández. Madrid: Castalia, 1996.

Weiger, John G. "Cervantes' Curious Curate." *Kentucky Romance Quarterly* 30 (1983): 87–106.

Whinnom, Keith. *Diego de San Pedro.* New York: Twayne, 1974.

Chapter 5

IDEAS

Don Quixote is a rich and complex work, impossible to assess in any simplistic way. In this chapter, some of Cervantes' major ideas and concepts will be examined, beginning with a brief review of many of the writers and works that most influenced the conception and creation of *Don Quixote*.

CERVANTES: LITERARY INFLUENCES

Don Quixote has been called a compendium, or anthology, of Spanish Renaissance literature, in the sense that almost every type of poetry, theater, and prose fiction written in Spain in the sixteenth century has some place in the novel. No attempt will be made here to prove such a case in detail, but it is clear that Cervantes knew well the literary traditions that preceded him and reflected many of them in his novel. Cervantes' formal education was uneven, but he was obviously very widely read and had a profound intellectual curiosity. Influence in literature is notoriously hard to document, as it is often best seen in subtle tonalities and patterns of imagery. On the other hand, what many want to see as a direct influence is sometimes no more than coincidence or independent similarity. In this chapter, attention will be called to some of the more obvious influences on the creation of *Don Quixote*.

First, it must be noted that Cervantes had an extensive background in Greek and Roman literature, history, mythology, and culture. Classical characters are often alluded to or actually appear in his works, usually with burlesque or comic connotations. Apollo and Mercury, for example, are actual characters in his *Viaje del Parnaso*. In a great comic scene in *Don Quixote* part 2, chapter 56, Cupid, son of Venus and the boy god of love, takes advantage of an opportunity to triumph over the soul of a lackey and makes Tosilos fall in love by shooting him through the heart with a golden arrow two yards long. Among the classical writers who appear to have most influenced Cervantes are the Greeks Homer and Heliodorus, and the Romans Virgil, Ovid, and Apuleius. Cervantes also knew the Bible very well, as biblical allusions, paraphrasings, and citations are frequent in *Don Quixote* and his other works (Monroy, *La Biblia en el "Quijote"*).

The most significant influences on Cervantes, however, are Spanish. First of all, *Don Quixote* would not be possible without the romances of chivalry, which Cervantes, like his protagonist, had read extensively and almost knew by heart. *Amadís de Gaula* was the most important of these romances for Cervantes. The late *Belianís de Grecia* (1547) by Jerónimo Fernández (?–ca. 1579), a work that initiated the second, more extravagant, wave of chivalric romances, ranks second in importance, and at least a dozen other romances influence the novel in some way. The names Don Quixote invents, his consciously archaic chivalric rhetoric, his descriptions of chivalric plots and adventures, his frequent invocation of his lady, his transformation of prosaic reality according to the models in his favorite romances, and much more, are all in accord with his chivalric vision. Don Quixote's concept of chivalry and his understanding of the romances of chivalry are the point of departure for everything else in the novel.

Cervantes knew the pastoral romance tradition well, was intimately familiar with *La Diana* and other works in the genre, and had written his own pastoral tale in *La Galatea*. Don Quixote's speech on the Golden Age (part 1, ch. 11), the episode involving the pseudo-shepherds Grisóstomo and Marcela (part 1, ch. 12–14), the story of Leandra (part 1, ch. 51), the shepherds of the feigned Arcadia (part 2, ch. 58), and the plans made by Don Quixote and Sancho to take up the pastoral life (part 2, ch. 67), are some of the most obvious expressions of the pastoral in *Don Quixote,* and, implicitly as well as explicitly, the pastoral informs much of the novel (Finello, *Pastoral Themes and Forms*).

The picaresque novel fascinated Cervantes, and in *Don Quixote* the galley slave Ginés de Pasamonte (part 1, ch. 22), who later becomes the puppeteer Maese Pedro (part 2, ch. 26), is a *pícaro*. *Lazarillo de Tormes* and *Guzmán de Alfarache* are the only picaresque novels that were in print when *Don Quixote* was published in 1605, but even at that early point in time, in the discussion between Don Quixote and Ginés about the latter's autobiography, Cervantes recognized that a literary genre was taking shape (Guillén, "Genre and Countergenre").

It is clear that Cervantes knew the tradition of romanticized historical fiction about Muslim Spain. In part 1, chapter 5, he has Don Quixote identify with Abindarráez, the Muslim hero of the popular anonymous sixteenth-century short story titled *El Abencerraje y la hermosa Jarifa, (The Abencerraje and the Beautiful Jarifa)*. Another obvious prose influence on Cervantes is the sequel to *Don Quixote* by Alonso Fernández de Avellaneda. Cervantes repeatedly pokes fun at his rival's book, changing the course of Don Quixote's travels (part 2, ch. 59), describing how devils in hell play tennis with the book (part 2, ch. 70), and making one of the principal characters in that novel sign an affidavit that Avellaneda's Don Quixote and Sancho are imposters (part 2, ch. 72).

Cervantes most admired the poetry of Garcilaso de la Vega, and he cites, paraphrases, and parodies Garcilaso's famous work on several occasions in *Don Quixote* (Rivers, "Cervantes y Garcilaso"). As a poet himself, and as a writer active in meetings of literary academies, Cervantes had contact with and may have been influenced by a number of other poets, particularly Francisco de Herrera, Luis de Góngora (1561–1627), the Argensola brothers Bartolomé (1562–1631) and Lupercio (1559–1613), and, of course, Lope de Vega. One of the most profound poetic influences on Cervantes, however, was the vast—and vastly popular—corpus of traditional *romances,* or ballads (Eisenberg, "The *Romance*"). The very first words of the first chapter of the 1605 *Don Quixote* are "En un lugar de la Mancha" ("In a village of La Mancha"), an octosyllabic line from a popular ballad.

Not only did Cervantes write extensively for the theater, he also dramatized in a theatrical fashion many key scenes in *Don Quixote,* such as Camila's feigned suicide attempt in order to deceive her husband (part 1, ch. 34); the staged enchantment of Don Quixote by the priest and barber (part 1, ch. 46); Maese Pedro's puppet show (part 2, ch. 26); and many of the events that take place at the palace of the duke and duchess (part 2, chs. 30–57) (Syverson-Stork, *Theatrical Aspects*). In part 2, chapter 11, Don Quixote and Sancho have an encounter with an acting troupe traveling from one village to another dressed in costume. In addition, the theater is discussed on occasion by characters such as the priest Pero Pérez, the canon of Toledo, and Don Quixote (part 1, ch. 48).

Two important nonliterary influences on Cervantes were religious reformer Desiderius Erasmus of Rotterdam, discussed briefly in chapter 1, and the Spanish physician Juan Huarte de San Juan. Huarte's influential medical treatise *Examen de ingenios para las ciencias* (1575; *Scientific Examination of Men's Wits*) set forth a classic statement of the theory of bodily humors that was one of the cutting-edge medical theories of the time. If we conceive of Don Quixote's madness as consisting in an imbalance among these humors, we might say that his brain is hot and dry from his excessive reading and lack of sleep, which leads to a predominantly choleric personality, together with an imaginative and inventive intelligence. But if choler is dominant early in the novel, by the time of Don Quixote's death melancholy becomes more prominent (Green, "El *ingenioso* hidalgo"). A third writer who influenced Cervantes was Alonso López Pinciano, whose work on aesthetics will be discussed later in the section on literary theory.

Cervantes drew heavily upon a vast store of folklore to create characters such as Sancho Panza and others in *Don Quixote*. There are, in fact, over a dozen folktales, folk characters, and folk scenes in the novel (Barrick, "The Form and Function of Folktales"). As Mikhail Bakhtin has studied at length *(Rabelais and His World),* an extremely important part of the folk tradition of the Middle Ages and Renaissance was the celebration of carnival and the carnivalesque nature of everyday life. Sancho, again, best represents the carnivalesque tradition of mockery, role reversal, bawdy humor, and reveling in food and drink. And Cervantes may well have had first-hand contact with the Arabic tradition of storytelling, especially during his years of captivity in Algiers. The figure of the Arabic historian Cide Hamete Benengeli, supposed author of the adventures of Don Quixote and Sancho, could have been inspired by this tradition (see chapter 1).

Among foreign influences, several Italian writers were of undeniable importance to Cervantes, who was stationed in Italy during his years in the army, considered Naples the most beautiful city in the world, and probably spoke and read Italian quite well. First and foremost among the Italian influences are the epic chivalric poems of Matteo Maria Boiardo (1441–94) and, especially, Ludovico Ariosto (1474–1533). Ariosto's *Orlando Furioso* (first edition 1516, complete edition 1532; *The Madness of Orlando*) was one of major importance for Cervantes in the writing of *Don Quixote,* not far behind *Amadís de Gaula* itself. Allusions to, paraphrasings of, and quotations from *Orlando Furioso,* and references to its major characters (Orlando, Angelica, Mambrino, Reinaldos, Brunelo, Sacripante, and others) are found throughout Cervantes' novel. Ariosto also provided a model of the intermingling of noble chivalry and burlesque humor, the marvelous and the real, and the lofty and the prosaic (Hart, *Cervantes and Ariosto*). Other important Italian influences on Cervantes include the lyric poetry of Francesco Petrarca (see chapter 4) and *Morgante Maggiore* (1483; *Morgante the Great*), the work of Luigi Pulci (1432–84), as well as the short story tradition represented by the previously mentioned Boccaccio, Bandello, and Giraldi Cinzio. The stories of Cardenio-Dorotea-Fernando-Luscinda, the *Curioso impertinente,* and Leandra's tale, all reflect the Italian tradition of short fictions.

There is not a single English or French author whose work noticeably influenced Cervantes' *Don Quixote.* English and French themes and characters, however, play a significant role in the form of characters from the Arthurian chivalric tradition, such as Arthur, Guinevere, Lancelot, and Merlin, and from the Carolingian chivalric tradition, especially Charlemagne and Roland (Williamson, *The Half-Way House*). It is interesting that when the Spanish adapted these English and French medieval legends and tales, new, uniquely Spanish, characters and episodes were introduced. One is Quintañona, Guinevere's lady-in-waiting who has no equivalent in the original English stories but who became a folkloric figure in Spain (see *Don Quixote* part 1, chs. 13, 16, 49 and part 2, ch. 23). This process was even more extensive in the Spanish adaptations of the French stories, and many of the Carolingian chivalric characters most popular in Spain in general and in Cervantes in particular are purely Spanish creations: Belerma, Bernardo del Carpio, Calaínos, Durandarte, Gaiferos, Melisendra, Montesinos, and others.

CERVANTES: LIFE AND LITERARY CREATION

Cervantes lived a full, rich, and exciting life, and it is only natural that many of his life experiences should also find their way into his work. Several of his plays, short stories, and interludes (all described briefly in chapter 1) directly reflect his life as a soldier, captive, itinerant commissary, and tax collector. The same is true of *Don Quixote.* Don Quixote is about the same age as Cervantes when he wrote the beginning of part 1 of *Don Quixote.* In the prologue to his *Novelas ejemplares* Cervantes describes a portrait of himself that is not far from the image of Don Quixote that emerges from the novel. The military career of the captive Ruy Pérez de Viedma, who tells his story in part 1, chapters 39–41, is very similar to that of Cervantes, and his age and appearance upon release from captivity is very similar to that of Cervantes at the same point in his life. On several occasions in the novel Don Quixote expresses opinions that are consistent with what Cervantes is known to have believed: wounds received in battle confer honor (part 1, ch. 15; part 2, prologue), liberty is a precious gift from heaven (part 2, ch. 58), and so forth. Don Quixote is not Cervantes, but they do share certain characteristics. In other cases, some descriptions and events in *Don Quixote* probably would not have been written without the author's personal experiences. For example, Cervantes' life as a soldier and captive certainly enrich not only the captain's story (part 1, chs. 39–41), but also Don Quixote's remarks about the hardships of the soldier's life in his arms and letters speech (part 1, chs. 37–38; also in part 2, ch. 24), and the military adventure that begins aboard the galley in Barcelona harbor (part 2, chs. 63–65).

The description of Don Quixote's household and other scenes of village life, including the home life of Sancho Panza and his wife, probably recall life as he saw and lived it in Esquivias and other small villages in La Mancha and Andalusia. The inn scenes undoubtedly reflect the many inns in which Cervantes must have stayed in during his travels throughout Spain. His descriptions of shepherds, goatherds, muleteers, soldiers, *pícaros,* criminals, and other types from the lower socioeconomic strata of life are drawn from his extensive contacts with such people during his military service, travels in southern Spain, and sojourns in prison. Don Quixote's personal library described in part 1, chapter 6, is probably a reflection of books read, and maybe even owned, by Cervantes himself; and the opinions expressed by the priest and barber, and later by the canon of Toledo may reflect, at least to some extent, Cervantes' own literary estimates (but see Forcione, *Carvantes, Aristotle*). The many scenes involving technological innovation and accomplishment—printing press, windmills, fulling mill, watermill, firearms, talking head, naval technology—may well reflect Cervantes' own personal interest in and curiosity about such matters. Cervantes creates some of the strongest, most independent, most articulate women characters in Golden Age literature: Marcela, Dorotea, Camila, Doña Rodríguez, and others. We can only speculate that his experiences with the women in his life—mother, lover, wife, daughter, sisters, niece—with whom he lived much of the time may have enabled him to write of women's sense of self and agency in such an original way.

Cervantes also appears to have drawn some of his characters, or at least their names, from personal experience. For example, residents of the town of Esquivias and the family and friends of his wife, Catalina, who lived there seem to have found their way into *Don Quixote*. Esquivias is a small town in the province of Toledo known in the Renaissance for its wines and located on the border of La Mancha. Cervantes first went there on personal business in 1584, and there he met and married Catalina. Esquivias is not technically located in La Mancha, but it is close enough (and located in a region sometimes referred to as *la Manch alta,* the upper area or region of La Mancha) and it is of such importance in Cervantes' life, that it has often been proposed as the major rival to Argamasilla del Alba as the "village of La Mancha" that was Don Quixote's home. The case for Esquivias rests on two factors: Cervantes' familiarity with the town (he lived there for short periods of time beginning in 1584) and the documented presence of a number of people with names identical (or at least very similar) to those of characters in *Don Quixote.* There was, for example, a family of *hidalgos* with the surname Quijada (suggested as the possible surname of Don Quixote in part 1, ch. 1), a deceased relative of Cervantes' wife named Alonso Quijada, another relative named Gabriel Quijada de Salazar, a parish priest named Pedro Pérez (the name of the priest so prominent in part 1 of *Don Quixote*), a Mari Gutiérrez (a name once used for Sancho Panza's wife in part 1, ch. 7), and others with names like Ricote (a friend of Sancho's who appears in part 2, chs. 54–55, 63, 65), Carrasco (the bachelor who is very prominent throughout part 2 of the novel), and Lorenzo (both the last name of Aldonza and the first name of Don Diego's son in part 2, ch. 18). So perhaps at least some of the fictional characters of *Don Quixote* may have been based, at least to some degree, on real historical figures. Also, there was a man named Diego de Miranda (the name of the *hidalgo* with whom Don Quixote and Sancho spend time in part 2, chs. 16–18) living in the building where Cervantes and his family lived in Valladolid in 1604–6. Literature is always a remake of previous literature, but in many instances, and specifically in Cervantes' case, it is also something drawn from lived experience.

THE CONCEPT OF CHIVALRY

Don Quixote is a comic tale of a man who believes in chivalry, thinks that fictional characters such as Amadís de Gaula and Belianís de Grecia are historical figures, and attempts to become a knight-errant himself. The romances of chivalry provide the point of departure for the novel; without a concept of chivalry, there is no novel. Therefore, it is inevitable that we should ask: What was Cervantes' attitude toward the idea of chivalry? One answer was made famous by the English romantic poet Lord Byron (1788–1824) when he wrote that "Cervantes smiled Spain's chivalry away" (Byron 364), reducing to a simple phrase the conception of *Don Quixote* as a comic satire and perhaps implying that such gaiety is ultimately sad. But it probably is not accurate to reduce what must have been a complex set of ideas to a satiric laugh (or smile).

On four occasions in the prologue to part 1 of the novel Cervantes or his friend say or imply that the sole purpose in writing the novel is to criticize and satirize the romances of chivalry. The most explicit of these is when the friend says that "your book has no other aim but to undo the authority and influence that the romances of chivalry have in the world and with the undiscerning readers [*el vulgo*]," (part 1, prologue). At no point does Cervantes ever say that he had any other specific aim in mind when he wrote his novel. There is something a little odd in this, however, for at least three reasons.

First, by the late sixteenth century the romances of chivalry were no longer the most popular type of literary entertainment in Spain. The pastoral romances had been in vogue since the end of the 1550s and these books were read more than those of chivalry. This is not to say that the romances of chivalry were not read at all, for they were (as a second, more fantastic, wave of chivalric romance was initiated by *Belianís de Grecia* in 1547), but they were less dominant than they had been earlier in the century and less popular than the newer vogue of pastoral stories. Furthermore, the greatest entertainment genre in the final decades of the century was not books of fiction, but the theater. People from all ranks of society frequented the theater in greater numbers than read books of any kind. If Cervantes wanted to make fun of contemporary literature, he would have been more likely to make his protagonist a shepherd (an idea that occurs to Don Quixote in part 1, ch. 67) or a fanatical theater-goer.

Second, literary parody usually implies more than sneering contempt for what is being parodied. Literary parody is, at heart, a matter of style (see chapter 6) and consists of a comic exaggeration of characteristic aspects of the writing style of an author or group of authors. But one often parodies to chide and laugh both at and with the object of parody. Most of the time there is a certain degree of admiration or respect for the object of parody, for one rarely takes the effort to call attention to excess in something that is simply disdained or rejected out of hand (Riewald, "Parody as Criticism"). There is no question that *Don Quixote* is, among other things, a parody of the style of the romances of chivalry, but that in no way implies that Cervantes did not have a certain admiration for these books.

Cervantes could never have written *Don Quixote* if he had not read, and read attentively, dozens of romances of chivalry, and one does not read dozens of any type of fiction one dislikes; something held an attraction for him in the books his hero devours. The fact that five chivalric romances are praised (at least to some degree) and not burned in the examination of Don Quixote's library in part 1, chapter 6, suggests that the author must have found something of value in these books. A critic of the romances of chivalry as perceptive and articulate as the canon of Toledo also admits (in part 1, ch. 48) that he has already drafted about a hundred pages of a romance of chivalry that he thinks would be an improvement over what has already been published. Again, this suggests that there must be something of value there, and writing a chivalric romance would be a good thing to do, but only if it were done well rather than badly.

Third, to criticize the romances of chivalry is not to criticize the concept of chivalry itself. There is no reason to believe that Cervantes—patriot, proud soldier, courageous prisoner, both a staunch defender and a sharp critic of his times—was disdainful of the idea of chivalry. Don Quixote's reasons for choosing to become a knight-errant in part 1, chapter 1, are to gain fame and serve his nation, precisely the things that motivated Cervantes both as a soldier and as a writer. Byron was wrong: Cervantes did not smile away Spain's chivalry, he merely poked fun at some exaggerated and extravagant literary stories of chivalry.

REALITY AND APPEARANCE

American critic Lionel Trilling has stated that the basic theme of all literature is "the old opposition between reality and appearance, between what really is and what merely seems" (*The Liberal Imagination* 207). Therefore, he concludes, since this theme is nowhere explored earlier or better than in Cervantes' novel, "all prose fiction is a variation on the theme of *Don Quixote*" (209). In chapter 7 we will look at how and why *Don Quixote* might be considered the prototype of the novel in general, but here it seems appropriate to pause and consider the theme of reality versus appearance in Cervantes' novel.

As Trilling suggests, the theme is not original with Cervantes. We can see perfect examples of the reality-appearance conflict in the earliest works of ancient literature, as in Homer's *Odyssey* (eighth century BCE), where Odysseus' absence appears to signify his death, but in reality does not; where Penelope's relationship with her suitors appears to signal her interest in them, but in reality does not; and so forth. If everything in life were in fact exactly as it seems to be, there would be no literature of any kind, for who would be interested in reading something where everyone is in agreement about all things and there is no conflict, no aspiration, no hopes for something better? The appearance-reality relationship is as foundational to all literature as is language itself: without it there is no literature (nor is life itself very interesting any more). In Cervantes' Spain, the theme is obvious in *La Celestina,* where Melibea appears to be a virtuous young woman but is in reality the lover of Calisto; in *Lazarillo de Tormes,* where the squire appears to own a comfortable home, dress well, and eat well, but is in reality an impoverished and starving man. Of course, virtually everything else in these works and others also depends on the tension between what seems to be and what is.

So, if Cervantes did not invent the theme, why is he given so much credit for its importance in literature in general and the novel in particular? The answer may be, as Trilling suggests, that Cervantes brought the concept to the fore in a way no one had before or has since. What Don Quixote believes are historical records are in reality fictional tales; what he perceives as a castle is actually an inn; what he thinks are ladies are prostitutes; giants are windmills; armies are flocks of sheep; Mambrino's helmet is a barber's shaving basin. The supposedly cruel and disdainful Marcela is in fact a strong, independent, honest young woman; what appears to be a young man bathing his feet in a stream is a beautiful young woman in search of the man who betrayed her; Anselmo is convinced that his wife is faithful when in fact she is Lotario's lover; and so on throughout the novel.

At every point, Don Quixote and all other characters perceive reality through the filter of their own experiences, values, ideas, memories, and hopes. But this should hardly be surprising, as that is exactly what all of us do in every aspect of our daily lives. The theme of reality versus appearance has always been at the heart of literature and the human condition in general. We trace the idea back to Cervantes because not only did he place it at the central core of his novel in a way that no one ever had before, but his novel then became the most read, admired, and imitated work of literature in Europe for centuries (see chapter 7).

LITERATURE AND LIFE

The relationship between literature and life might be considered a subset of the theme of reality and appearance. For the middle-aged *hidalgo* who lives in a village of La Mancha, literature, and specifically the romances of chivalry, provides something far more exciting, more interesting, and more attractive than his boring life. Much literature, especially prose fiction, begins with an alternate vision of reality supplied by the protagonist's reading of books or, in more modern times, movies or television: Emma Bovary in Gustave Flaubert's *Madame Bovary* (1856–57); Maggie Tulliver in George Eliot's *The Mill on the Floss* (1860); Eugene Henderson in Saul Bellow's *Henderson the Rain King* (1959); and Chance in Jerzy Kozinski's *Being There* (1971). Sometimes, in both literature and life, the inspiration is not fiction but a political theory or religious conviction. Two prime examples of this are Raskolnikov in Fyodor Dostoevsky's *Crime and Punishment* (1866) and Julien Sorel in Stendhal's *The Red and the Black* (1830), both inspired in large part by their reading about Napoleon. All the Christian saints—Santa Teresa de Avila is an obvious example— who have imitated Christ or famous saints and martyrs of the past are, in an obvious way, little different from Don Quixote.

Not surprisingly, this common theme in literature is also a reflection of a frequent occurrence in life. Psychologist Theodore Sarbin first began to explore the quixotic syndrome as an organizing theme for psychology: "It is clear that the reading of literary works can serve as an antecedent condition for the enactment of roles based on involvement in one's imaginings. Cervantes provides the paradigm case" ("The Quixotic Principle" 172). For Sarbin, this is a common occurrence, always involving "(a) the phenomenology of book reading, and (b) the discovery of empirical correlates" (176). Perhaps one of the main reasons why the character of Don Quixote has had such resonance with people in all cultures, historical periods, and languages, is that the basic premise of the novel is an integral part of the human condition.

More recently, psychiatrist and biographer Jay Martin has continued this line of thought by defining the so-called fictive personality as

> the disease that so disturbed the man who became known as Don Quixote de la Mancha that he replaced his own personality with the fictions that he derived from extensive readings in the tales of chivalric romance. He lost or suspended his own unsatisfactory self and replaced it with the characters, thoughts, feelings, and actions created by others. Something splendid, as well as something frightening, happened to him as a result. (*Who Am I This Time?* 12)

Martin finds examples of the fictive personality throughout literature and history, citing, for example, Mark David Chapman, murderer of John Lennon; John W. Hinckley, Jr., who attempted to assassinate President Ronald Reagan; terrorist Carlos the Jackal; French philosopher and novelist Jean-Paul Sartre; the quixotic World War II general George S. Patton; novelist William Faulkner; and many others. But, significantly, Martin considers the first "full portrait" as "given in one of the world's enduring literary characters, Don Quixote. In this outstanding character Cervantes gives us a remarkable, full exhibition of the fictive personality, and he helps thereby to enlarge our sense of the way fictions become imbedded. In its most general sense, the theme of the book is the confusion between illusion or fantasy and reality" (79).

Life consists of dealing with the perceived differences between reality and appearance. One way in which we attempt to cope with the complexities of life is to imitate models that come from history or literature. What difference is there, after all, between attempting to live in imitation of Jesus Christ or Napoleon and attempting to live in imitation of Amadís de Gaula or Travis Bickle (the Robert De Nero character in the film *Taxi Driver* who was John Hinckley's model)? No one has explored this universal feature of human life in fiction more than Cervantes, and for this alone he fully deserves the recognition he has been accorded.

THE MYTH OF THE GOLDEN AGE: ARMS AND LETTERS

If, like the concept of chivalry, the reality-appearance and its variant the literature-life theme are primary in *Don Quixote,* there are other themes and concepts of interest in the novel, although on a less all-encompassing scale. Two such ideas that were common in Cervantes' time are the myth of the Golden Age and the idea of the relationship between arms and letters. These are the topics of two of the longest and most interesting of Don Quixote's discourses, both cases, delivered as after-dinner speeches.

The myth of an Edenic past had its origins, and was very popular, in Greek and Roman culture, and had its greatest expression in the works of Ovid, Hesiod, and Virgil. According to Hesiod, history was divided into four ages, those of gold, silver, bronze, and iron. The age of gold was always identified as being some ill-defined time in the distant past. Every historical period has a vision of a long-gone golden age of peace and harmony. The idyllic pastoral world of poetry (Garcilaso's eclogues, Góngora's *Soledades*) and prose romance (Montemayor's *La Diana,* Cervantes' *La Galatea*) are fundamental expressions of the values of the age of gold. The Garden of Eden is the foundational Golden Age myth for Christianity. Modern expressions of a concept of a Golden Age may be expressed by cultural conservatives in terms of "the good old days" of the early American settlers or even the idyllic times of the 1950s when television shows like *Leave it to Beaver* supposedly captured the spirit of the happily married, traditionally heterosexual, Christian family. Those on the cultural left, however, might seek a Golden Age in the pre-Colombian pristine purity of native American societies or in the nostalgia for a never-realized pure Marxist state.

The topic was a popular one in the Renaissance, and Don Quixote's speech on the subject when he is with the goatherds (part 1, ch. 11) is one of the finest expressions of the myth. In an ancient time of abundance and harmony, says Don Quixote, women feared no threat to their virtue, but with the passing of time, and as we approached our current age of iron, the order of chivalry was instituted to provide necessary defense for innocent people, especially women. Thus it is that Don Quixote links his own chosen profession with one of the great cultural myths of all time. An irony of the presentation of this topic in *Don Quixote* is that the illiterate goatherds understand little of Don Quixote's elegant speech, and so the effect is lost on his audience, even if it is not on the reader (Levin, *The Myth of the Golden Age*).

The arms versus letters debate also has its roots in antiquity, where it is best illustrated in the comparison between Achilles (representing arms, military valor taken to the highest level) and Odysseus (representing letters, the power of discourse, tact, and cunning). In medieval Christendom, the debate was often formulated in terms of *fortitudo* (strength) and *sapientia* (wisdom). In Spain, a typical medieval expression of the theme is the thirteenth-century debate poem titled *Disputa de Elena María (Debate between Helen and Mary)* in which the former defends her lover, a knight, and the latter speaks for hers, a cleric. Cervantes burlesques this genre in *La guarda cuidadosa,* where the servant maid Cristina must choose between a poor soldier and a subsacristan (assistant to the person in charge of maintaining church property; probably little more than a janitor). One of the most frequent themes of the Renaissance was that the ideal courtier should be equally accomplished at arms, the practice of knighthood and warfare, and letters, which can refer either to law or to creative writing. The prototype of this ideal in Spain was the great poet Garcilaso de la Vega, who died bravely in battle.

Cervantes' life also illustrates the pattern, as his career as a soldier in the 1570s led to a certain glory before he turned to writing in the 1580s. Don Quixote also endorses the ideal, especially in the speech, considered by many to reflect Cervantes' own views, that he gives to an illustrious company after dinner at the inn of Juan Palomeque in part 1, chapters 37–38, in which he argues most strongly for arms over letters. It is probably no accident that Don Quixote's speech comes between the reading of the manuscript of the *Curioso impertinente* (part 1, chs. 33–35) representing letters, and the story the captain tells of his life and adventures (part 1, chs. 39–41), representing arms; or that Ruy Pérez de Viedma (arms) is reunited with his brother Juan (letters) in part 1, chapter 42. In Don

Quixote's discussion with the page who is going off to join the army in part 2, chapter 24, he again extols the virtues of arms over letters and describes the life of the soldier in terms that seem to recall aspects of Cervantes' own military experiences.

SOCIAL CRITICISM

It has often been stated that the gentle Cervantes never engages in serious social criticism in *Don Quixote*. Such is not the case, but the social criticism in the novel is not always explicit. Probably the most profound episode of social critique comes during Don Quixote's stay with the duke and duchess in part 2 of the novel. There he encounters the figure of Doña Rodríguez, thc highest-ranking *dueña* (*dueña de honor;* usually an elderly widow, referred to only by her last name) in the duchess's retinue. At first, she is simply a comic character who gets into a name-calling squabble with Sancho when he and Don Quixote first arrive at the castle (part 2, ch. 31), and it appears that she will be no more than a stock figure, the comic *dueña* about whom so much satiric literature was written.

But later she becomes a real lady in distress (even though her tale always retains comic aspects) and as such appeals to Don Quixote to help marry her daughter to the neighbor who has dishonored her, bravely confronting the duke, her master (part 2, ch. 48). She reveals, among other things, that the duke refuses to take action to help her daughter because he owes money to the young seducer's father and that the duchess has two running sores on her legs that purge her of the evil humors in her body. She is beaten and paddled by the duchess and another of the maidens at the castle who overhear what she tells Don Quixote. Then, when Don Quixote fails to take action, Doña Rodríguez confronts him in the presence of the duke, a daring move that forces the duke to act (part 2, ch. 52).

The duke's scheme is to have his lackey Tosilos, in the guise of the seducer, defeat Don Quixote (thus obviating the marriage and having some fun at the same time), but this is thwarted when Tosilos suddenly falls in love and agrees to marry the young woman. After getting over their initial outrage because the real seducer is not present, both the wronged young woman and her mother accept the proposed marriage (part 2, ch. 56). Later, we learn that after Don Quixote leaves the duke's castle, the lackey is beaten for disobeying orders, the daughter enters a convent, and Doña Rodríguez returns to Castile a broken woman (part 2, ch. 66). Doña Rodríguez thus is crucial in revealing the social and moral corruption of the duke and duchess, and her hopes of marrying her daughter are thwarted by the duke, whose actions result in the destruction of her family. The shift by Doña Rodríguez from comic *dueña* to victim of aristocratic arrogance and abuse of power makes her a key figure in what may be the most significant and substantial example of social criticism in *Don Quixote*. Throughout the sojourn with these noble and powerful representatives of the upper rank of the social hierarchy, both the duke and the duchess are consistently presented as frivolous, callous, and even cruel.

In general, the representatives of the upper classes and clergy are presented as being the same sort of insensitive and self-centered people as the duke and duchess. Vivaldo makes fun of Don Quixote's chivalric vocation (part 1, ch. 13); the canon of Toledo laughs and jumps with joy when Don Quixote is in a bloody fight with the goatherd Eugenio (part 1, ch. 52); the officious house priest, described by the narrator as a "grave ecclesiastic," who lives with the duke and duchess, ridicules and insults Don Quixote (part 2, chs. 31–32); and Don Antonio Moreno and his wife take advantage of hosting Don Quixote in Barcelona to play tricks on him (part 2, chs. 62–65).

On the other hand, poor peasants and others not so high on the social scale are much more likely to treat Don Quixote with respect and deference. Pedro Alonso is kind and considerate with the raving mad Don Quixote when he finds him following the encounter with the merchants and takes him home, waiting until dark to enter the town in order not to embarrass the pathetic knight (part 1, ch. 5). The goatherds share their food and lodging with Don Quixote and Sancho, listen politely to his speech on the Golden Age, and cure the knight's bleeding ear (part 1, chs. 11–13). Juan Palomeque and his family receive and care for Don Quixote when he first arrives at their inn (part 1, chs. 16–17). Then in part 2, the newlyweds Basilio and Quiteria host Don Quixote and Sancho for three days after their marriage (ch. 22). Don Diego de Miranda, admittedly a low-level nobleman, an *hidalgo* like Don Quixote, but one who lives comfortably, if far from the centers of power and influence, and his wife and son generously host Don Quixote and Sancho for four days (part 2, chs. 17–18); and finally, the Catalonian bandits, led by Roque Guinart, treat Don Quixote and Sancho with respect and some degree of deference when they spend three days with them on the way to Barcelona (part 2, chs. 60–61). In many ways, the single most sensitive and humane character in the novel is the simple peasant Sancho Panza.

The cumulative effect of all these interactions is that the reader gets the impression that the degree of humanity decreases as one goes up in the social hierarchy (to judge by early twenty-first American society, some things seem never to change). This is hardly surprising in a novel written by a man who knew poverty and instability in his family during his youth, suffered the hardships of a soldier in warfare, endured years of imprisonment and punishment in Algiers, suffered bureaucratic rebuke when he attempted to secure a post in the colonies, was rewarded more with frustration and hardship (including excommunication, prison, and bankruptcy) than with income or respect during his years as a commissary and tax collector, lived in (or at least near) squalor in a few rooms with the women of his family in Valladolid, and died in poverty. All this, while he saw daily the opulence of the court and the high nobility, the lavish lifestyle of his rival Lope de Vega, the way riches from the New World flowed into Spanish coffers and yet made little real contribution to the nation's well being, the ornate tomb erected to the deceased king Felipe II in the Seville cathedral, and the decadence and corruption of Felipe III, the last king to rule during his lifetime, and much more. Cervantes may not shout his protest at the top of his voice in *Don Quixote,* but it is hard to read the novel and come away with much respect for the powers that ruled and enjoyed privilege during his lifetime. Life was not kind to Cervantes, and his response could well have been one of frustration, resentment, and bitterness. Instead, he maintained a sense of dignity, sensitivity, and generosity right through to the end. *Don Quixote* is not the product of a bitter or angry man, but a reflection of its creator's profound humanity.

There is one more occasion on which Cervantes deals with a major social issue of the time, and here the ambiguity is even greater than in the case with the duke and duchess. When Sancho abandons his governorship and returns to the duke's palace (part 2, ch. 54), he has a chance encounter with an old friend named Ricote. Ricote is one of the hundreds of thousands of *moriscos* (Muslims converted to Christianity or their descendants) who were forced to leave Spain in a series of laws issued beginning in 1609. He is back in Spain, in disguise as a pilgrim, in order to return to his village and dig up a large quantity of money he has hidden there. He and Sancho talk about the forced exile that separated him from his wife and daughter and what hardship this has been for what was obviously a decent family. This would seem to be an indictment of the royal policy of exclusion, but then Ricote incongruously praises the royal decree of banishment that broke up his family and destroyed his life, lauding both the king, Felipe III, and his minister, Don Bernardino de Velasco, who made the decisions. Later in the novel (part 2, chapters 63, 65) Ricote reappears and is reunited with his daughter, but again he lauds the decision to drive the *moriscos* out of the country and his family's fate is left undecided. The race of *moriscos* is also criticized by the dog Berganza in the *Coloquio de los perros,* and there is another ambiguous (more critical than sympathetic) episode involving *moriscos* in Cervantes' *Persiles* (part 3, ch. 11).

The scenes involving Ricote and his family have alternatively been read as a stinging satire on the subject and an awkward but sincere expression of Cervantes' belief that the country was better off without this pernicious group. How should the reader take these scenes? The hardships suffered by Ricote and his family are presented as unjust—but the man most affected by the events praises the policy that brought about the hardships. Are Ricote's comments ironic? They seem not to be. Are these comments placed in his mouth by an author afraid of official authorities? Perhaps, but this is not Cervantes' practice on other occasions when dealing with sensitive matters, such as religion. Did Cervantes have conflicting and self-contradictory feelings about the matter? Again, perhaps, but, ultimately, who knows? The expulsion of the *moriscos,* following the expulsions of the Jews and Muslims a century earlier, continued the process of making Spain both more homogeneous and less capable. It was a major social issue, and its presentation in *Don Quixote* calls attention to the issue, but in the most ambiguous of ways (for more on the *morisco* problem in Spain, see Chejne, *Islam and the West*).

RELIGION

There is probably no subject more contentious in Cervantes studies than that of his views on religion, and there is no way to make a convincing argument about Cervantes' true feelings about religion. In *Don Quixote* alone, there are over a hundred citations of, or references or allusions to, the Bible. At times, Cervantes' works have been read as those of a faithful Catholic, even an ultra-conservative supporter of the Counter-Reformation. Nowhere in his work is there an explicit statement of criticism of the Church—nor could there be in the age of the Inquisition. At other times, some of his works, especially *Don Quixote,* have been read as religious parody or freethinking iconoclasm. Both of the extreme views are probably just that: extreme. It is highly unlikely that Cervantes was ultra-orthodox or reactionary, and it is equally unlikely that he was a freethinker or an atheist.

In one of his earliest known works, the play *Los tratos de Argel,* the sublime virtues of Christianity and Christians are contrasted with the degenerate evil of Islam and Muslims, in a crudely propagandistic and simplistic binary way. And at the end of his life he finished writing an allegorical, symbolic and very orthodox novel *Los trabajos de Persiles y Sigismunda,* which ends when the pilgrims reach Rome, the center of Christianity, and marry happily. Following the lead of his sisters and his wife, Cervantes joined the Third Order of Saint Francis shortly before his death. The Franciscan Order was structured into three divisions. The First Order was that of the fully-ordained priests. The Second Order, known as the Poor Claires *(las Clarisas),* was for cloistered women. The Third Order was a devotional association of laymen, which was joined by many noblemen and literary figures of Cervantes' day, often for social as much as, if not more than, spiritual ones. Cervantes' sisters Andrea and Magdalena, as well as his wife Catalina, all joined this order before Cervantes did. After a three-year period in which he had been a novice in the order, he took his final vows on April 2, 1616, and died some three weeks later. All of this suggests that Cervantes was a very devout and traditional Roman Catholic.

On other occasions, however, Cervantes seems to take a much more reserved, even slightly ironic, attitude toward the Church. Many of his references to or statements about the Church, the clergy, and religious practices are ambiguous and highly suggestive. The book-burning in part 1, chapter 6 of *Don Quixote* may be a criticism of the Inquisition's autos-da-fe. The scene in which Don Quixote, Sancho, and the humanist cousin visit a hermitage in part 2, chapter 24—after Don Quixote's remarks about how hermits today are not what they used to be, they arrive at the hermitage and find that the hermit himself is absent but his female assistant (!) is there to greet them—has been read as a commentary on the corruption and decadence of the clergy. Some would see in the priest's donning of a woman's dress in part 1, chapters 26–27, and standing by, crying out, and wringing his hands with the women present in the inn during the free-for-all fight in part 1, chapter 45, as implicit anticlerical statements. Some have perceived Don Quixote as blasphemous when he says "more than 80 Our Fathers and the same number of Hail Marys, Salve Reginas and Creeds" as he concocts the balm of Fierabrás in the inn in part 1, chapter 17, and again when he tears off a piece of his shirt-tail in order to fashion a makeshift rosary in part 1, chapter 26, and then says "a million Ave Marias." However, some believe these scenes were included simply for comical purposes. There was apparently no problem with these scenes in the first edition of *Don Quixote,* but in the second printing the rosary was made from some galls from a cork tree and the exaggerated number of prayers was eliminated. The changes may have been made by Cervantes himself. Later, in 1624, the Portuguese inquisition censored the reference to the torn-off shirt-tail.

One of the most famous phrases in the novel occurs in part 2, chapter 9, when Don Quixote and Sancho search for Dulcinea at night in El Toboso and, thinking they are approaching her palace, find that the building is in fact the town church, and Don Quixote says "We have come upon [*hemos topado con,* which can be read more as "come up against" or "run into"] the church, Sancho," a remark that many believe is a warning not to meddle in matters that the Church (i.e., the Inquisition) might criticize, but that many others insist means only that the building is the church and not the palace. During a discussion with Sancho in part 2, chapter 36, about the lashes he is to inflict on himself, the duchess makes the comment that "works of charity that are done in a lukewarm and half-hearted manner have no merit and are not worth anything," a comment that was censored by the Inquisition in some later editions of the novel, but which could also be seen simply as a harmless passing remark.

There are many more such ambiguous and tantalizing statements concerning the Church, the Inquisition, the clergy, prayers, and other aspects of religion throughout *Don Quixote.* The fact of Cervantes' youthful studies with Juan López de Hoyos, an open follower of Erasmus, has led scholars to detect strong Erasmian currents in his work (see chapter 1). Overall, Cervantes impresses readers as more secular than most, if not all, of his contemporaries. After all, important and influential writers like Francisco de Herrera, Lope de Vega, Luis de Góngora, Tirso de Molina, Pedro Calderón de la Barca, and others, were all ordained priests. It is quite possible that religious skepticism was a central feature in the younger and mature Cervantes' ideology, but that he became more conservative and orthodox as he aged.

CERVANTES' LITERARY THEORY

Cervantes never wrote a work on aesthetics or literary theory, but there is no question that he was very familiar with both classical theory and with much of the more modern Italian and Spanish theories of his day. His works abound with examples, and sometimes discussions, of some of the key features of Aristotelian literary theory: *admiratio, imitatio,* unity, verisimilitude, poetic versus historic truth, decorum, the legitimized marvelous, rhetorical display, moral edification, and instructive erudition, among others. Cervantes' understanding of Aristotle probably came in large part from his certain familiarity with one contemporary Spanish theorist: Alonso López Pinciano, known simply as El Pinciano. His major publication was *Philosophia antigua poética* (1596; *Ancient Poetic Philosophy*), written in the form of a dialogue and presenting an original and coherent version of Aristotelian poetics (Canavaggio, "Alonso López Pinciano").

Other important concepts in Cervantes' works can also be discerned. First, there is the Horatian doctrine of *ut pictura poesis* (as in painting, so in poetry; or as is painting, so is poetry), the idea that one can paint a picture in words, or, at least, convey with words an image (or an impression) of reality in the way that a painting can. Another is *tropelía* (confusion), the science of making something change its appearance or seem to be other than what it is. A third is *ekphrasis,* a concern in literary texts with visuality, the visual arts, and visual perception. Noteworthy, also, is Cervantes' attitude toward digressions, which he criticizes, as in a comment by Don Quixote during the presentation of the puppet show in part 2, chapter 26, when he tells the boy narrating the story that he should tell his story in a straight line and not go off on tangents, and in the *morisco* translator's comment in part 2, chapter 18, that certain descriptive details have been omitted because they were not related to the principal purpose of the history but merely "cold digressions." In both of these cases there is no small amount of irony in the comments of these comic characters (and we should always remember that an opinion expressed by a character should not automatically be assumed to be the opinion of the author, at least unless there are other reasons to believe such to be the case). But on other occasions, as in the *Coloquio de los perros,* there are other, more serious, comments about digressions, and certainly Cervantes' narrative practice in all his works is far different from the digression-laden technique of Mateo Alemán in *Guzmán de Alfarache* (see Mancing, "Embedded Narration"). Just as he was not fond of digressions, Cervantes warns against an affected style of writing, as when Don Quixote tells the narrating puppeteer's assistant that "all affectation is bad" (part 2, ch. 26).

Finally, it is worth pointing out that throughout his works, Cervantes consistently places poetry at the pinnacle of the literary arts. Don Quixote's long discussion with Don Diego de Miranda about the latter's son's obsession with poetry and about the nature of poetry itself in part 2, chapters 16 and 18, is characteristic: "Poetry, señor *hidalgo,* is, in my opinion, like a young, tender, and extremely beautiful maiden, whom many other maidens—which are all the other sciences—should enrich, perfect, and adorn. She should be served by all of them, and they should all are derive their authority from her" (part 2, ch. 16). This is consistent with Cervantes' personification of poetry in his story *La gitanilla,* in his allegorical defense of good poetry in *El viaje del Parnaso,* and in other comments scattered throughout his works.

To illustrate but a single example of classical theory, we can use the concept of *imitatio,* or imitation, a key to our understanding of Cervantes' (and Don Quixote's) aesthetics. The idea of imitation first comes up in the prologue to part 1 of the novel. There, when Cervantes is discussing with his friend how to write the prologue, the friend notes that not much adornment is needed, and that a writer should always imitate good models, "for the more perfect that imitation is, the better your writing will be." Then, in his proposed penance in Sierra Morena, Don Quixote explains to Sancho the importance of imitating great models in a passage that deserves to be quoted at length:

> Sancho, I want you to know that the famous Amadís de Gaula was one of the most perfect of all knights-errant. I didn't speak well when I said *he was one:* he was the only one, the first, the unique, the lord of all who lived in his time in the world. To hell with Don Belianís and all those who claim to have equaled him in something, because I swear they are wrong. I also say that when a painter wants to become famous in his art he attempts to imitate the originals of the best painters he knows; and this same rule applies to all other trades and professions of importance that serve to adorn a state. Anyone who wants to achieve the name of prudent and long-suffering should, and does, imitate Ulysses, in whose person and travails Homer paints us a living portrait of prudence and patience, just as Virgil shows us, in the person of Aeneas, the valor of a dutiful son and the wisdom of a brave and successful general. They do this, not by painting or describing them as they were, but as they should have been, in order to leave an example of their virtues for future generations. In this same way, Amadís was the north star, the morning star, the bright sun of brave and loving knights, and all of us who enlist under the banner of love and chivalry should imitate him. So, Sancho my friend, if this is so, as it is, I find that the knight-errant who best imitates Amadís will come closest to achieving perfection in chivalry. (part 1, ch. 25)

Although here couched in terms of chivalric perfection, the concept of imitation is at the heart of Cervantes' aesthetic values. Mimesis, imitation, and verisimilitude all address aspects of *imitatio* in the sense of reproducing a kind of literary realism—not in the stricter sense in which that term is used in later centuries, particularly the nineteenth, but in the way Cervantes understood the writing of fiction (Riley, "Don Quixote and the Imitation of Models").

It seems clear that Cervantes both admired and was critical of aspects of contemporary, especially Italian, theory. He knew and respected the classical position of theorists like Torquato Tasso, but he also knew and found interesting the less formal, freer, more popular practices of Ludovico Ariosto and others. The fact that he was able to criticize and satirize the pastoral, the chivalric, and the picaresque on one hand, and exemplify them in a very sympathetic light on the other hand, makes clear how subtle and thoughtful his own theorizing and practice were (see Riley, *Cervantes's Theory,* and Forcione, *Cervantes, Aristotle*).

Almost all of Cervantes' works deal with literary theory to at least some extent, and there are scenes like the examination of Don Quixote's library in part 1, chapter 6, and the literary conversations among the priest, the canon of Toledo, and Don Quixote in part 1, chapters 47–50, which are virtual essays in theory. Equally interesting are the scenes of dramatized implicit literary theory and criticism: the conversation Cervantes has with his friend in the prologue to part 1; the dialogue between Don Quixote and Sancho as the latter tells a story in part 1, chapter 20; the discussions during the presentation of the puppet show by Maese Pedro in part 2, chapter 26; and various comments by the editor-narrator concerning the manuscript of Cide Hamete Benengeli throughout the novel.

Finally, it should be noted that as proud as Cervantes was as an author, he recognized that he could not dictate his readers' understanding his work. In line with modern reader-response theory based in cognitive science (see, for example, Gerrig, *Experiencing Narrative Worlds*), Cervantes recognizes, and even celebrates, the interpretative authority of the reader. There is a passage in the prologue to part 1 of the novel that is one of the clearest and purest expressions of the reader's interpretive authority of all time:

> But, although I seem to be Don Quixote's father, I am his stepfather, and I don't want to follow today's custom and beg you, almost with tears in my eyes, as others do, my dear reader, to pardon or overlook the shortcomings that you may see in this child of mine. For you are neither his relative nor his friend, and you have your soul in your body and your free will as much as the next person, and you are in your own house, where you are lord of it, just like the king is lord of his taxes, and you know the common proverb, "Underneath my cloak I kill the king" [more or less the equivalent of "A man's home is his castle"]. All of this exempts you and makes you free of any responsibility or obligation, and so you can say anything you want about the story, without fear that you will be criticized for your criticism or that you will be rewarded for your praise. (part 1, prologue)

The author cannot tell the reader how to read the book—and much less can the text itself determine how it is to be understood, a concept that Cervantes would have found incomprehensible. Reading is not a passive act of receiving information, deciphering a code, or discovering meaning, but an active and creative one. As Bakhtin has rightly insisted (and as cognitive psychologists and linguists today would agree), meaning does not exist already *in* an utterance or *in* a text, waiting to be discovered by a listener or a reader; rather, meaning—or understanding—must be *actively constructed* by the listener or the reader. According to Bakhtin, all true understanding is "sympathetic" (*Art and Answerability* 102–3) and "creative" (*Speech Genres* 7):

> In the actual life of speech, every concrete act of understanding is active: it assimilates the world to be understood into its own conceptual system filled with specific objects and emotional expressions, and is indissolubly merged with the response, with a motivated agreement or disagreement. *To some extent, primacy belongs to the response, as the activating principle:* it creates the ground for understanding, it prepares the ground for an active and engaged understanding. Understanding comes to fruition only in the response. Understanding and response are dialectically merged and mutually condition each other; one is impossible without the other. (*Dialogic Imagination* 282; emphasis added)

For Bakhtin, understanding is never a passive process, as it is conceived in Saussurean linguistics and the critical and interpretive theories and practices derived from or grounded in Saussure's work: "A passive understanding of linguistic meaning is no understanding at all" (*Dialogic Imagination* 281). What is quite amazing is that Cervantes clearly intuited all this some four centuries earlier.

NARRATIVE THEORY AND PRACTICE: METAFICTION

Cervantes experimented frequently with narrative technique and structure in his novels and short stories. A comprehensive study of his practice throughout his works is outside the purview of this book, but it is important to look closely at what he did in *Don Quixote* and why. Since the literary genre that Cervantes used as a point of departure was that of the romances of chivalry, he naturally selected an overall narrative structure comparable to the one seen in all those works. Beginning with *Amadís de Gaula,* the romances of chivalry were presented as historical narratives, translations of ancient texts written in exotic languages. The standard practice was for the author to explain in the prologue that he had discovered the precious historical text, had it translated, and edited it for the contemporary audience.

Absurdities and anachronisms abound in the romances of chivalry. Montalvo, for example, claims that the events in the life of Amadís took place "not many years after the passion of our Redeemer and Savior, Jesus Christ" (*Amadis of Gaul* 21), but of course there was nothing comparable to knight-errantry at that time in history. In this and other chivalric romances characters are magically transported great distances by benevolent (or, sometimes, evil) enchanters or a knight might ride in a few days' time from, say, England to Turkey. Time, geography, and logic are all violated on a regular basis, especially in the romances written in the latter part of the sixteenth century, and thus have little significance in the books Don Quixote was so fond of reading.

Cervantes takes great advantage of the narrative structure of the romances of chivalry and parodies it throughout his novel. In the prologue to part 1, he and his friend discuss his efforts to locate documents pertaining to Don Quixote in the Archives of La Mancha. These nonexistent archives, supposedly located in a relatively backward and minor region of Spain rather than in some great ancient city, would have been perceived by the novel's first readers as an enormous literary joke. In the opening chapters of the novel the narrator (whom we can identify as Cervantes) continues his search in these archives and is frustrated when the last document he has located comes to an end and cuts short the battle between Don Quixote and the Basque squire in part 1, chapter 8.

The next chapter opens with a diligent but fruitless search for more archival material that finally comes to an end when Cervantes the narrator accidentally meets a young boy with some notebooks and manuscripts he is going to sell to a silk merchant. Curious, Cervantes looks at the papers, sees that they are written in Arabic, and has someone who reads that language examine them for him. It turns out that the boy is selling a work called the *"History of Don Quixote of La Mancha. Written by Cide Hamete Benengeli, an Arabic Historian"* (part 1, ch. 9). Delighted to find a lengthy historical source for the story of Don Quixote, Cervantes has the entire work translated into Spanish, and he edits it for publication. Proof that the work is edited and not merely passed along as the translator prepared it can be seen in the fact that the title of the novel is changed and some details, such as names, are regularized; for example, *Zancas* is supposedly used for *Panza* sometimes in the Arabic manuscript but that form of the name never appears in the edited Spanish version; furthermore, on several occasions the editor interrupts the historian's narrative in order to comment on the story or its presentation. The remainder of part 1 of the novel is supposedly a translation of Cide Hamete's work. One thing, however, worries the narrator: the fact that the historian is Arabic, "since all the people of that nation are liars" (part 1, ch. 9).

From this point on, the absurdity of the supposed source of the story becomes a constant source of humor. Throughout the novel, the events that are narrated are referred to as a *verdadera historia,* a "true history," which means that the "true" narrative of the life of Don Quixote is something that has been written by a congenital liar. Importantly, the word *historia* in Spanish serves for two concepts which have different words in English: (truthful) *history* and (fictional) *story* (Wardropper, *"Don Quixote"*). Furthermore, the supposedly omniscient historian Cide Hamete turns out to be very fallible at times and, curiously, he seems to be a contemporary historical person who is, among other things, a native of La Mancha and apparently a relative of the mule driver with whom Don Quixote gets into a fight in the inn (part 1, ch. 16). Cervantes also adds to the narrative from time to time his own commentary and observations or opinions made by other people.

Unfortunately, Cervantes claims, after Don Quixote's return home in part 1, chapter 52, Cide Hamete's manuscript and the historical sources from the Annals of La Mancha containing further information about him have all been exhausted, although local informants there maintain that the knight sallied forth again and went to the city of Zaragoza where a chivalric tournament was held. However, Cervantes claims to have received from an elderly physician a decaying lead box that the physician had found in the ruins of an old hermitage that was under renovation. The box contained some decomposing parchment manuscripts in Gothic script in which further adventures of Don Quixote, including his death, were described. Evidently these papers had existed for a very long period of time, perhaps centuries, a curious phenomenon since the events of Don Quixote's life took place "not long ago" (part 1, ch. 1), clearly in contemporary Spain. (It is an absurdity worthy of a chivalric romance that the documents describing the events were written very long before the events themselves actually took place.) Foremost among these papers were some poems written by the members of the Academy of Argamasilla del Alba, a town in La Mancha. Cervantes promises to keep looking for material with which to write a continuation of the story.

After all this mock concern about manuscript sources, one would expect that the 1615 continuation of the novel would open with a description of how the continuation of the reliable historical manuscript was located. But no, the first words of the sequel are simply "Cide Hamete Benengeli, in the second part of this history, which contains the third sally of Don Quixote, says that . . ." But this perhaps disappointing opening belies the fact that Cide Hamete and his manuscript become much more important in part 2 than they were in part 1. In fact, much of the humor of the continuation is generated by playful metafiction consisting of commentary about the manuscript of the true history.

At the end of part 2, chapter 2, Sancho announces to Don Quixote that a book has been written about their adventures, that the author is a Muslim named *Berenjena* (eggplant, Sancho's mispronunciation of *Benengeli*), and that a local resident, one Sansón Carrasco, who has just returned from the University of Salamanca with his bachelor's degree, has read the book. Don Quixote, worried (as was Cervantes earlier) that the book may not be a truthful account since the author is a Muslim and therefore a natural liar, invites Sansón to discuss the book with him. Thus it is that the literary characters Don Quixote and Sancho Panza become aware of the fact that they are literary characters. This scene so impressed the archetypal postmodern fiction writer Jorge Luis Borges that he devoted one of his most famous essays to it: "Partial Enchantments in the *Quixote*," perhaps the most celebrated essay in his *Other Inquisitions*.

It is difficult to overstate the originality of Cervantes' accomplishment in this profound metafictional ploy. Earlier Spanish writers had engaged in ample experimentation with the technique of blending real and fictional spaces, commenting on the origins of the text within the text itself, and by having the author enter into his own text. Romances and novels as different as Diego de San Pedro's *Cárcel de amor* (1492), Garci Rodríguez de Montalvo's *Las sergas de Esplandián* (1510), Francisco Delicado's *La Lozana andaluza* (1528), Mateo Alemán's *Guzmán de Alfarache* (1599, 1604), and Francisco López de Ubeda's *La Pícara Justina* (1605), among others, all make innovative use of aspects of self-consciousness: the author as character, direct address to the reader, discussions of how the text being read came into being, introduction of competing fictions into the text, and so forth. All these efforts pale in comparison with what Cervantes does in *Don Quixote*.

The metafictional play in part 2 of the novel greatly expands the possibilities of the technique of literary self-consciousness. Cide Hamete does not simply write his true history, he also comes repeatedly to the fore to provide comic relief throughout the novel:

in part 2, chapter 5, he is criticized by his translator for writing an inauthentic scene in which Sancho speaks in a way that is far beyond his abilities;

in part 2, chapter 8, he pauses to utter praise for Allah;

in part 2, chapter 10, he says he cannot believe what Don Quixote does in this chapter but considers it his duty to write it as it happened;

in part 2, chapter 12, it is thought by some that he wrote a long comparison of the friendship between Rocinante and Sancho's ass to the classical friendship between Pilades and Orestes;

in part 2, chapter 17, he has trouble finding the words to describe Don Quixote's madness when facing the lion;

in part 2, chapter 18, he has his description of the home of Don Diego de Miranda edited out by the translator;

in part 2, chapter 24, he cannot believe what Don Quixote says happened to him in the Cave of Montesinos but writes it as a good historian should, even though there is a rumor that some people say that he retracted the statement on his death bed;

in part 2, chapter 27, he swears like a Catholic Christian;

in part 2, chapter 31, he lies (or at least misleads the reader) when he says that when Don Quixote is received with honor at the palace of the duke and duchess this he believes, for the first time in his life, that he truly is a real knight-errant, but the subsequent discussion between Don Quixote and Sancho demonstrates that such is far from the truth;

in part 2, chapter 38, he lies to the reader in saying what the "real" name of the Countess Trifaldi was when a page dresses in disguise as part of a joke being played on Don Quixote, but the whole scene is a fake and so, by definition, there is no "reality" behind the character's name;

in part 2, chapter 40, he is praised, with heavy irony, by the narrator;

in part 2, chapter 44, some people say that he complains in the original manuscript that the translator did not translate it correctly (or, perhaps, that he would not in the future when it would be translated);

in part 2, chapter 44, also, he makes a long exclamation about the nature of poverty (but this passage is also described as Don Quixote's thoughts on the subject);

in part 2, chapter 48, he makes the comment that he would give the best of his two cloaks to see the scene involving Don Quixote and Doña Rodríguez;

in part 2, chapter 53, he waxes philosophic about the passage of time, but—Muslim philosopher that he is—he mistakenly gets the order of the seasons of the year backward;

in part 2, chapter 70, he offers his own opinion about the motivation of the people who make fun of Don Quixote and Sancho; and

in part 2, chapter 74, he hangs up his pen, telling his writing instrument
what to say if another author should attempt to use it—and then seeming
to blend into Cervantes himself.

Don Quixote himself is a less comic and more pathetic character in part 2
of the novel than he was in part 1, but overall the humor in the novel con-
tinues to a high degree because of the comedy provided by Cide Hamete.
In fact, one could go so far as to say that in part II Cide Hamete replaces
Don Quixote as the single most frequent source of comedy in the novel
(Mancing, *The Chivalric World*).

   A second sustained line of metafictional play begins in part 2, chapter 59,
when Don Quixote learns that another author has written a sequel to the
original book of his adventures. He leafs through a copy of the book and
criticizes it on several accounts. Most importantly, since the apocryphal
author has him go to Zaragoza (as was suggested at the end of Cervantes'
part 1 and as has been Don Quixote's destination so far in part 2), he will
"prove" the inauthenticity of the book by changing his plans and going
to Barcelona instead. Upon arrival in Barcelona in part 2, chapter 61, the
knight and squire are greeted as the authentic Don Quixote and Sancho
and not the false ones of the other sequel. The next day (in part 2, ch. 62),
he visits a print shop where books are made, sees that a new edition of the
other book is being prepared, and warns that the book's "Martinmas [tra-
ditionally, Saint Martin's Day, Nov. 11, was when pigs were taken to be
slaughtered] will come, as it does to all pigs." In part 2, chapter 70, when
Don Quixote and Sancho are taken back to the palace of the duke and
duchess, Altisidora, who had earlier feigned love for Don Quixote, pretends that she has died of love and descended briefly into hell before being
brought back to life. In hell, she says, she saw two devils playing tennis, but
using Avellaneda's book in place of a tennis ball and commenting on how
bad the book is, one devil actually saying that it is so bad "that if I myself
tried to make it worse, I couldn't." In part 2, chapter 72, Don Quixote
and Sancho meet Don Alvaro Tarfe, a major character from Avellaneda's
sequel, and convince him to swear and sign a notarized statement that the
people he spent time with were not the "real" Don Quixote and Sancho.
And finally, in the last chapter of the novel, Cide Hamete hangs up his pen
and warns all other potential authors to leave Don Quixote dead and buried
and not write any more false sequels of his adventures.

   When Mateo Alemán learned that another writer had written a sequel to
his first volume of *Guzmán de Alfarache*, he brilliantly brought his rival's
protagonist into his own sequel, made him a poor imitation of Guzmán,

and then had him commit suicide. In this way, he both killed off his rival's literary creation and proved the superiority of his own work (McGrady, *Mateo Alemán*, 113–29). Alemán thus provided Cervantes with an example of how to deal with one's literary rival and unauthorized continuer of his work. Cervantes begins his criticism of Avellaneda in the very first words of the prologue to his own part 2, when he says:

> By God, how anxious you must be waiting for this prologue, my illustrious (or perhaps plebeian) reader, thinking that you will find in it revenge, argument, and abuse directed against the author of the second *Don Quixote,* that is, the book by the man they say was engendered in Tordesillas and born in Tarragona! Well, in truth I am not going to give you that satisfaction; for although insults awaken anger even in the humblest of bosoms, mine is to be an exception to this rule. You probably want me to call him an ass, stupid, and insolent; but such thoughts have not even occurred to me: let him live with his sin, let him eat his own bread, and let him worry about it. (part 2, prologue)

Alemán's revenge is probably as brilliant as Cervantes', but the latter's is funnier, more extended, and more varied. Along with the metafiction based on Cide Hamete Benengeli, it is a highlight of part 2 of the novel.

Another metafictional theme in *Don Quixote* is the presence of Cervantes himself in the novel in several ways. First of all, Cervantes can be seen as the primary narrator of the fiction. Most theorists of narrative, especially those who work within the framework of structuralist narratology, maintain that the flesh-and-blood author can never enter into the ontological plane of the fiction, and hold that at best there can only be an implied (or inferred) authorial presence in the work. These theorists also insist that the narrator must be an anonymous fictional voice or structure—or, in the case of a novel like *Don Quixote,* there may be multiple fictional voices, but none of them can belong to the author (the best representative of this position writing in English is Parr, *"Don Quixote": An Anatomy;* but see also the more recent books by Paz Gago, *Semiótica del "Quijote,"* and Stoopen, *Los autores, el texto, los lectores*).

Sometimes, however, theory gets in the way of simple logic, an example of what Bakhtin calls "theoreticism" *(Toward a Philosophy)*. There is no reason why—as countless readers down through the centuries have assumed—*Don Quixote* should not be understood as a story told (i.e., narrated) by Cervantes. And in fact, that assumption seems more warranted here than it might in other situations. After all, in the prologue to part 1, Cervantes writes of his research in the archives of La Mancha in order to find material for the story. There is no shift in tone or voice as the narrator begins the tale in part 1, chapter 1, and in these early chapters the narrator says he continued his research in the Manchegan archives. It is still the voice of Cervantes who makes these statements, and the primary narrator of the remainder of the novel is the same voice. The mere fact that Cervantes *says* (i.e., is identified as the voice we hear) certain things in his fiction does not mean that we are expected to believe it, or believe that he presents it, as historical truth. A father can tell his children a wild story about being with cowboys and rustlers in the old west and everyone knows that it is understood as a fiction. But it is the father who *tells* the story; the historical, flesh-and-blood father is the narrator, but what he says is a fiction. For millennia, that format has probably been the prototype of fictional narrative: a real person orally tells or, in more modern times, writes a fiction (for an extended defense of this position, see Mancing, "Cervantes as Narrator," together with the critique by Parr, "On Narration and Theory" and the "Response to Jim Parr" by Mancing).

So recognizing Cervantes as the narrator of his novel should present no problem. This in itself is not particularly metafictional. But it is when the author enters as a character, along with his fictional characters. And Cervantes does indeed pull off this metafictional slight-of-hand. First of all, when the priest and barber examine Don Quixote's library in part 1, chapter 6, the barber comes across "*La Galatea,* by Miguel de Cervantes." The priest then comments, "This Cervantes has been a good friend of mine for many years, and I know that he is more versed in misfortunes than in verses." If Pero Pérez, the priest in the village of La Mancha, is a good friend of Miguel de Cervantes, author of *La Galatea* (1585; Cervantes' first book) the historical and fictional worlds are paradoxically fused.

Later, in part 1, chapter 40, when the escaped captive Ruy Pérez de Viedma recounts his adventures in Algiers, he comments on "a Spanish soldier, a certain Saavedra, who, although he did things that will remain in the memory of those people for many years, and all in order to gain freedom, yet he was never beaten by his master, nor was any such order ever given, nor was any harsh word spoken to him." Recall that Saavedra was the second surname that Cervantes started to use for himself in the 1580s, and that he did in fact make heroic efforts to escape slavery, that he was not severely punished for such efforts, and that he was recognized and admired by his contemporaries (see chapter 4). So not only was the historical Cervantes a friend of the priest's, he was also a companion to the brave soldier who tells his story.

And finally, it should be noted that in part 1, chapter 47, when Don Quixote leaves the inn to return home, the innkeeper presents the priest with the manuscript of a story titled *Rinconete y Cortadillo*. It had been left in the inn, along with the story of the *Curioso impertinente* that the priest had read in part 1, chapters 33–35, by a previous traveler who had spent the night there, and the innkeeper suggests that both works might be by the same author. Since Cervantes is in fact the author of *Rinconete* (it was published in his 1613 collection of *Novelas ejemplares*) he may also be the author of the *Curioso*. This suggests that perhaps Cervantes stayed in Juan Palomeque's inn at some time in the past. Like the great nineteenth-century Spanish novelist Benito Pérez Galdós (1843–1920), Cervantes is a part of his own fictional world, mingling and talking with the other characters, as much at home in fiction as he is in reality.

EMBEDDED NARRATIVES

Embedding fictions within fictions is as old as storytelling itself. Nothing is more archetypal than the structure of the ancient Arabian *Thousand and One Nights,* the story of King Shahryar, who takes a new wife each day and, after spending just the one night with her, has her put to death the next day. The beautiful Scheherazade, however, becomes the king's wife and that night tells him a story but leaves it incomplete. Her execution the next day is postponed so that the king can hear the end of the story the next night. The same thing is repeated that night and every night until the king gives up on the idea of ever killing his wife. In other words, the whole story is about storytelling, with one story after another told within the framework of the story. In medieval Europe, such framed collections of narratives were also common—Chaucer's *Canterbury Tales* in England and Don Juan Manuel's *Conde Lucanor* in Spain are classic examples. The great Italian Renaissance storytellers like Boccaccio used the same technique.

Longer and more coherent narratives also included shorter narrative sequences within them. Romances from ancient Greece (Heliodorus' *Ethiopian History*) to the late middle ages (Malory's *Le Morte Darthur*) always included within them first-person narratives told by other characters or episodes that were at best tangential to the main action. The chivalric and pastoral romances so popular in Renaissance Spain and the rest of Europe continued the practice of telling stories that contained other stories embedded within them. In effect, the intertwined stories of various ongoing chivalric adventures or of a series of chronic lovers' complaints that characterize these romances are little more than one embedded tale after another, usually with the resolution taking place as part of the primary narrative thread. The picaresque novel *Guzmán de Alfarache* (1599, 1604) is primarily a first-person narrative of the protagonist's life and opinions, but there are also five other stories told by other characters and embedded in the primary narrative. Such secondary stories provide a change of pace, theme, tone, and narrative voice. In general, such embedded narratives were much appreciated by contemporary readers.

Like most writers of his time, Cervantes sought variety within a work and did not hesitate to include one narrative within another. Part 1 of *Don Quixote* contains three obviously embedded narratives: the story of the *Curioso impertinente* (part 1, chs. 32–34), the captive's tale of his adventures and escape from Algiers (part 1, chs. 39–41), and Eugenio's story about the deceived Leandra (part 1, ch. 51). Each is unique in its presentation. The *Curioso* is the most artificial intrusion into the story of Don Quixote and Sancho. It is an anonymous manuscript read by one character, the priest, to the assembled guests in the inn. It is an independent literary work, a fiction, and none of its characters exists on the same ontological plane as those of Cervantes' novel. The captive Ruy Pérez de Viedma tells his own story in an extended first-person narrative. It is grounded in verifiable history, and its first part parallels the life of Cervantes himself. Whereas the *Curioso* is brought to an absolute end, the story of the captain and the lovely Zoraida is not quite complete, as she has yet to gain sufficient instruction in the Christian religion and be baptized so that the two can marry. Although a happy ending is anticipated by everyone, the characters disappear from the novel without our actually learning what eventually happens to them. Eugenio's story of Leandra is far shorter then the two others, but it shares something of them both. Like the *Curioso,* it is a story heard by a group of characters in Cervantes' novel, but this is an impromptu oral telling, not the reading of a manuscript. Like the captive's tale, the story told by Eugenio is narrated in first-person, but the primary interest is not in the teller, but in Leandra. The resolution is somewhere between the two earlier models in that the story is basically complete, with the deceived Leandra placed in a convent by her father, but with some opening left for Eugenio and other jilted lovers left to lament their fate.

Much more original and experimental is the story of Cardenio, Dorotea, Fernando, and Luscinda. The story is told by no fewer than three different narrators over a space of 14 chapters and is seamlessly integrated into the primary narrative of the adventures of Don Quixote. The tale begins in part 1, chapter 23, when Don Quixote and Sancho enter the Sierra Morena and learn from a goatherd about the mad nobleman who rode a mule to death there some six months previously and since then has alternated between lucid states and periods of madness. At times this man cryptically alluded to his betrayal by a certain Don Fernando. Then Don Quixote has a face-to-face encounter with the man, named Cardenio, who offers to tell his story. In part 1, chapter 24, Cardenio tells how the wealthy and powerful Don Fernando, supposedly in love with a rich peasant woman named Dorotea, deceived Cardenio and began to court Cardenio's beloved, Luscinda. But a passing reference to *Amadís de Gaula* gives Don Quixote the occasion to interrupt the story and talk about romances of chivalry. Cardenio lapses back into madness, beats Don Quixote, Sancho, and the goatherd, and flees.

In part 1, chapter 27, the priest and barber run into Cardenio, who tells them his story beyond the point where Don Quixote had interrupted him. Barely has he finished, when, in part 1, chapter 28, the three men hear a voice that turns out to be that of Dorotea, who tells them the story from her point of view. Cardenio and Dorotea both agree to help with Don Quixote, and are present at the inn when Fernando and Luscinda arrive there in part 1, chapter 36, and Dorotea convinces Fernando to honor his word to her. All four characters continue to be factors in Don Quixote's life through part 1, chapter 46, when he is taken away in a cage, supposedly under enchantment. The fragmentation of the story into several narrative units, the alternation among multiple narrators, the fact that no one hears the complete story as a coherent whole, the way the characters take on important roles in Don Quixote's life that have nothing to do with their own concerns, and the way the definitive ending of the story takes place wholly within the primary narrative, all combine to make this perhaps the single most interesting experiment in narrative embedding in all of Renaissance prose fiction.

Something similar, but on a much smaller scale, is the story of the death of the student-shepherd Grisóstomo in part 1, chapters 12–14. First, the goatherd Pedro arrives with the news that Grisóstomo has died of love for the beautiful Marcela and is to be buried the next day. Don Quixote urges Pedro to tell him the whole story, but as he does so, Don Quixote interrupts several times to correct his pronunciation, but Pedro speaks more eloquently as the story goes on. The beautiful and wealthy Marcela, adored by many of the men in the village, felt affection for no one and took to solitude, dressed as a shepherdess, in order to avoid men. Grisóstomo, his friend Ambrosio, and several others dressed as shepherds and went out to roam the hills lamenting their unrequited love. Now Grisóstomo has died because of Marcela's cruelty. The next day, the burial takes place, but suddenly the cruel Marcela herself appears high on the cliff at whose foot the burial is taking place. There she delivers a brilliant, long, rhetorical speech in self-defense: she recognizes that she is beautiful and that beauty inspires love, but this in no way obliges her to love in return; she insists that "I was born free, and in order to live free I chose the solitude of the countryside" (part 1, ch. 14); therefore, Grisóstomo's death is in no way her fault. After she finishes speaking, Marcela disappears in the forest and is never seen again. In this case, much of the interest comes in the way Marcela recontextualizes the version that the men have told about her. In their version she is cold and cruel, in hers she is determined and independent. This embedded narrative is noteworthy for the way it emphasizes the importance of context and point of view, as well as for its presentation of the closest thing to a proto-feminist female character to be found in Spanish Golden Age literature.

There is one more narrative in part 1 of the novel that merits more recognition as an embedded narrative than it has received. This is the story told by Sancho in part 1, chapter 20. Frightened by the mysterious pounding noise they hear, Sancho tells Don Quixote a story to help take his mind of the idea of going away at once to investigate the adventure: the goatherd Lope Ruiz, loved by the shepherdess Torralba, takes his flock and flees his pursuer, but has to cross a river where there is but a small boat in which the boatman can ferry only one goat at a time. Here Sancho warns Don Quixote that he should keep an accurate count of the goats as they reach the other side of the river. And so the process begins: one goat, another, and another. Don Quixote insists that they have all crossed and that Sancho should get on with the story, but, when he cannot say exactly how many goats have crossed, Sancho declares the story over. Don Quixote cannot believe that the tale has been brought to an end and asks incredulously if it is really over. And Sancho replies, "It's as over as my mother's life" (for an analysis of the scene, see Halevi-Wise, *Interactive Fictions* 21–49).

Some consider Sancho's tale an example of popular, folkloric narrative with the structure of the sort of repetitive bedtime story parents tell their children to put them to sleep, complete with the counting of sheep (here, goats), while others see it as a kind of shaggy-dog story, an elaborate joke. The scene is a brilliant presentation of traditional oral storytelling (for two differing readings, see Mancing, "La retórica," and Shipley, "Sancho's Jokework"). Sancho's story is formulaic, full of clichés, repetitions, and conventions. Don Quixote interrupts no fewer than six times and criticizes the way Sancho is telling the story, demonstrating the fundamental difference between an oral story and a written one: you can interrupt, and thus directly influence the course, and even the outcome, of an oral tale, but the written story is already complete and cannot be modified. Sancho's natural folktale stands at the opposite pole from the artifice of the artfully written *Curioso impertinente.* (It might be objected that the *Curioso* is indeed interrupted by Don Quixote's dream that he is fighting with the giant, but it is the *reading* of the story that is interrupted, not the story itself; nothing changes the written narrative.)

Overall, in part 2 of the novel, Cervantes is more cautious and less experimental than he was in part 1. Probably his main narrative experiment in the 1615 *Don Quixote* is the long period during the stay with the duke and duchess when he separates the knight and the squire (part 2, chs. 44–53). Don Quixote stays in the ducal palace where he is manipulated, tricked, and humiliated, while Sancho takes over the governorship of Barataria and comes to the fore as perceptive, decisive, and successful, clearly demonstrating his moral and ethical superiority over those who constantly try to manipulate and laugh at him.

Before separating the two characters, there is some editorial commentary on Cide Hamete's explicit recognition of the criticism some readers level at the inclusion of embedded narratives:

> a kind of complaint that the Moor had about himself, for having taken in his hands a history that was so dry and so limited as is this one about Don Quixote, because it seemed to him that he had to limit himself to talking about him and Sancho, without daring to include other digressions and episodes that were more serious and more entertaining. And he said that to go on with his mind, his hand, and his pen writing about a single subject and speaking through the mouths of so few persons was an intolerable job, whose result would not redound to the benefit of its author, and that in order to avoid this problem he had made use of the artifice of some *novelas* in the first part . . . (part 2, ch. 44)

The report of the wise historian's complaint continues for a while, and then the narrator concludes as follows:

> And thus, in this second part he didn't want to include any more independent or add-on *novelas,* but some episodes that might seem like tales, developed out of the very events of the true history—but only a few of these, and told as succinctly as possible. And, since he stays within the narrow limits of the narration, even though he has the ability, capacity, and intelligence needed to treat the whole universe, he asks the reader not to disparage his work but to give him some praise, not for what he writes, but for what he refrained from writing. (part 2, ch. 44)

Then, in the very next paragraph, Sancho goes off to take possession of his governorship, leaving Don Quixote behind at the duke's palace. It seems clear that in Cervantes' mind there was some sort of conceptual link between the inclusion of embedded narratives and the separation of the two main characters. There are some embedded narratives in part 2 of the novel, but none of them is as long as *Curioso,* the captain's story, or the Cardenio affair. All the episodes of the sequel that have some trappings of being an embedded story—Camacho's wedding (part 2, chs. 20–21), the braying aldermen (part 2, ch. 25), the Claudia Jerónima story (part 2, ch. 60), etc.—are very brief and thoroughly integrated in the primary narration.

Cervantes' text in both parts is further complicated by other types of narration, particularly those invented and staged for the purpose of deceiving Don Quixote in terms of his chivalric madness: Dorotea's tale of Micomicona (part 1, chs. 29–30); Sancho's story of his supposed visit to Dulcinea (part 1, chs. 30–31), the "enchantment" of Don Quixote by the priest and barber (part 1, chs. 46–47); Sancho's "enchantment" of Dulcinea (part 2, ch. 10); Sansón's tale of his love for Casildea de Vandalia (part 2, ch. 14); the procession of "enchanters" that follows the hunt with the duke and duchess (part 2, ch. 34); the long Trifaldi episode that culminates in the ride on Clavileño (part 2, chs. 36–41); the story of Altisidora's supposed descent into hell after her "death" (part 2, ch. 70); and other, briefer episodes.

In addition, Don Quixote himself narrates chivalric adventures (often more archetypal than particular): the tale of the armies of Alifanfarón and Pentapolín (part 1, ch. 18); the life-cycle of a knight-errant (part 1, ch. 21); the episode of the Knight of the Lake (part 1, ch. 50); the events of the Cave of Montesinos (part 2, ch. 23); and others. In addition, there is the story of how Cervantes the narrator searched for and found Cide Hamete's manuscript in Toledo (part 1, ch. 9). Finally, there is the obviously fictional extratextual scene between Cervantes and a supposed friend on the nature of literary prologues that comprises the majority of the prologue to part I. The very concept of embedded narratives in *Don Quixote* is a problematic one.

The wide variety of techniques Cervantes uses throughout *Don Quixote* to embed one narrative within another is a major facet of his narrative theory and practice. The art of narrative embedding is a highlight of the novel and illustrates Cervantes' complete mastery of the storyteller's art.

WORKS CITED

Bakhtin, M. M. *Art and Answerability: Early Philosophical Essays by M. M. Bakhtin.* Ed. Michael Holquist and Vadim Liapunov. Trans. and notes Vadim Liapunov. Supplement trans. Kenneth Brostrom. Austin: U of Texas P, 1990.

——. *The Dialogic Imagination: Four Essays.* Ed. Michael Holquist. Trans. Caryl Emerson and Michael Holquist. Austin: U of Texas P, 1981.

——. *Rabelais and His World.* Trans. Hélène Iswolsky. Bloomington: Indiana UP, 1984.

——. *Speech Genres and Other Late Essays.* Trans. Vern W. McGee. Ed. Caryl Emerson and Michael Holquist. Austin: U of Texas P, 1986.

——. *Toward a Philosophy of the Act.* Ed. Michael Holquist and Vadim Liapunov. Trans. and notes Vadim Liapunov. Austin: U of Texas P, 1993.

Barrick, Mac E. "The Form and Function of Folktales in *Don Quijote.*" *Journal of Medieval and Renaissance Studies* 6 (1976): 101–38.

Borges, Jorge Luis. "Partial Enchantments of the *Quixote.*" In *Other Inquisitions.* Trans. Ruth L. Simms. Intro. James E. Irby. Austin: U of Texas P, 1964; original Spanish ed. 1952.

Byron, George Gordon. *Byron's Don Juan: A Variorum Edition.* Vol. 3, 2nd ed. Ed. Truman Guy Staffan and Willis W. Pratt. Austin: U of Texas P, 1971.

Canavaggio, Jean. "Alonso López Pinciano y la estética literaria de Cervantes en el *Quijote.*" *Anales Cervantinos* 7 (1958): 13–107.

Chejne, Anwar G. *Islam and the West. The Moriscos, a Cultural and Social History.* Albany: State U of New York P, 1983.

Eisenberg, Daniel. "The *Romance* as Seen by Cervantes." *El Crotalón, Anuario de Filología Española* 1 (1984): 177–92.

Finello, Dominick. *Pastoral Themes and Forms in Cervantes' Fiction.* Lewisburg: Bucknell UP, 1994.

Forcione, Alban K. *Cervantes, Aristotle, and the Persiles.* Princeton: Princeton UP, 1970.

Gerrig, Richard J. *Experiencing Narrative Worlds: On the Psychological Activities of Reading.* New Haven: Yale UP, 1993.

Green, Otis H. "El *ingenioso* hidalgo." *Hispanic Review* 25 (1957): 175–93.

Guillén, Claudio. "Genre and Countergenre: The Discovery of the Picaresque." In *Literature as System: Essays Toward the Theory of Literary History.* Princeton: Princeton UP, 1971. 135–58.

Halevi-Wise, Yael. *Interactive Fictions: Scenes of Storytelling in the Novel.* Westport, CT: Praeger, 2003.

Hart, Thomas R. *Cervantes and Ariosto: Renewing Fiction.* Princeton: Princeton UP, 1989.

Levin, Harry. *The Myth of the Golden Age in the Renaissance.* New York: Oxford UP, 1969.

Mancing, Howard. "Cervantes as Narrator of *Don Quijote.*" *Cervantes* 23.1 (2003): 117–40.

——. *The Chivalric World of Don Quijote: Style, Structure, and Narrative Technique.* Columbia: U of Missouri P, 1982.

————. "Embedded Narration in *Guzmán de Alfarache.*" In *"Ingeniosa Inven-ción": Essays on Golden Age Spanish Literature for Geoffrey L. Stagg in Honor of His Eightieth Birthday.* Ed. Ellen M. Anderson and Amy R. Williamsen. Newark, DE: Juan de la Cuesta, 1999. 69–99.

————. "Response to Jim Parr." *Cervantes* 24.2 (2005), 135–54.

————. "La retórica de Sancho Panza." In *Actas del Séptimo Congreso de la Asociación Internacional de Hispanistas.* Ed. Giuseppe Bellini. Rome: Bulzoni Editore, 1982. 717–23.

Martin, Jay. *Who Am I This Time? Uncovering the Fictive Personality.* New York: W. W. Norton, 1988.

McGrady, Donald. *Mateo Alemán.* New York: Twayne, 1968.

Monroy, Juan Antonio. *La Biblia en el "Quijote."* Madrid: V. Suárez, 1963.

Montalvo, Garci Rodríguez de. *Amadís of Gaul.* Trans. Edwin B. Place and Herbert C. Behm. Lexington: UP of Kentucky, 1975.

Parr, James A. *"Don Quixote": An Anatomy of Subversive Discourse.* Newark, DE: Juan de la Cuesta, 1988.

————. "On Narration and Theory." *Cervantes* 24.2 (2005): 117–33.

Paz Gago, José María. *Semiótica del "Quijote": Teoría y práctica de la ficción narrativa.* Amsterdam: Rodopi, 1995.

Riewald, J. G. "Parody as Criticism." *Neophilologus* 50 (1966): 12–48.

Riley, Edward C. *Cervantes's Theory of the Novel.* Oxford: Clarendon P, 1962.

————. "Don Quixote and the Imitation of Models." *Bulletin of Hispanic Studies* 31 (1954): 3–16.

Rivers, Elias L. "Cervantes y Garcilaso." In *Homenaje a José Manuel Blecua.* Madrid: Gredos, 1983. 565–70.

Sarbin, Theodore. "The Quixotic Principle: A Belletristic Approach to the Psychological Study of Imaginings and Believings." In *The Social Context of Conduct: Psychological Writings of Theodore Sarbin.* Ed. Vernon L. Allen and Karl E. Scheibe. New York: Praeger, 1982. 169–86.

Shipley, George. "Sancho's Jokework." In *Quixotic Desire: Psychoanalytic Perspectives on Cervantes.* Ed. Ruth El Saffar and Diana de Armas Wilson. Cornell: Cornell UP, 1993. 135–54.

Stoopen, María. *Los autores, el texto, los lectores en el "Quijote" de 1605.* Mexico City: Facultad de Filosofía y Letras, UNAM, 2002.

Syverson-Stork, Jill. *Theatrical Aspects of the Novel: A Study of "Don Quixote."* Valencia, Albatros, 1986.

Trilling, Lionel. *The Liberal Imagination: Essays on Literature and Society.* New York: Viking P, 1950.

Wardropper, Bruce W. "*Don Quixote:* Story or History?" *Modern Philology* 63 (1965): 1–11.

Williamson, Edwin. *The Half-Way House of Fiction: "Don Quixote" and Arthurian Romance.* Oxford: Clarendon P, 1984.

Chapter 6

NARRATIVE ART

Spanish is often called *la lengua de Cervantes*—the language of Cervantes—in recognition of the elegance and sobriety of Cervantes' style, especially in *Don Quixote.* But whereas some devotees idealize and revere everything Cervantes did as perfect and morally righteous, others have called him a sloppy, inconsistent, and error-prone writer. Representative of the latter group is Jorge Luis Borges, for whom Cervantes appears to be just about the only Spanish writer for whom he had much respect. Even so, he described Cervantes' works in general as mediocre, praising only *Don Quixote*—but even here Borges criticized the novel as boring, repetitious, and poorly written, offering the opinion that numerous writers of less talent often wrote better Spanish (see Rodríguez-Luis, "El *Quijote* según Borges"). The truth is somewhere in between, but there is no question that Cervantes was in many ways a consummate artist, frequently striving for specific effects in his prose. This chapter is concerned with the style(s) of *Don Quixote,* aspects of characterization in the novel, and other facets of Cervantes' narrative art.

LEVELS OF STYLE

One thing that is probably not apparent to many readers today is just how modern Cervantes' prose is. Spanish is a much more conservative language than is, for example, English. Cervantes' exact contemporary, William Shakespeare, wrote an English that can at times seem impenetrable to twenty-first-century readers. Shakespeare sounds archaic, stilted, artificial—yet supremely elegant and beautiful, of course—but even moderately educated Spaniards today can read and understand Cervantes directly and easily, because Cervantes writes what is essentially a very modern Spanish. Some of his vocabulary, imagery, and cultural references may be unfamiliar, and he often uses a more elegant, refined, and rhetorical syntax than is characteristic of much contemporary writing, but these are minor inconveniences at best. (For some twenty-first-century readers, even nineteenth-century writers such as Pérez Galdós or George Eliot seem stilted and difficult to read because of their large and sometimes antiquated vocabulary and their complex syntax.) Notes in Spanish editions of *Don Quixote* often explain cultural or historical matters more often than they do linguistic or stylistic ones.

Cervantes' works exhibit an extraordinarily wide range of stylistic register, much of which is inevitably lost in translation, as has been illustrated from time to time in previous chapters, and as will be seen again later in this chapter. One can identify several levels of style in *Don Quixote*. First and foremost there is the general narrative style, elegant yet simple and straightforward, which sets the overall tone for the novel. Many translators have remarked on the beauty, simplicity, and freshness of Cervantes' style. Edith Grossman, for example, describes Cervantes' writing as "a marvel: it gives off sparks and flows like honey. Cervantes' style is so artful it seems absolutely natural and inevitable; his irony is sweet-natured, his sensibility sophisticated, compassionate, and humorous" (xx). Skillful translators, like Grossman, convey this modern, natural, graceful style on every page of the book.

But occasionally the style of Cervantes' narrator and characters contrasts with the ongoing narrative and conversational style. For example, there are times when a character makes an utterance characterized by conscious rhetorical devices such as repetition, parallel structures, antithesis, and extended comparison. We see this when Don Quixote imagines how a future wise enchanter will write the story of his adventures (part 1, ch. 2), in Don Quixote's speech on the Golden Age (part 1, ch. 11), or in Marcela's elegant defense of her proto-feminist philosophy about love and agency (part 1, ch. 14), which is perhaps the single most impressive rhetorical display in the entire novel (Mackey, "Rhetoric and Characterization"). Related to this is the style of the more idealistic or Italianate narratives of upper-class lovers such as Cardenio (part 1, ch. 27) or Dorotea (part 1, ch. 28) and in the entire text of the *Curioso impertinente* (part 1, chs. 33–35). This prose is more stilted, artful, and slow-paced, and it stands well apart from the scenes of description or conversation between characters. The better-educated characters, such as the canon of Toledo and Sansón Carrasco, often speak in a discourse that is slightly more learned or academic and includes an occasional phrase in Latin, but it does not normally reach the very highest registers of consciously artificial and rhetorical prose.

Although some passages have a more elevated style, Cervantes also includes numerous instances of a lower, more colloquial, informal, even incorrect discourse. The primary example of a low style is the colloquial speech of peasants such as Sancho or the goat herd Pedro (at least at the beginning of his discourse in part 1, ch. 12). Probably the most distinguishing feature of Sancho's discourse is his frequent citation of proverbs, that inexhaustible font of popular wisdom, often spoken in great length (see Parker, *The Humor*). Sometimes this language is exaggerated for comic effect, as it is in the speech of the ignorant peasant woman presented by Sancho to Don Quixote as Dulcinea (part 2, ch. 10). Further variants, often producing a comic effect, are the broken Spanish of the Basque squire (part 1, ch. 8), the slang of thieves and rogues (part 1, ch. 22), the Frankish dialect of the *morisco* Ricote and his companions (part 2, ch. 54), and the Arabic-flavored style of the captain in the narrative of his military exploits and escape from Algiers (part 1, chs. 39–41).

Don Quixote's discourse consists of all of the above. At times he can be somewhat pompous and artificial, especially when he is lecturing Sancho about matters of chivalry, condescendingly beginning with a phrase like, "You should know, Sancho, that . . . " Most of the time, in his dealings with Sancho and other characters, he uses a straightforward, correct, polite discourse that resembles the overall narrative style of the novel. He can, however, descend into vulgarity and obscenity, as when he insults Ginés de Pasamonte (part 1, ch. 22), calling him a "son of a whore," or when Sancho makes his master angry, and Don Quixote responds with a series of insulting epithets and obscenities (see, for example, part 1, ch. 46).

There is one other feature of Don Quixote's discourse that is frequently completely obscured in translation: his conscious use of an artificially archaic style, called *fabla*. Since the romances of chivalry were always purported to be translations of old texts, several of them are written in a style that evokes an earlier state of the Spanish language. *Amadís de Gaula*, Don Quixote's favorite book, was actually a rewrite of a medieval text, and its modern adapter, Garci Rodríguez de Montalvo, states in his prologue that he modernized the language of the old text. At the same time, however, Montalvo deliberately retained an archaic flavor, both in the parts he kept or adapted from the medieval text and in those he himself wrote. The authors of several later romances of chivalry, even some from the very late sixteenth century, also consciously incorporate this archaic style into works, even though by that time it came across as even more stilted and artificial (see Lucía Megías, *De los libros de caballerías* 95). In order to imitate his literary heroes, Don Quixote often speaks in *fabla,* especially early in his chivalric career, employing a small repertoire of archaic phonological and morphological forms and a modest archaic vocabulary (see Mancing, *The Chivalric World*).

The effect of such archaic speech by Don Quixote, especially when combined with his archaic armor—it was not his father's, nor even his grandfather's, but his great-grandfather's armor—is comic, and attention is drawn to the fact that it evokes incomprehension and laughter from several characters in the novel. Don Quixote, in other words, both looks and sounds like someone from a century in the past. Don Quixote's archaic speech declines in frequency during the course of the novel; he uses none after part 2, chapter 32. Other characters, including Sancho and the priest Pero Pérez, quickly learn to use *fabla* in imitation of Don Quixote, often in order to deceive and manipulate him. The style is contagious, and there are even times when the narrator gets caught up in the comic chivalric and writes briefly in *fabla.* One example of how *fabla* works can be seen in Don Quixote's invocation of Dulcinea in part 1, chapter 2:

¡Oh princesa Dulcinea, señora deste *cautivo* [miserable] corazón! Mucho agravio me *habedes* [habéis] *fecho* [hecho] en despedirme y reprocharme con el riguroso *afincamiento* [apremio] de mandarme no parecer ante *la vuestra* [vuestra] *fermosura* [hermosura]. *Plégaos* [Plázcaos], señora, de *membraros* [recordar] *deste vuestro* [vuestro] sujeto corazón que tantas cuitas por vuestro amor padece. (121)

The underlined words (the modern forms of which are in brackets), and especially the ones that begin with *f-* and the *-edes* verb forms, would have been perceived at once by Cervantes' contemporaries as archaic, and therefore highly comic. Compare the obvious effect this language must have had on Cervantes' contemporary readers with the effect of the same passage in a good modern translation, in this case that of Edith Grossman:

O Princess Dulcinea, mistress of this captive heart! Thou hast done me grievous harm in bidding me farewell and reproving me with the harsh affection of commanding that I not appear before thy sublime beauty. May it please thee, Señora, to recall this thy subject heart, which suffers countless trials for the sake of thy love. (25)

The effect here may be somewhat stilted and old-fashioned sounding, but it still falls far short of the effect of the original. Grossman uses the archaic second-person form of address, *thou hast, thy,* and *thee,* quite regularly throughout the novel, so the impression it makes here is diluted by its appearance in contexts where no archaic effect is intended. Vocabulary like *grievous* and *reproving* also make some contribution to the tone, but these words in English are not absolute archaisms (no longer in use) as were the words Cervantes employs. And then there is the common mistake of understanding *cautivo* solely in its modern meaning of *captive.* That meaning was also current, and in fact was the most common usage during Cervantes' day, but in chivalric contexts *cautivo* specifically retains its archaic meaning of *miserable* or *unfortunate.* Don Quixote uses this archaic word more often than any other, largely because it survived longest in the romances of chivalry than in other types of discourse, and he knew that his readers would find its archaic usage comic. Translators' inability to convey accurately the specific humor involved in this type of speech by Don Quixote is far from a fatal flaw. The passage can be understood, and at least some of its linguistic humor may be approximated, as it is by Grossman here. However, this is a good illustration of Don Quixote's metaphor of reading a translation is like seeing a tapestry from the reverse side (part 2, ch. 62).

Overall, *Don Quixote* provides an excellent illustration of some of Bakhtin's major concepts about language: hybridization, the mixing of different linguistic consciousnesses in a single utterance; heteroglossia, a multiplicity of social voices and speech genres and their mutual interrelationships; and polyphony, multiple discourses reflecting multiple consciousnesses. According to Bakhtin, heteroglossia is what distinguishes the novel from all other genres, and he notes that "the classic and purest model of the novel as genre [is] Cervantes' *Don Quixote,* which realizes in itself, in extraordinary depth and breadth, all the artistic possibilities of heteroglot and internally dialogized novelistic discourse" (*Dialogic Imagination* 324).

DIALOGUE AND DESCRIPTION: REALISM

Throughout the novel, Don Quixote and Sancho talk to each other and to other characters in a natural, conversational way. Before Cervantes, no other fiction writer was able to convey such a sustained sense of realistic human dialogue in fiction (except perhaps Fernando de Rojas in *La Celestina,* where the dialogue often sparkles with a modernity that is astounding for a work first published in 1499). Characters in Italian short fiction, the lovers, knights, shepherds, and *pícaros* of sentimental, chivalric, pastoral, and picaresque fictions at best only rarely engage in dialogue; they tend to speak in alternating monologues. What is more, Cervantes as author/narrator rarely interprets, overrides, or otherwise contextualizes what the characters say.

In this sense, *Don Quixote* truly is one of the first examples of what Bakhtin (in *Problems of Dostoevsky's Poetics*) calls the polyphonic novel: a novel in which the narrator's (or author's) voice has no privilege over those of the characters, all of whom speak from within their own personal consciousness and with their own point of view. But we should not exaggerate or overstate the case here, for although Cervantes often achieves real polyphony in *Don Quixote,* there are still some significant differences between Cervantes' accomplishment and the fully polyphonic novels of Dostoevsky as understood by Bakhtin; there is a greater degree of authorial privilege in Cervantes than in Dostoevsky.

Perhaps the most significant role Sancho has to play in *Don Quixote* is that of interlocutor with Don Quixote. Sancho makes his master discuss everyday, mundane details of life; enables him to laugh at himself and others; and forces him to argue his position. In part 2 of *Don Quixote,* there is even more dialogue and conversation than in part 1, as the growing familiarity and degree of friendship of the two main characters comes more to the fore and as the plot becomes less action-oriented and consists more of conversations of all kinds.

There are relatively few descriptions in *Don Quixote,* as Cervantes prefers to evoke characters, settings, and actions more than describe them in detail. Character descriptions, particularly, usually consist of a few evocative and imprecise details, leaving it to the reader to fill in the gaps. For example, Don Quixote is described in part 1, chapter 1, as "approaching fifty years of age; he had a hearty constitution, his flesh was dry, his face gaunt; he was an early-riser and was fond of the hunt." Later, at various points in the narrative, there are brief descriptive comments that help fill in what Don Quixote looks like, but overall the reader's image of the character is based more on the reader's imagination. More often than not, however, today's reader already has a good idea of what Don Quixote looks like even before beginning to read the book. Illustrations in the text and on the book's cover reinforce an image already formed by famous artists such as Doré and Picasso, actors in film and theatrical versions of the novel, and pictures and drawings in magazines and cartoons (see Riley, "*Don Quixote:* From Text to Icon," and chapter 8). Sancho is introduced simply as a neighbor of Don Quixote's, "an honest man—if such a title can be given to one who is poor—but with very little salt in his mill" (part 1, ch. 7). Only later, and in passing, is it mentioned that he is fat (although that is already suggested in his name: *Panza,* belly) or that he has a beard.

Occasionally somewhat more descriptive information is provided. When Don Quixote and Sancho first arrive at Juan Palomeque's inn (part 1, ch. 16), they meet the innkeeper's daughter, described simply as "very good looking," and, in sharp contrast, the servant Maritornes:

> an Asturian girl: her face was broad, the back of her head was flat, and she had a snub nose; she was blind in one eye and not very healthy in the other. It is true that the loveliness of her body made up for her other faults: she was less than seven hand-spans from head to toe, and her shoulders, which weighed heavily upon her, made her look at the ground more than she would have wanted.

The object here, of course, is to draw a grotesquely comic picture, in large part just for the fun of it. In part 2, chapter 3, Sansón Carrasco is introduced as a man who, even if named after the Biblical Sampson, is described as "not a very large man, although he was a great joker; he had a sallow complexion, but a very good mind. He was about 24 years old, round-faced, with a flat nose, and a large mouth, all signs that he had a malicious nature and was fond of tricks and practical jokes." The point here is to underscore the character's frivolous nature, a feature that will be born out repeatedly in the novel. In one of Cervantes' more extended descriptions, the *hidalgo* Don Diego de Miranda is described in part 2, chapter 16, but almost exclusively in terms of what he is wearing, particularly his green cloak. Although the possible symbolism of the color green in this description has been much debated, the important thing is that the character's obvious material status and gentile demeanor stand in sharp contrast to the *hidalgo* Don Quixote. See also, for example, the descriptions of the galley slave Ginés de Pasamonte (part 1, ch. 22), the mad Cardenio in the Sierra Morena mountains (part 1, ch. 23), Dorotea (part 1, ch. 28), the captain and Zoraida (part 1, ch. 37), the peasant woman Sancho identifies as Dulcinea (part 2, ch. 10), the troupe of actors (part 2, ch. 11), Sansón Carrasco as the Knight of the Wood (part 2, ch. 14), the grotesque fake nose of Tomé Cecial as squire to Sansón (also part 2, ch. 14), the dancers at Camacho's wedding feast (part 2, ch. 20), the beautiful Quiteria and the gallant Basilio at the same wedding ceremony (part 2, ch. 21), the enchanted chivalric characters in Don Quixote's dream in the Cave of Montesinos (part 2, ch. 23), Ginés de Pasamonte as the puppeteer Maese Pedro (part 2, ch. 26), the Countess Trifaldi and her squire (part 2, ch. 38), Sancho when he sets out to become governor (part 2, ch. 44), Teresa Panza (part 2, ch. 50), and Roque Guinart (part 2, ch. 60), none of which is really particularly lengthy or detailed and which often stress clothing more than personal appearance or facial features.

Altisidora describes herself at some length in song (part 2, ch. 44), but the description is an incongruously grotesque one and is not verified in narration. The detailed description of Clara Perlerina (part 2, ch. 47) by the man posing as her fiancé's father is equally detailed and equally grotesque. These descriptions, along with those of Maritornes and Tomé Cecial's nose, suggest that Cervantes was particularly fond of describing the comic and grotesque. The other extreme, that of feminine beauty, is normally only described with general and conventional superlatives: Marcela, Camila, Dorotea, Luscinda, Zoraida, Doña Clara, Quiteria, the duchess. Don Quixote's detailed, poetic description of Dulcinea in part 1, chapter 13, is more a parody of Petrarchian conventions than anything else. In contrast to these relatively extended descriptions (relatively extended for Cervantes that is, not by the standards of many nineteenth-century realist novelists), there is no mention at all of the physical appearance of characters like Don Quixote's niece, his housekeeper, the priest Pero Pérez, the barber Maese Nicolás, Anselmo, Lotario, the canon of Toledo, Camacho, Basilio, the humanist cousin, the duke, the duke's majordomo, Don Antonio Moreno, Alvaro Tarfe, and many others.

External descriptions of buildings or settings are either minimal or expressed in terms of conventions such as the *locus amoenus,* as in the pleasant meadow, with a flowing brook, lush grass, shady trees, singing birds, and so forth. Cervantes in no way approximates the descriptive technique of many nineteenth-century novelists. And yet, perhaps surprisingly, the great nineteenth-century writers considered his work in *Don Quixote* as their point of departure. How can this be? Gustave Flaubert, for example, who is generally considered the prototype of the realist novelist, admired *Don Quixote* above all works of fiction, referring to it as the book he knew by heart even before reading it, and praising Cervantes' ability to evoke an image of the roads of Spain without ever actually describing them. It is the latter idea that gets right to the heart of what realism in literature is: all readers of *Don Quixote* experience the world Cervantes evokes; they see the roads and the inns, they see and hear characters, they take part in what is going on. *Real* realism does not consist in giving the reader every possible detail in order to make him or her see something as close as possible to what the writer sees or imagines. Rather, it consists in empowering the reader so that he or she can creatively imagine being there and performing the actions afforded by the text.

Richard Gerrig is a cognitive psychologist who has researched what happens when people read works of fiction. The results of his investigation is a book titled *Experiencing Narrative Worlds* (1993), perhaps the single most important contribution to narrative theory in the final quarter of the twentieth century. Gerrig has concluded that there are two (accurate) metaphors frequently used by readers to describe their experience of reading fiction: "readers are often described as *being transported* by a narrative by virtue of *performing* that narrative" (2). When we read a work of narrative fiction, we experience a kind of (biological or neurological) virtual reality. We have the experience of being there, of taking part in the action, of performing what takes place, and that is the fundamental difference between reading a book and seeing a play or film.

When we read *Don Quixote,* we do not *see* someone charge a windmill, we creatively *imagine* the scene. We imagine—see—the setting (road, hill, structure), we imagine—hear—Don Quixote's voice as he charges. In short, as Gerrig says, we are transported from our own time and space to that of Don Quixote, and we perform what happens: we actively create the roads, the figures of the characters, the intonation of their voices, and everything else. *That* is realism in literature—a private reality that makes the reading experience qualitatively different from all media in which we actually see someone or something created by another person or team of people (Mancing, "See the Play, Read the Book").

The reason nineteenth-century novelists like Flaubert, Dickens, Dostoevsky, Pérez Galdós, Melville, and so many others admire Cervantes' achievement is that they experience the reality of what happens in *Don Quixote.* It is not, as Félix Martínez-Bonati (*"Don Quijote" and the Poetics of the Novel*) has argued at length, that *Don Quixote* is formally a realist novel. The affinity that realist writers feel with Cervantes is not based on certain specific novelistic techniques, but on the sense of the real that comes through when reading his novel.

ELEMENTS OF STYLE: THE EFFECTS OF LANGUAGE

As has been suggested on several occasions in recent chapters, what gets lost in translation more than anything else is nuance of language. All translations of *Don Quixote,* in all languages, are much more monologic than is the original Spanish, for Cervantes is a master at changing, blending, modulating, and modifying the language of the text for (usually comic) effect. This is the essence of the heteroglossia Bakhtin posits as the defining characteristic quality of the novel as a genre. Much of the pleasure in reading *Don Quixote* in Spanish is in savoring subtle plays on words, following linguistic threads through the text, noting the surprising juxtaposition of words and ideas, laughing at neologisms (new words, or innovative modifications of common words), understanding the comedy of Don Quixote's consciously archaic chivalric speech (the *fabla* discussed previously), understanding the humor behind the etymology of a name, enjoying contrasting styles in a given passage, noting the hybrid nature of some passages, appreciating what Bakhtin calls "double-voiced" discourse, catching an erotic or obscene connotation in an image, or comprehending the humor in a joke or a word mispronounced by Sancho. This is a subject that cannot be pursued in detail in this chapter, but that deserves some consideration in order to give the reader further reason to pause and consider what the front side of the textual tapestry might really look like. Because of space limitations, only a few examples will be examined here: neologisms, humorous names, and erotic imagery.

Neologisms

Cervantes is a master at inventing words appropriate to his needs in context. Brief mention has already been made (in chapter 2) of *baciyelmo* (basin-helmet), when Sancho combines both *bacía* (basin), and *yelmo* (helmet), thus producing a hybrid word that acknowledges both realities at the same time. In part 1, chapter 43, when the innkeeper's daughter and the servant Maritornes trick Don Quixote by tying his hand to a window and making him spend the entire night standing on his horse, they are referred to in narration as *dos semidoncellas,* "two semi-virgins." But, of course, virginity (like pregnancy), is one case where binaries are appropriate: one either is or is not; there is no partial state. Therefore, the word might suggest that the innkeeper's daughter is a virgin while Maritornes certainly is not, so that they average out to two semi-virgins; but another possibility is that the daughter is less pure than was believed.

Baciyelmo and *semidoncellas* may be two of the most obviously comic neologisms in *Don Quixote,* but there are dozens of others. Here are just a few other examples (emphasis throughout is mine):

> in part 1, chapter 3, Don Quixote's dinner the previous evening in the inn
> is referred to in narration as "su *venteril* y limitada cena": "his *innly* and
> limited meal";

in part 1, chapter 7, when Don Quixote and Sancho (on his ass) first sally forth together, Don Quixote tries to recall if any knight-errant had ever "traído escudero caballero *asnalmente*": "brought along a squire riding *assnally*";

in part 2, chapter 46, Don Quixote is badly scratched by a cat (with a bell tied to its tail) in a joke that gets very much out of hand; the chapter title includes the phrase "temeroso espanto *cencerril* y *gatuno*": "fearful *belline* and *catine* [not *feline*, a perfectly proper word that also exists in Spanish and specifically was not chosen for use by Cervantes] frightening"; and at the end of the chapter we have the phrase "aquella canalla *gatesca*, encantadora y *cencerruna*": "that *catesque* [not the same as the *gatuno* of the chapter title, and, again, not simply the normal *feline*], enchanting, and *belled* [not the same as the *cencerril* of the chapter title, and therefore not quite the same as the previously acceptable *belline*] rabble";

in part 2, chapter 68, the chapter title announces that Don Quixote has a "*cerdosa* aventura": "*pigly* [not quite *porcine*, a good, if not common and perhaps a little funny-sounding, word in English] adventure."

It might be objected that words like innly, assnally, belline, catine, catesque, belled, and pigly are not real adjectives—but that is the point: neither are the words that Cervantes wrote. Translating them by acceptable variants in English completely misses the point: these are invented words designed to evoke laughter.

Finally, there is the scene in the castle of the duke and duchess in part 2, chapter 38, when the supposed Countess Trifaldi (a role played by the duke's majordomo dressed in drag) implores the aid of the famous knight-errant Don Quixote and is answered by Sancho Panza. Trifaldi's utterance is supposedly made very funny by her/his use of a series of superlatives formed by the addition of the augmentative suffix -*ísimo* (connoting exaggeration) and because the passage is loaded with words with stress on the third syllable from the last, an awkward rhythm in Spanish. Thus we have: *señor poderosísimo* (very powerful lord), *hermosísima señora* (very beautiful lady), *discretísimos circunstantes* (very discreet company), el *acendradísimo caballero* (very distinguished knight), and *valerosísimos pechos* (very valiant bosoms). But, to exaggerate the intended comedy, Trifaldi deliberately misuses the -*ísimo* suffix by applying it to three nouns, thus forming words that are absolutely ungrammatical, and therefore (intentionally) absurd in Spanish: *don Quijote de la Manchísima* (Don Quixote of the very Mancha), *su escuderísimo Panza* (his very squire Panza), and *mi cuitísima* (my very misfortune). The passage is funny, even if its linguistic comic effect is either completely or partly lost in *all* English translations.

But what is even funnier is the reply made by Sancho:

—El Panza—antes que otro respondiese, dijo Sancho—aquí está, y *el don Quijotísimo* asimismo; y así podréis, *dolorosísima dueñísima*, decir lo que *quisieridísimis;* que todos estamos prontos y *aparejadísimos* a ser vuestros *servidorísimos.* (emphasis added)

"The Panza is here," said Sancho before anyone else could respond, "and *the Don very Quixote* also; and thus you can, *very painful very dueña,* say whatever *you should very want;* for we are all ready and *very prepared* to be your *very servants.*

Sancho here uses the suffix correctly with adjectives twice, but he also deliberately misuses the form three times by applying it ungrammatically to nouns and, to top off the whole passage, once to a conjugated verb form: *quisieridísimis.* The correct grammatical form of this verb would be *quisierais,* imperfect subjunctive of *querer,* meaning "that you might like." But notice how the word is deformed in multiple ways. First, the - *ais* ending is modified with the insertion of *d* (in what must be an attempt to approximate Don Quixote's archaic *-ades* type of second-person verb) and, at the same time, the substitution of *i* for *a.* But then, Sancho further modifies the ending by adding a variant of the *-isimo* adjectival suffix in which the final *-mo* is changed to *-mis: -ísimis.* The result is a completely meaningless verb-like word with six repetitions of the vowel *i.* It may be the funniest single word in the novel. How is it possible to even begin to capture something like this in English?

Cervantes' contemporary Spanish readers must have found the novel—sprinkled throughout with comic new or deformed words and phrases—to be supremely funny on a stylistic or linguistic level that even modern Spaniards sometimes have difficulty appreciating. The impossibility of conveying this comic word play in translation—and it must be impossible, since no English-language translation (or translation into any other language), however brilliant, has ever succeeded in conveying adequately the comedy involved—means that by definition, as mentioned earlier, a reading of *Don Quixote* in translation is always like looking at the reverse side of the tapestry.

Humorous Names

Cervantes engages in an ongoing comic play with proper names throughout *Don Quixote.* Not every name in the novel is comic, by any means, but many of them are, and virtually all the names associated with the romances of chivalry carry comic connotations. Much of the humor throughout the novel comes from the names of giants and knights-errant in imitation of the names found throughout the chivalric romances (some earlier examples were cited in chapter 2). In *Don Quixote,* chivalric names invented by Cervantes include: Caraculiambro (part 1, ch. 1), whose name derives from *cara* (face) and *culo* (ass) and perhaps *ambos* (both); Timonel de Carcajona (part 1, ch. 18), from *timonel* (rudder) and *carcajada* (belly laugh); the Princess *Micomicona* from *Micomicón* (part 1, ch. 30), from *mico* (monkey, repeated twice); and many more (see Mancing, "The Comic Function").

Further humor comes when Sancho Panza and other uneducated and illiterate peasants mispronounce chivalric names. For example, Sancho demonstrates a chronic inability to pronounce correctly the name *Mambrino* (he of the golden helmet). He confuses it with *malandrín* (scoundrel) and says *Malandrino* (part 1, ch. 19); he mixes it with the common name *Martín* and says *Martino* (part 1, ch. 21); and he corrupts it with *maligno* (evil person) to get *Malino* (part 1, ch. 44). He has similar problems with other names, such as the queen Madásima and the surgeon Elisabat, mentioned by Cardenio in part 1, chapter 24, and deformed in part 1, chapter 25, by Sancho into *Magimasa* (something like Magic-dough) and *aquel abad* (that abbot). Similarly, in part 1, chapter 7, the niece and housekeeper cannot quite get the name of the wicked enchanter *Frestón,* the former calling him *Muñatón* (from the folkloric figure of Muñatones de la Sierra), and the latter calling him *Fritón* (from *frito,* fried), an understandable error by the housekeeper and cook.

Even more interesting are the multiple connotations of the names of the major characters, especially those of Don Quixote de la Mancha, Sancho Panza, and Dulcinea del Toboso. Don Quixote's name, especially, carries with it a number of comic connotations. First (as noted in chapter 5), there were people living in small towns in La Mancha (and specifically in Esquivias, the home of Cervantes' wife, Catalina, and in which he lived off and on for some years) who had the surname Quijana. But beyond the suggestive historical sources for the name, it is clear that the depreciatory suffix *-ote* connotes inappropriate size and awkwardness. At the same time, however, the ending recalls the name of one of the most famous of all knights-errant, Lanzarote—Lancelot of the Lake from the Arthurian tradition—an association that Don Quixote proudly makes in part 1, chapter 2, when he recites a ballad about Lancelot, but substitutes his own name. Perceptive Renaissance readers, however, might well have recalled another knight whose name had the same ending—Camilote, a comic character in the romance of chivalry *Primaleón* (1512) and in the Gil Vicente play *Dom Duardos* based on that romance, who defended the beauty of his unattractive lady.

The Spanish word *quijote* (from the Catalan *cuixot*) is used for the piece of armor that covers a knight's thigh (in English, *cuisse*), and some readers have seen in its use a connotation of sexuality, perhaps prudery or an unconscious desire to sublimate sexual desire. The first part of the name in Spanish, *Quij-*, carries with it various comic images also elicited by some of the names the narrator's supposed sources (in part 1, ch. 1) suggest for the *hidalgo* who becomes Don Quixote: Quijada, Quesada, Quejana, which evoke *quijada* (jaw; some have even perceived here a subtle allusion to the famous, outsized jaw of the Hapsburg line), *queso* (cheese), and *queja* (complaint). The uncertainty about the specific form of the character's surname is compounded in part 1, chapter 5, when Pedro Alonso calls him "Señor Quijana," another new variant. The same thing happens in part 1, chapter 49, when Don Quixote claims to be a direct descendant from Gutierre Quijada. In each of these cases, the most recent suggestion seems more authoritative than the last, but in part 2, chapter 74, on his deathbed, Don Quixote refers to himself as "Alonso Quijano," which is generally taken to be the definitive form of his name.

The addition of the phrase *de la Mancha* is a parody of the practice of fictional knights who adopt the name of their country as part of their name: *de Gaula, de Grecia, de Inglaterra,* and so forth. But La Mancha was a relatively impoverished and infertile section of Spain, rather than a glorious nation. The entire name, however, does carry a certain lyrical hint in that it forms an octosyllabic line that would fit perfectly into a ballad or lyric poem, as in the previously-mentioned ballad about Lancelot cited in part 1, chapter 2. His new name was important to Don Quixote, as he spent no less than a week pondering it so that it would be musical, lofty, and significant, like the one he had chosen for his horse—Rocinante (a name derived from *rocín,* nag, and *antes,* before: before, he was just a nag; now, he is the foremost nag in the world). Don Quixote's self-baptism should also recall the Judeo-Christian practice of assuming a new name as a sign of a new status in life: Saul of Tarsis becomes Saint Paul, Samuel L. Clemens becomes Mark Twain, Clark Kent becomes Superman. New name, new identity, constant linguistic and conceptual comedy: Don Quixote's name is all this throughout the novel.

Sancho Panza, too, is replete with comic connotations. *Sancho,* as well as being the name of a series of medieval kings, is derived from *santo* (saint), which gives the proverb *Al buen callar llaman Sancho* (Sancho is

the name for not speaking; or, it is saintly not to speak). *Panza* means belly
or paunch which gives Sancho the name of Holy Belly, personifying his
joy in eating and clearly designating his role as a symbol of carnivalesque
revelry. There was, furthermore, a carnival celebration among students at
the University of Salamanca which featured a grotesque figure named Santo
Panza: Saint Belly (the definitive study of the carnivalesque in literature,
very helpful in understanding Sancho's folkloric roots, is Bakhtin's *Rabelais
and His World;* see also Márquez Villanueva, "Sobre la génesis literaria,"
and Molho, "Raíz folklórica"). Supposedly, his name is sometimes given
in Cide Hamete's Arabic manuscript as Sancho Zancas, but in Cervantes'
edited version Zancas never appears (see chapter 5).

Finally, Dulcinea del Toboso also conforms to the same pattern of multiple
images and connotations. In part 1, chapter 1, Don Quixote transforms the
name of Aldonza Lorenzo into Dulcinea, modifying the first name in order
to make it sound more poetic. But Aldonza itself is of Arabic origin, and
it was particularly common among the lower classes. In some instances,
it was used as an epithet in place of a proper name for a woman who is
unattractive and of easy virtue, as suggested by the proverbial *A falta de
moza, buena es Aldonza* (If there's no woman around, Aldonza will do).
Don Quixote's transformation of the reality of Aldonza into the ideal of
Dulcinea is a prototypical act in his systematic transformation of base reality into poetic fantasy. Don Quixote presumably based his version of the
name on the assumption that the meaning of Aldonza was *dulce* (sweet).
The *-ea* suffix is in keeping with the poetic names of idealized women of
the lyric and pastoral traditions: Astrea, Dorotea, Finea, Galatea, Melibea,
and others. There is a shepherd named Dulcineo in Antonio de Lofrasso's
pastoral romance *Las fortunas de amor* (1573; *The Fortunes of Love*),
which may be another possible source for Don Quixote's invention. The
addition of *del Toboso* is a *reductio ad absurdum* of the chivalric tradition
of incorporating the name of the country of origin into the knight's name.
Don Quixote at least adds the name of a region of his country, La Mancha,
but El Toboso is only the name of a small and insignificant village. Furthermore, El Toboso was known to be populated mainly by *moriscos,* which
adds a further level of richness to Don Quixote's choice of a title.

Erotic Imagery

Those who would idolize Cervantes and his works as representing the
finest, purest, and most sublime aspects of Spanish, if not universal, culture, or those who make use of fictional works for doctrinaire purposes,

tend not to be aware, or to deny the existence of the erotic and, at times, obscene connotations of some words and deeds of Cervantes' characters and narrators. Similarly, issues of sexuality and gender, including what is now called queer theory, often tend to pass unnoticed, particularly among more naïve and traditional readers. No work of Cervantes' would ever be classified as pornographic, but it would be a mistake not to recognize that many of his works contain erotic and obscene words, phrases, and allusions. Part of the problem of nonrecognition is the dated nature of some of the imagery Cervantes uses: what sometimes carried an erotic connotation in the Renaissance is often not recognized as such in our day.

An example of the erotic undertones of Cervantes' texts can be seen in *Don Quixote* part 1, chapters 27 and 32. These passages deal with the oxtail borrowed from the inn of Juan Palomeque by the priest and barber as they prepare to dress as a damsel in distress and her squire in order to trick Don Quixote into giving up his penance in Sierra Morena and return home. The oxtail is first mentioned at the beginning of part 1, chapter 27, when the barber fashions a beard out of *una cola rucia o roja de buey* ("a grayish or reddish oxtail, where the innkeeper would stick his comb"), on the surface, an innocent and incidental reference. But when Don Quixote and those traveling with him reach the inn, the innkeeper's wife hurries to recover her tail from the barber so that she can again put her husband's comb back in it. *Peine* (comb) in Spanish cannot, in a context like this, fail to evoke *pene* (penis), while *pelo* (hair) and *cola* (tail) have similar connotations in both English and Spanish for women's pubic hair and genitals.

Another example can be seen in the confession of Sansón Carrasco (i.e., the Knight of the Mirrors) when he is defeated by Don Quixote in part 2, chapter 14. Carrasco admits that Dulcinea is more beautiful than his own Casildea de Vandalia, but in these terms: "I confess that the dirty tattered shoe of Señora Dulcinea del Toboso is worth more than the badly combed, but clean, beard of Casildea." The foot-shoe (penis-vagina) imagery is common in Renaissance literature, especially in some erotic and pornographic anonymous poetry of the period, and the beard-pubic hair analogy is the same as the one described in the previous paragraph. Furthermore, the erotic value of all the cross-dressing and undressing scenes in Cervantes' works—especially the strongly implied homoeroticism when the priest, the barber, and Cardenio spy upon the voluptuous naked feet of the young man who turns out to be Dorotea dressed as a man (part 1, ch. 28)—is hard to deny (on erotic themes in Cervantes' work, see El Saffar, "Sex and the Single Hidalgo;" Fuchs, "Border Crossings;" and Cerezo Aranda and Eisenberg, eds. "Selected Papers").

WINDMILLS

Don Quixote is a novel filled with unforgettable scenes, such as the book-burning, the windmills, the numerous inn scenes, Sancho's blanketing, the armies of sheep, and the galley slaves in part 1; and the enchantment of Dulcinea, Don Quixote's encounter with the lion, the Cave of Montesinos, Maese Pedro's puppet show, Sancho's island Barataria, and the death of Don Quixote in part 2. Even material items such as the enchanted helmet/shaving basin and the windmills have become cultural icons and have taken on symbolic value. In the first original illustration of *Don Quixote,* the frontispiece of the 1618 French edition, Don Quixote wears Mambrino's helmet and there is a windmill in the background.

The windmill scene (part 1, ch. 8) deserves particular consideration, as it, more than anything else, has come to represent Don Quixote's madness. This is the first adventure Don Quixote has with Sancho at his side, and it can legitimately be considered the prototype of a quixotic adventure, of which the most important features are:

- the statement of reality in narration;
- Don Quixote's transformation of this reality;
- Sancho's pointing out what the reality is;
- Don Quixote's rejection of Sancho's advice;
- the attack (combat, encounter);
- the result, which is either a victory for Don Quixote or some sort of unfortunate outcome (usually a fall, beating, or stoning); and
- Don Quixote's rationalization of his defeat; usually he blames things on the intervention of an enchanter who changed reality (see the longer discussion of the quixotic adventure in these terms in Mancing, *The Chivalric World* 112–17).

The iconic value of a man attacking a large machine, together with its strategic early placement in the novel (what is known in psychology as the primacy effect), have made it the standard for graphic interpretations of Don Quixote. One definition of a quixotic character or person is one who "tilts at windmills." Further, the windmill, with its arms that turn round and round but go nowhere, is itself a symbol of madness (usually seen in the clown's pinwheel or the circular motion we make with our finger pointing at our temple in order to indicate craziness). The windmills may also recall the image of Satan in the frozen depths of Dante's *Inferno* flailing his arms around and generating a great wind. It is not hard to see how

Don Quixote might perceive from a distance several windmills on a hilltop as gesticulating giants. Even the modern tourist who travels through La Mancha and sees the windmills of Consuegra, Mota del Cuervo, or Campo de Criptana when approaching these villages can imagine how one could mistake them for giants. A trip to one of these sites today allows twenty-first-century readers of the novel the opportunity to go into the mills, see how they were constructed and how grain was milled for flour, and imagine Don Quixote in their midst.

CHARACTERS

Don Quixote's image is more easily recognized than that of any other literary character ever created (see chapter 7), in spite of the fact that Cervantes presents his characters less by description than by what they do, as discussed previously. No one who reads the novel fails to form an impression—and a mental image—of Don Quixote. What is interesting, however, is that although the visual impression of the character has changed little throughout four centuries, the way that image is interpreted in psychological terms has undergone a great deal of modification. In the seventeenth and eighteenth centuries, both in Spain and in the rest of Europe, *Don Quixote* seems to have been read and understood almost universally as a satire, a burlesque, a funny book. Certainly it appears that the characters in part 2 of the novel who have read part 1—Sansón Carrasco, the duke and duchess, Don Juan and Don Jerónimo, Don Antonio Moreno—all react to Don Quixote in these terms. In part 2, chapter 3, when Don Quixote asks Sansón what episodes from his earlier exploits are most discussed, the answer is a list of comic adventures that took place in the first, more comic, half of the novel, part 1, chapters 8–22. Avellaneda, the anonymous author of the apocryphal continuation, also consistently stresses the comic and the burlesque. The Don Quixote who appears on stage and in the poetry of the period is always comic, usually ridiculous; other contemporary references to Don Quixote are in the same spirit. An often-cited anecdote relates that King Felipe III once saw a student reading a book and laughing, and remarked that either the man was crazy or he was reading *Don Quixote*. He was in fact reading Cervantes' novel.

Although there are some subtle indications that Cervantes himself may have seen something more than humor in his own work (see Weiger, *The Substance*), it is clear that a major (if not the only) conscious aim Cervantes had was to write a comic fiction. But by the eighteenth century in England there was a growing sense that *Don Quixote* was more than just a funny book (Tave, *The Amiable Humorist*) and that Cervantes was one of the greatest of all writers. Later in the century the German romantics completely reoriented readers' understanding of the protagonist, seeing him as noble and misunderstood. Overall, this romantic reading, or variants of it, have been dominant in the nineteenth and twentieth centuries (for a comprehensive review of this process, see Close, *The Romantic Approach*). Whether the opposition is stated in terms of comic versus romantic, cautionary versus idealist, fool versus hero, or hard versus soft, however, there are two polar opposites that mark the spectrum across which almost every conceivable understanding of Cervantes' novel has been expressed (see chapters 7 and 8).

If pressed, many readers would probably say that Don Quixote is most typically conceived as the madman who attacks windmills thinking they are giants. That is, he is a kind of absurd idealist who does impractical things that can be funny and noble at the same time. This is what it means to be "quixotic"—a term (along with its variants: quixotism, quixotical, and quixotically) that has become commonplace in English. In fact, Don Quixote has had more influence on the English language and culture than any other work of (non-British) literature. Along with quixotic and its variants, the phrase "tilting at windmills" also obviously derives from Cervantes' novel.

There are some readers who believe Don Quixote is always and only a funny figure, the butt of jokes, and should constantly be laughed at. Others believe that from the very beginning he is noble and idealistic, morally superior to other characters and social values in general (see the discussion of hard and soft critics in chapter 8). Most readers, however, perceive both comic and serious aspects of the character throughout the novel, often with the comic most prominent in part 1 (and especially the first half of part 1) and the more serious aspects of his character becoming more apparent as the novel progresses.

At the beginning of the novel Don Quixote is in control of almost everything that happens. He convinces the first innkeeper to treat him as a knight-errant and to bestow the order of chivalry upon him, and, for the most part, the world in general seems to conform to his interpretation of it throughout the first half of the 1605 novel. But when the priest and barber reenter the scene in part 1, chapter 26, they (along with Dorotea, Cardenio, and others) begin to take control of the action. Most of what happens in the second half of part 1 is initiated by other characters, a process that culminates in Don Quixote's "enchantment" by the priest and barber (part 1, ch. 46), who then take him home in a cage. During the same period of time other characters—Cardenio, Dorotea, Anselmo, Camila, the captive, his brother, Don Luis, Doña Clara, the canon of Toledo, and others—become the focus of the reader's attention, as Don Quixote is relegated to a secondary role.

Throughout part 2, Don Quixote displays less of the authentic enthusiasm he had in part 1. He is not even sure if he should make another sally until he is urged to do so by Sancho, Rocinante's whinnies, and Sansón Carrasco's discussion of the published book about his adventures. In part 2, chapter 4, Don Quixote, who does not know what to do, asks Sansón if the author of part 1 has plans to write a sequel, and Sansón assures him that he does. And so Don Quixote rides out again, not of his own volition, but because it is to be written—which leaves him no choice. At no point in part 2 of the novel does he transform reality as he did consistently early in part 1. It might seem that on at least one occasion Don Quixote does transform reality the way he did in part 1: the adventure of the enchanted boat and the watermills in part 2, chapter 29. But even when he claims that the mills are a city, castle, or fortress where someone is held captive and waits to be rescued, he admits that "they seem to be watermills." At no point in part 1 of the novel did he ever say anything like "they seem to be giants" or "they appear to be sheep," but he always insisted that things were in fact what they appeared to him to be. In part 2, Don Quixote consistently sees reality, or the "reality" presented to him by others; he pays for his adventures; he spends time relaxing and enjoying the hospitality of others; he controls his urge to intervene or interrupt; he spends much more time talking than he does attacking; he becomes dejected, melancholy, and pessimistic; and he acts more like a tourist than a knight-errant during his visit to Barcelona. It seems that Don Quixote's extended relationship with Sancho Panza and his repeated and often painful encounters with material reality are the primary factors that bring about the evolution of his character. By the time of his death in part 2, chapter 74, when the now apparently sane Alonso Quixano disavows his identity of Don Quixote and apologizes for all that he has done, few readers are still laughing at him (see Mancing, *The Chivalric World,* for an extended analysis of the novel in the way briefly described here).

It is only necessary to compare the Don Quixote of the early chapters of part 2 with the Don Quixote of the beginning of part 1 to see clearly that he is already a very different person. The encounter with the troupe of actors in part 2, chapter 11, makes clear the way Don Quixote's character has evolved. In part 1, chapter 8, when the innocent friars of Saint Benedict try to explain who they are, Don Quixote responds by saying

"No soft words with me, for I know who you are, you lying rabble." But in part 2, chapter 11, he listens patiently to a reasonable explanation from men dressed as king, knight-errant, and even Death itself and fully accepts what they say. In part 1, chapter 8, Don Quixote's will is supreme—"what I say is true"—but after encountering the actors he thinks that nothing is certain: "and now I say that you have to touch appearances with your hand in order to avoid being deceived." At the beginning of his career he charged into battle with little regard to his personal safety and confident of his own prowess, as in part 1, chapter 15, when he says "I am worth a hundred." But when he has to face the actors, armed with stones and awaiting his attack, he pauses "to think about how to attack them with the least danger to his person," and after Sancho advises him not to deal with actors, he gladly agrees and says "let us leave these phantasms and search again for better and more qualified adventures." It is hard to read this chapter and not admit that Don Quixote has indeed undergone considerable change. By part 2, chapter 29, the episode of the enchanted boat, Don Quixote has virtually given up: "I can do no more." Only the chance encounter with the duchess in the next chapter keeps the novel going.

Although Don Quixote evolves during the course of the novel, Sancho undergoes an even greater change. At first, Sancho seems to be the polar opposite of Don Quixote. He is a short, fat, ignorant, pragmatic, realistic, cowardly peasant who finds wisdom in the wealth of proverbs that he knows by heart, whereas Don Quixote is a tall, thin, well-educated, impractical, idealistic, and (foolishly) valiant *hidalgo* and knight-errant who finds inspiration in the many romances of chivalry he has read. Cervantes may well have conceived of Sancho as the inverse of Don Quixote in every way, but if so he modified his concept as he continued to write.

The literary origins of the character of Sancho are in the medieval and Renaissance folkloric and carnivalesque traditions, the buffoons of Roman theater, and the wise fool. Sancho's role in *Don Quixote* is largely to be reality instructor to Don Quixote, as well as to provide comic relief, beginning with his name. The way in which he makes Don Quixote talk about things other than knight-errantry, prosaic things like eating and drinking, also very subtly serves to undermine Don Quixote's chivalric mission. It seems clear that Sancho grows in self-confidence, worldly wisdom, and moral stature throughout the course of the novel (a process sometimes called quixotization; see chapter 8). In part 2 of the novel, he speaks more frequently than Don Quixote, achieves success while Don Quixote goes into decline, and survives the novel as a generally positive figure.

The highlight of Sancho's career is his brief stint as governor of the island of Barataria. In part 1, chapter 7, when Don Quixote first recruits Sancho as his squire, he promises someday to name him ruler of an island—he uses the Latinate *ínsula,* rather than the regular *isla* in Spanish, since that is the term often used in chivalric romances—as a reward for his good services. The very first words Sancho speaks when he rides out with Don Quixote in part 1, chapter 7, are: "Look your grace, señor knight-errant, please do not forget what you have promised me about the *ínsula,* for I'll know how to govern it, no matter how big it is." Just two chapters later, in part 1, chapter 10, after the encounter with the friars of Saint Benedict, Sancho immediately requests his island, but Don Quixote assures him that this was a mere crossroads adventure, and that the island reward will come later after he has gained fame as a knight-errant.

Throughout the novel, Sancho's future governorship becomes a running joke, as it is clear that Don Quixote can never gain the fame and power he strives for and that there is no possibility of his ever bestowing a governorship on his squire. Thus it comes as a surprise when, in part 2, chapter 32, a brief mention of the promised island inspires the duke's offer to make Sancho the governor of a "spare" island under his purview. That Sancho receives his ultimate reward from the idle, pleasure-seeking duke rather than after the culmination of Don Quixote's chivalric career is a point of embarrassment and humiliation for the knight-errant. The duke's aim in this gesture is to set Sancho up as the butt of a series of practical jokes and provide laughs for everyone involved, as Sancho is separated from Don Quixote in part 2, chapters 44–53 and goes off to take possession of his (landlocked) island, apparently a small village called Barataria (see Allen, "The Governorship of Sancho" and Jones, "The Baratarian Archipelago"). But Sancho turns the tables on the tricksters and acts as an intelligent, compassionate, generous, and fair ruler. By the time he renounces his governorship in part 2, chapter 53, and departs with only a bit of bread and cheese as his reward, the scene is one of regret and admiration: "They all embraced him, and he, weeping, embraced all of them, and he departed, leaving them marveling not only at his words but at his decision, which was so firm and so discreet."

Dulcinea del Toboso is perhaps the greatest absent character in the history of literature. Neither she nor the woman upon whom she is based, the peasant Aldonza Lorenzo, ever appears in the novel, yet her presence is everywhere and her name is constantly on the lips of the characters. Much of the best comedy in the novel takes place in scenes in which Dulcinea is involved. Probably the episode with the most far-reaching consequences in

Don Quixote is the one in which Sancho presents to his master three peasant women as Dulcinea and two of her ladies and Don Quixote believes that his beloved has been enchanted (part 2, ch. 10). Dulcinea is simultaneously a parody of courtly love conventions and Petrarchian imagery, as well as an unobtainable ideal. This mere figment of a writer's and a character's imagination has, however, become almost real in the readers' minds and in popular culture. Dulcinea was personified in public celebrations in Spain beginning in 1605, just months after the novel was first published, and she has been brought to life on stage, in fiction, and in song repeatedly over the centuries (for more on Dulcinea, see Close, "Don Quixote's Love for Dulcinea;" Herrero, *Who Was Dulcinea?*; and Mancing, "Dulcinea del Toboso").

The Arabic historian Cide Hamete Benengeli is as much a character as he is a narrator. As discussed at some length in chapter 5, he comes to the fore in part 2 of the novel as a comic figure. Rocinante, the aging nag who becomes Don Quixote's peerless steed, is perhaps the most famous horse in literature, perhaps the only one with his own personality. Like his master, Sancho, and Dulcinea, he became so popular that his name and his figure immediately entered popular culture. Sansón Carrasco is right in part 2, chapter 3, when he notes that "as soon as people see a skinny nag, they say, 'There goes Rocinante.' " There is a running joke throughout the novel about Rocinante's inability to move swiftly, his erotic interests, and his friendship with Sancho's ass. Aging, bony, inadequate Rocinante is a reflection of his aging, lean, pretentious master, just as the well-fed, pragmatic ass is a perfect match for Sancho.

The gallery of other characters in Don Quixote runs into the hundreds and includes the memorable priest, Pero Pérez, and his friend the barber, Maese Nicolás, who in part 1 sally forth quixotically apparently to attempt to rescue their friend Alonso Quixano who has gone mad and is doing crazy things. Their motivation becomes suspect, however, when they decide to play along with Don Quixote's madness in order to laugh at him and Sancho (Mancing, "Alonso Quijano y sus amigos"). In part 2 of the novel, their role is largely taken over by Sansón Carrasco, who is even more overtly frivolous, insensitive, and envious of Don Quixote. The duke and duchess are the highest-ranking members of society who appear in the novel, and they are consistently criticized for the often cruel jokes and tricks they play on the knight and squire. Other memorable characters include the generous goatherds, the proto-feminist Marcela, the grotesque Maritornes, the *pícaro* Ginés de Pasamonte, the discrete Dorotea, the clever Basilio, the courteous Don Diego de Miranda, the unfortunate Doña Rodríguez, the anguished

Ricote, and the brave bandit Roque Guinart. Most of these characters have only brief appearances in the novel but are remembered long after the book has been read.

One of the marvelous things about *Don Quixote* is that many readers feel that they are in the presence of real people: Don Quixote, Sancho, and the rest seem *alive,* almost palpable. It is the creation of a fictional text that affords this sense of intermingling with real people, of being a part of actual life, that may be Cervantes' greatest achievement. Laurence Sterne writes that he would have traveled farther to see Don Quixote than any hero of antiquity. Herman Melville called Don Quixote one of the greatest sages who ever lived. It is the ability to evoke reactions such as these that is one of the primary reasons why *Don Quixote* is a novel, in every significant sense of that term, and not a stylized romance or simple satire.

WORKS CITED

Allen, John J. "The Governorship of Sancho and Don Quijote's Chivalric Career." *Revista Hispánica Moderna* 38 (1974–75): 141–52.

Bakhtin, M. M. *The Dialogic Imagination: Four Essays.* Ed. by Michael Holquist. Trans. by Caryl Emerson and Michael Holquist. Austin: U of Texas P, 1981.

———. *Problems of Dostoevsky's Poetics.* Ed. and Trans. Caryl Emerson. Intro. Wayne C. Booth. Minneapolis: U of Minnesota P, 1984.

———. *Rabelais and His World.* Trans. Hélène Iswolsky. Bloomington: Indiana UP, 1984.

Cerezo Aranda, José Antonio, and Daniel Eisenberg, eds. "Selected Papers from the International Colloquium on Eroticism and Witchcraft in Cervantes." Special issue of *Cervantes* 12.2 (1992).

Close, Anthony J. "Don Quixote's Love for Dulcinea: A Study of Cervantine Irony." *Bulletin of Hispanic Studies* 50 (1973): 237–56.

———. *The Romantic Approach to "Don Quixote": A Critical History of the Romantic Tradition in "Quixote" Criticism.* New York: Cambridge UP, 1977.

El Saffar, Ruth. "Sex and the Single Hidalgo: Reflections on Eros in *Don Quijote.*" In *Studies in Honor of Elias Rivers.* Ed. Bruno M. Damiani and Ruth El Saffar. Potomac, MD: Scripta Humanistica, 1989. 76–93.

Fuchs, Barbara. "Border Crossings: Transvestism and 'Passing' in *Don Quixote.*" *Cervantes* 16.2 (1996): 4–28.

Gerrig, Richard. *Experiencing Narrative Worlds: On the Psychological Activities of Reading.* New Haven: Yale UP, 1993.

Grossman, Edith. "Translator's Note to the Reader." In *Don Quixote.* By Miguel de Cervantes. Trans. Edith Grossman. New York: Ecco, 2003. xvi–xx.

Herrero, Javier. *Who Was Dulcinea?*. New Orleans: Graduate School of Tulane U, 1985.

Jones, Joseph R. "The Baratarian Archipelago: Cheap Isle, Pourboire Isle, Chicanery Isle, Joker's Isle." In *"Ingeniosa Invención": Essays on Golden Age Spanish Literature for Geoffrey L. Stagg in Honor of His Eighty-Fifth Birthday.* Ed. Ellen M. Anderson and Amy R. Williamsen. Newark: Juan de la Cuesta, 1999. 137–47.

Lucía Megías, José Manuel. *De los libros de caballerías manuscritos al "Quijote."* Madrid: Ensayo, 2004.

Mackey, Mary. "Rhetoric and Characterization in *Don Quijote.*" *Hispanic Review* 42 (1974): 51–66.

Mancing, Howard. "Alonso Quijano y sus amigos." In *Cervantes: Su obra y su mundo. Actas del I Congreso Internacional sobre Cervantes.* Ed. Manuel Criado de Val. Madrid: Edi-6, 1981. 737–41.

———. *The Chivalric World of "Don Quijote": Style, Structure and Narrative Technique.* Columbia: U of Missouri P, 1982.

———. "The Comic Function of Chivalric Names in *Don Quijote.*" *Names* 21 (1973): 220–35.

———. "Dulcinea del Toboso—On the Occasion of Her 400th Birthday." *Hispania* 88.1 (2005): 53–63.

———. "See the Play, Read the Book." In *Cognition and Performance.* Ed. F. Elizabeth Hart and Bruce McConachie. London: Routledge, in press.

Márquez Villanueva, Francisco. "Sobre la génesis literaria de Sancho Panza." *Anales Cervantinos* 12 (1958): 123–55.

Martínez-Bonati, Félix. *"Don Quijote" and the Poetics of the Novel.* Trans. Dian Fox in collaboration with the author. Ithaca: Cornell UP, 1992.

Molho, Maurice. "Raíz folklórica de Sancho Panza." In *Cervantes: Raíces folklóricas.* Madrid: Gredos, 1976. 217–355.

Parker, Alexander A. *The Humor of Spanish Proverbs.* Cambridge: Heffer and Sons, 1963.

Riley, E. C. *"Don Quixote:* From Text to Icon." *Cervantes* Special Issue (Winter, 1988): 103–15.

Rodríguez-Luis, Julio. "El *Quijote* según Borges." *Nueva Revista de Filología Hispánica* 36 (1988): 477–500.

Tave, Stuart. *The Amiable Humorist: A Study in the Comic Theory and Criticism of the Eighteenth and Early Nineteenth Centuries.* Chicago: U of Chicago P, 1960.

Weiger, John J. *The Substance of Cervantes.* Cambridge: Cambridge UP, 1985.

Chapter 7

RECEPTION

The reception history of *Don Quixote* is long and rich. This chapter can only outline in briefest form how the single most popular and influential work in the history of world literature has been received by four centuries of readers and, especially, writers. We will begin with a brief look at contemporary reactions, trace the novel's presence and influence in subsequent centuries, assess Cervantes' achievement and the place of *Don Quixote* in the literary canon, look briefly at *Don Quixote* in other arts, and end with some comments on *Don Quixote* and Don Quixote in popular culture and with some remarks on the 2005 celebration of the 400th anniversary of the first publication of the novel. At no point will we do more than scratch the surface. Emphasis in this survey is more on the aesthetic reception of Cervantes' novel than it is on the critical and scholarly reception of the novel. Aspects of how readers throughout the centuries have understood Don Quixote and Sancho have been touched upon throughout the previous chapters, and the final chapter will deal substantively with the scholarly reception.

DON QUIXOTE IN THE SEVENTEENTH CENTURY

Cervantes apparently finished part 1 of *Don Quixote* and delivered it to his publisher Francisco de Robles in the fall of 1604. Then it was submitted for review by governmental agencies—a primitive version of the copyright process, as well as a censorship procedure—and the appropriate approvals were granted between September 26 and December 20. The book was printed in the shop of Juan de la Cuesta in Madrid and went on sale in the early months of 1605. The book sold extraordinarily well, and was frequently reprinted: six times in 1605 alone, and 11 times by 1617. After part 2 was published in 1615 (and reprinted alone twice more by 1617), the two parts were published together more than a dozen times in the seventeenth century.

Immediately the figures of Don Quixote, Sancho, Dulcinea, and even Rocinante and Sancho's ass became popular figures in Spanish culture (see chapter 1). Few public parades, processions, or festivities were complete without their appearance. Everyone from the king down to the lowliest peasant knew who the tall, thin knight-errant and his short, fat squire were. As early as 1605 or 1606 dramatist Guillén de Castro (1569–1631) staged a play titled *Don Quijote de la Mancha,* but it was less about the comic antics of knight and squire than about the love plot involving Cardenio, Dorotea, and others. Between 1605 and 1615 Francisco de Quevedo wrote a burlesque poem titled "Testamento de don Quijote" ("Don Quixote's Will"), which consists of Don Quixote's writing of his will and his death. Cervantes' friend, Alonso Jerónimo de Salas Barbadillo (1581–1635) was the first to imitate *Don Quixote* in prose fiction with his novel *El caballero puntual* (1614; *The Punctilious Gentleman*). Shortly after the publication of part 2 of the novel, Francisco de Avila staged a short, comic farce titled *Entremés famoso de los invencibles hechos de Don Quijote de la Mancha* (1617; *Famous Interlude of the Invincible Deeds of Don Quixote de la Mancha*). The farce takes advantage of the comic figure and madness of Don Quixote, depicting scenes where he takes an inn for a castle and has encounters with *pícaros* who make fun of him, presenting a serving maid as Dulcinea—probably the first fusion of the prostitutes (Maritornes, Aldonza, Dulcinea) that becomes a staple in many subsequent versions of the novel. Throughout the remainder of the century there are frequent evocations of Cervantes' novel and his characters in works of fiction and, especially, in the theater (see the brief comments on Calderón de la Barca in chapter 4).

An interesting and significant indication of Cervantes' influence can be seen in the 1615 novel titled *Engaños deste siglo* (1615; *Deceits of This World*) published in Paris by the exiled Spanish Protestant Francisco Loubayssin de Lamarca (ca. 1588–ca. 1660). In it, Cervantes and his novel are mentioned together with several classical authors, thus suggesting that *Don Quixote* was already seen as something special. The fact that a Spaniard living in France was already treating Cervantes like a classical author within a decade of the publication of *Don Quixote* part 1, and in the same year that *Don Quixote* part 2 appeared, is a strong testimony to the immediate influence and popularity of Cervantes' novel, together with the admiration and respect accorded to it. This, however, was an isolated incident, as the important elevation of Cervantes to classical status came in the eighteenth century, and not in Spain but in England.

The fame and influence of *Don Quixote* was not limited to Spain and Spanish possessions in Europe and the Americas, however. A copy of part 1 of *Don Quixote* was already in England in 1605, and soon thereafter Thomas Shelton began his translation of the work. This translation was complete by 1608 and was published in 1612; Shelton's translation of part 2 appeared in 1620. In France, César Oudin published a translation of part 1 in 1614, and this was followed by François Rosset's translation of part 2 in 1618. The two parts were translated into Italian by Lorenzo Franciosini in 1622 and 1625. Later in the seventeenth century the novel was also translated into Dutch (1676–77) and German (1683). (Subsequently, *Don Quixote* has been translated, in whole or in part, into more languages than any other work of literature.)

Don Quixote became the work most frequently adapted to theater and imitated in fiction in seventeenth-century Europe, particularly in England and France. At the same time, the stories in Cervantes' *Novelas ejemplares* were also adapted and imitated dozens of times throughout the rest of Europe; overall, Cervantes provided more plots for European writers than anyone else. Quite consistently, the two aspects of *Don Quixote* that attracted most attention were the comic, slapstick, bawdy, and satiric antics of Don Quixote and Sancho (especially during the latter's governorship) and the embedded stories of love and intrigue, particularly Cardenio-Dorotea et al and the *Curioso impertinente*. Just as the first translation of *Don Quixote* was into English, so the most significant influences of Cervantes' novel are to be found in England.

It was on stage that *Don Quixote* first had an impact on English culture. Virtually all the major Elizabethan dramatists—Francis Beaumont, William Davenant, John Fletcher, John Middleton, William Shakespeare—wrote, either individually or in collaboration, plays based on material from Cervantes' novel. Of these, of course, the most fascinating is the case of Shakespeare. In 1613 a collaborative work by Shakespeare and Fletcher titled *The History of Cardenio,* or just *Cardenio,* based on events from *Don Quixote* part 1, chapters 23–46, was staged in the Royal Palace. It was long thought that the play was lost, but recently it has been suggested that the work known as *The Second Maiden's Tragedy,* long attributed to other writers, particularly John Middleton, is in fact the lost Shakespeare-Fletcher collaboration (see Hamilton's edition of the play and his accompanying critical material). Unfortunately, the play is a rather ghastly revenge drama that ends in multiple deaths; if it is at least partly Shakespeare's, it is far from his best work. Whether or not *The Second Maiden's Tragedy* is the lost *Cardenio,* it is interesting to contemplate the association of the two greatest writers of the time. Later in the seventeenth century, the most significant of several theatrical works inspired by *Don Quixote* was Thomas D'Urfey's three-part musical comedy *The Comical History of Don Quixote*—parts 1 and 2, 1694, and part 3 with the subtitle *With the Marriage of Mary the Buxome,* 1696—which featured music by Henry Purcell and John Eccles. Overall, this is probably the best musical *Don Quixote* that appeared in the same century in which the novel was published.

A similar process of cultural assimilation of the comic *Don Quixote* occurred in France. In about 1614, the same year that the first French translation of the novel was made, there was an anonymous *Ballet de Don Quichot,* probably the first dance version of Cervantes' novel, and around 1620 there was an anonymous French masquerade with the title *L'Entrée en France de Don Quichot de la Manche (The Entry of Don Quixote de la Mancha into France).* Like the English, French dramatists, such as Charles Dufresny, Bonaventure Fourcroy, Guyon Guérin de Bouscal, and Le Sieu Guyon Pichou, frequently adapted *Don Quixote* to the theater, often featuring scenes from Sancho's governorship. French fiction, too, showed the influence of Cervantes in a number of satires and romance novels, among others: Charles Sorel's *L'Histoire comique de Francion* (1623; *The Comic History of Francion*), Gilbert Saulnier Du Verdier's *Le Chevalier hypocondiraque* (1632; *The Hypochondriac Knight),* Paul Scarron's *Roman comique* (1651–57; *The Comical Romance*), Antoine Furetière's *Le Roman bourgeois* (1666; *The Bourgeois Romance*), and Adrien-Thomas-Perdou de Subligny's *La fausse Clélie, histoire française, galante et comique* (1670; *The False Clélie, a Gallant and Comic French Story*).

But perhaps the most interesting, and influential, rewrite of Cervantes in France came late in the century with the translation of *Don Quixote* with the title *Histoire de l'Admirable Don Quichotte de la Manche* (4 vols., 1677–79; *History of the Admirable Don Quixote de La Mancha*) by François Filleau de Saint-Martin (?–ca.1695). Filleau omitted Cervantes' final chapter, in which Don Quixote dies, in order to continue the story himself in vol. 5 (1695) of the work. The sequel begins with an Arabic narrator named Zulema who reports that Cide Hamete Benengeli was incorrect about the death of Don Quixote and who claims to have investigated the activities of Don Quixote and Sancho after their return home in part 2, chapter 73. Filleau's sequel was very popular in France and was translated to German within a year.

Within half a century after Cervantes' death, *Don Quixote* was an established European phenomenon, particularly in England and France, by then the two most important nations in Europe. While there was some interest in *Don Quixote* in Italy and Germany, the novel simply did not have the impact there that it did elsewhere. Meanwhile, Spain had already fallen so far into cultural, intellectual, and historical decline that the novel was published, read, adapted, and imitated more abroad than at home. While *Don Quixote* was enjoying great popularity abroad, there was not a single new edition of the novel in Spain between 1674 and 1704. This state of affairs would continue into the eighteenth century.

DON QUIXOTE IN THE EIGHTEENTH CENTURY

In the eighteenth century England was again the nation that lead the way in the reception of *Don Quixote,* but by the end of the century it was in Germany where Cervantes' novel had the most profound and lasting effect. While most Enlightenment readers still perceived *Don Quixote* more as a funny book, a broad comedy, and a satire than anything else, it is possible to perceive a subtle shift to a more nuanced and serious response, first in England and then in Germany.

While English dramatists of the late-seventeenth and the entire eighteenth century—Thomas Augustine Arne, James Ayres, Aphra Behn, George Colman, John Crowne, George Farquhar, Henry Fielding, Frederick Pilon, Nicholas Rowe, Richard Steele, Lewis Theobald—continued to entertain the public with the comic antics of Don Quijote, Sancho as a governor, and the tales of romance from *Don Quixote* (and, again, from the *Novelas*), it was in the new (to England) genre of the novel that Cervantes' influence was most profound. This influence is best seen in the work of the two greatest novelists of the century, Henry Fielding (1707–54) and Laurence Sterne (1713–68), as well as in a number of relatively minor novelists.

Fielding's first important novel was *The History of the Adventures of Joseph Andrews, and His Friend Mr. Abraham Adams: Written in Imitation of the Manner of Cervantes* (1742). Among the narrative techniques Fielding employs that are also characteristic of *Don Quixote* are the "true history" device, the intrusive narrator, the search for sources, comic character names, comic chapter titles, links from one chapter to the next, and a variety of embedded narrations. Some of the comic inn scenes, with naughty romps in the sack, mistaken identities, and brawls, are directly modeled on the adventures of Don Quixote and Sancho in the inn of Juan Palomeque (especially in part 1, chs. 16–17), and Parson

Adams is one of the great Don Quixote figures in literature. Many of the same characteristics are also found in Fielding's best-known novel, *The History of Tom Jones, a Foundling* (1749).

Laurence Sterne is the second novelist who most profoundly assimilated Cervantes' achievement in prose fiction. His monumental novel *The Life and Opinions of Tristram Shandy* (in nine installments, 1759–67) is clearly related in theme, structure, and technique to both *Don Quixote* and the Spanish picaresque novel tradition. The "Cervantick" (Sterne's neologism) element in the novel is seen in different ways in almost all the characters. Yorick is a sort of elegiac Don Quixote whose horse is a referred to as a new Rocinante. Both Walter Shandy and Uncle Toby have their own "hobby-horse," Sterne's term for a harmless quixotic obsession, while Corporal Trim is the Sancho of the novel, and the Widow Wadman is a singular Dulcinea figure. The narrator Tristram makes his own quixotic effort to bring his narrative, with all its overtly Benengelian tone and many references to *Don Quixote,* up to the present, always slipping further and further behind his goal.

Sterne and Fielding, different as they are, are the first two truly great writers to fully integrate the accomplishments of Cervantes into their own novels. The other two major English novelists of the eighteenth century, Daniel Defoe and Samuel Richardson, are somewhat less beholden to Cervantes. Works like Defoe's *Moll Flanders* (1722) owe more to the Spanish picaresque than to *Don Quixote,* although the comparison between *Robinson Crusoe* (1719) and *Don Quixote* has often been made, beginning in Defoe's lifetime. Richardson's sentimental, epistolary romance novels are farther in spirit from Cervantes' novel than the works of almost any other writer of the time, even if the theme of testing a woman's virtue had been made popular through the tale of the *Curioso impertinente* (part 1, chs. 33–35) and its many adaptations and variations in seventeenth- and earlier eighteenth-century English literature.

In addition to these writers, the works of several other English novelists are clearly and explicitly inspired by Cervantes: Charlotte Lennox's *The Female Quixote; or, The Adventures of Arabella* (1752), Tobias Smollett's *The Adventures of Sir Launcelot Greaves* (1760–62), Henry Brooke's *The Fool of Quality; or, The History of Henry Earl of Moreland* (5 vols., 1765–70), Richard Graves' *The Spiritual Quixote; or, The Summer's Ramble of Mr Geoffry Wildgoose; a Comic Romance* (3 vols., 1773), the anonymous *Philosophical Quixote; or, Memoirs of Mr. David Wilkins* (2 vols., 1782), and the anonymous *Amicable Quixote; or, The Enthusiasm of Friendship* (4 vols., 1788). The example of Smollett is particularly interesting, as, in addition to his *Launcelot Greaves* (a *greave* is a piece of leg armor, just as *quixote* is), he wrote several other novels—*Roderick Random* (1748), *Peregrine Pickle* (1751), and, especially, *Humphry Clinker* (1771)—all of which display the presence of both *Don Quixote* and the Spanish picaresque novel. Furthermore, Smollett published a controversial translation of *Don Quixote* (1755), which was widely read for more than a century.

Don Quixote was probably the most read and most influential book in England in the seventeenth and eighteenth centuries (see Paulson, *Don Quixote in England*). Given the fact that it had been on the English scene for more than a century before the writers discussed in the previous paragraphs began their work, Cervantes' novel may overall have even exceeded the popularity of works such as Samuel Richardson's *Pamela* (1740) and *Clarissa* (1747–48); it certainly had a more profound influence on the formation of the English novel than did the work of any English writer. The novel's establishment as a major genre in England in the eighteenth century, the first major flowering of the genre after its emergence in Renaissance Spain, would not have been possible—at least in the form that it assumed— without *Don Quixote*.

Furthermore, the English demonstrated an appreciation for Cervantes' novel that was unprecedented. Whig politician Lord Carteret made possible the first deluxe and (almost) critical edition of the novel, which was published in 1738 and included as a preface the first biography of Cervantes ever written, by the respected Spanish scholar Gregorio Mayáns y Síscar. The work was embellished with excellent engravings by John Vanderbank (who beat out William Hogarth for the honor) and was a truly elegant book. Particularly interesting is Vanderbank's frontispiece, which presents a young, handsome, virile Cervantes as a prototypical classical figure, a sort of modern Hercules. Arguably, this is the moment when Cervantes passes from the ranks of a popular writer to those of a classic; with this edition Cervantes becomes—in English eyes, at least—part of the canon of great writers. The English respect for Cervantes continued with the meticulous edition prepared by the Rev. John Bowle (1781), the first annotated, scholarly edition of the novel, and the first person to call Cervantes a "classic" writer (see Cox, *The Rev. John Bowle* and *The Tragedy of John Bowle*).

In Spain, there was a reaction to the fact that one of their most prized writers was lionized more in England than at home, and the first pretentious Spanish edition was the four-volume work, illustrated by six different artists (Goya was not among them; the sample he submitted was rejected!), published in 1780 by the Royal Spanish Academy and edited by Vicente de los Ríos. This was followed in 1797–98 by a five-volume edition, also

with Royal Academy sponsorship, by Juan Pellicer. Neither of these editions surpasses the achievements of Carteret or Bowle. What is clear is that
by the late eighteenth century Cervantes had been elevated to a level well
above most writers, a position he would never relinquish.

The situation in eighteenth-century France was comparable to that of
England. *Don Quixote* remained a preferred source for dramatic material, as is seen in the work of Philippe Néricault Destouches, Florent
Carton Dancourt, Charles-Antoine Coypel, Charles-Simon Favart,
Philidor, and Jean Guillaume Antoine Cuvelier de Trye. The French
novel of the century also made strides over the satiric and didactic fic-
tions of the previous century, even though many comparable works
continued to be written: Laurent Bordelon's *L'Histoire des imagina-
tions extravagantes de Monsieur Oufle . . .* (1710; *The History of the
Extravagant Imaginations of Monsieur Oufle . . .*), Guillaume Hyacînthe
Bourgeant's *Le voyage merveilleux de Prince Fan-Férédin* (1735; *The
Wonderful Travels of Prince Fan-Férédin*), Pierre Carlet de Chamblain
de Marivaux's *Pharsamon ou Les nouvelles folies romanesques* (1737;
Pharsamon, or The New Romance Follies, often printed with one of two
subtitles: *Le Don Quichotte français* or *Le Don Quichotte moderne—The
French Don Quixote* or *The Modern Don Quixote*), and Denis Diderot's
Jacques le fataliste et son maître (1796; *Jacques the Fatalist and His
Master*). Of these, Diderot's novel is particularly outstanding and may
be considered one of the best novels of the eighteenth century.

Some of the finest French fiction writers of the century—Choderlos
de Laclos, Graffigny, Marivaux, Montesquieu, Prévost, Rousseau, Sade,
Voltaire, and others—seem less obviously related to Cervantes. Their work
tends toward the sentimental, the erotic, the courtly, the philosophic, the
autobiographical, and (like the novels of Samuel Richardson) are often as
closely related to the romance tradition as they are to the novel tradition of
Cervantes and the picaresque.

In some ways, it is not in the arena of new fiction that *Don Quixote* was
most significant in France, but it was in translations, editions, and continuations of the novel itself that attracted most interest. Fillcau de Saint-
Martin's translation and continuation remained popular throughout the
eighteenth century, but it had strong competition. In 1704 Alain René
Lesage (1668–1747) translated Avellaneda's 1614 sequel to Cervantes' novel
to French as *Nouvelles Aventures de l'admirable Don Quichotte* (1704;
New Adventures of the Admirable Don Quixote), and maintained that it
was superior to Cervantes' two volumes. Lesage, by the way, translated
and adapted numerous Spanish picaresque novels, and his own *Gil Blas*

de Santillane (1715–35)—partly original, partly in imitation of Spanish models, partly a translation/adaptation of Vicente Espinel's *Marcos de Obregón* (1618)—became the most popular picaresque novel in Europe for two centuries. In 1711, Robert Challes (1659–1711) wrote a sequel to Filleau's sequel to Cervantes' own sequel: *Continuation de l'histoire de l'admirable Don Quichotte de la Manche* (1711; *Continuation of the History of the Admirable Don Quixote of La Mancha*). After that appeared an anonymous imitation/continuation of *Don Quixote* titled *Le Désespoir amoreux, avec Les nouvelles visions de Don Quichotte, histoire espagnole* (1715; *Amorous Desperation, with The New Visions of Don Quixote, a Spanish History*). And then, in 1722, another anonymously published sequel appeared titled *Suite nouvelle et veritable de l'histoire et des avantures de l'incomparable Don Quichotte de la Manche. Traduite d'un Manuscrit Espagnol de Cide-Hamet Benengely son veritable historien* (6 vols., 1722–26; *New and Truthful Sequel to the History and Adventures of the Incomparable Don Quixote de la Mancha. Translated from a Spanish Manuscript by Cide Hamete Benengely, His Truthful Historian*), the final volume of which is titled *Histoire de Sancho Pansa, alcade de Blandanda (History of Sancho Panza, Mayor of Blandanda)*. This work, too, was widely read and often republished throughout the century. Overall, Cervantes' novel (in the original and in the translations by Oudin and Rosset), Lesage's version of Avellaneda's sequel, the sequels by Filleau, Challes, and the anonymous writers of *Désespoir amoreux* and the *Suite nouvelle* were, together, some of the most frequently read fictions in Enlightenment France. It is interesting to note that, while the English were lionizing Cervantes, the French mostly continued to laugh at him through facile and superficial imitations and sequels. Recall also that in the French *Enciclopédie* it was affirmed that Spain had never contributed anything to the world (see chapter 4). Cervantes may have been omnipresent in France in the eighteenth century, but it was in England and Germany that he received the most respect and admiration.

Cervantes hardly made an appearance in Germany in the seventeenth century, and his popularity didn't increase until the rise of the Romantic writers and philosophers in the latter part of the eighteenth century. Until then, *Don Quixote* was known primarily through French translations, imitations, and adaptations. But in the second half of the century, Cervantes rivaled Shakespeare as a source of inspiration for Johann Wolfgang von Goethe (1749–1832), Friedrich Schiller (1759–1805), August Wilhelm von Schlegel (1767–1845) and his brother Friedrich (1772–1829), Ludwig Tieck (1773–1853), Christoph Martin Wieland (1733–1813), and others. For these writers, Don Quixote began to be perceived not as a mere comic madman and butt of satire, but as a man more admirable than his contemporaries, a noble and tragic figure. It is difficult to overstate the importance of these writers in viewing Don Quixote as a serious and respectable figure and definitively reorienting our understanding of Cervantes' novel.

And while German philosophy and literary criticism was reorienting readers' understanding of the novel, German dramatists and novelists— Johann Karl August Musäus, Christoph Martin Wieland, Johann Karl Wezel, Johann Gottwerth Müeller—wrote works that reflected this position. Of these, Wieland's *Die Abentheuer des Don Sylvio von Rosalva* (2 vols., 1764; *The Adventures of Don Sylvio of Rosalva*) is the most original and interesting, a Bildungsroman and a quixotic novel at the same time. Goethe's own literary works, especially his novels *Die Leiden des jungen Werthers* (1774; *The Sorrows of Young Werther*) and *Wilhelm Meisters Lehrjahre* (1795–96; *Wilhelm Meister's Apprenticeship*) are infused throughout with themes, characters, and metafictional narrative techniques derived from his beloved Cervantes. Ludwig Tieck's superb translation of the novel (1799–1801) became the version most Germans read for over a century and is still considered by many to be the best German translation of all time.

During the Enlightenment, the English assimilated Cervantes' achievement and created the first great post-Renaissance novelistic tradition with Fielding, Sterne, and others. The English also elevated Cervantes to the status of a classic with the first great editions of his work. France entertained itself with multiple editions, translations, and continuations of the *Don Quixote*. Germany reinvented Don Quixote as a romantic, noble figure. And Spain? As indicated above, the Spanish reacted to the English glorification of Cervantes by belatedly imitating their achievements. Spanish fiction throughout the century is mediocre at best, and the novels that most reflect Cervantes' achievement—by Jacinto María Delgado, Pedro Gatell, and José Francisco de Isla—are weak, sometimes pathetic, efforts that pale in comparison with what was being written in other countries (but for the metafictional achievement of Delgado, see Mancing "Jacinto María Delgado and Cide Hamete Benengeli").

DON QUIXOTE IN THE NINETEENTH CENTURY

By the nineteenth century the novel had became the dominant genre in world literature; previously, poetry and theater always had more prestige, and the novel (or the romance) was generally looked upon as being less serious, less refined, and less artistic. But with the emergence of great novelists in England in the eighteenth century and the realization of the potential of long fiction as a vehicle for aesthetic, social, and philosophical thought and practice, the novel came to the fore, and the best and most prominent writers of virtually every major literature included novelists. Not surprisingly, with the increased prominence of the genre so dominated by Cervantes, his influence and presence became ubiquitous. Therefore, it will not be possible, given the space limitations of this book, to continue to review in detail the reception of Cervantes and his novel throughout the world. Therefore, this section and the next one will be much more schematic and selective in nature; furthermore, because of the presumed interests of many readers of this book, some emphasis will be placed on the English and American traditions of the novel. Readers interested in pursuing further some of the following examples may do so by consulting the appropriate entries in my *Cervantes Encyclopedia,* where nearly all of them are discussed at greater length (albeit, still quite briefly) and further bibliography is provided.

The British novel in the nineteenth century opens with two very different writers whose work, especially their earliest efforts, owes much to Cervantes: Jane Austen (1775–1817) and Walter Scott (1771–1832). Austen's *Northanger Abbey* (written at the end of the eighteenth century but only published posthumously in 1818) is the story of Catherine Morland, a female Don Quixote who sees the world in terms of her preferred literary texts, in this case, gothic romances. Meanwhile, Scott is a romantic writer in the grand Cervantine tradition, and in no work of his is this seen better than in *Waverley* (1814) itself, where Edward Waverley is by all standards a quixotic character, who reads his way through a sea of books and perceives reality in terms of *Don Quixote* and other favorites. Among the important quixotic novelists later in the century, Charles Dickens (1812–70) and George Eliot (1819–80) are particularly prominent. In *The Posthumous Papers of the Pickwick Club* (1836–37), Dickens presents an amiable Quixote in Mr. Pickwick, with a very English Sancho named Sam Weller. Eliot's heroines Maggie Tulliver in *The Mill on the Floss* (1860) and Dorothea Brooke in *Middlemarch* (1871–72) are obviously quixotic, and in the latter novel the Reverend Casaubon is quixotic (and explicitly identified as such) in his search for the key to the understanding of all mythologies. Other novelists whose works fall within the tradition of Cervantes include Mary Shelley, William Makepeace Thackeray, Elizabeth Gaskell, and Lewis Carroll.

In the emerging literature of the United States, Cervantes is present from the beginning. Two of the best (a relative term here) early novels written in

America are those of Hugh Henry Brackenridge (1748–1816) and Tabitha Tenney (1762–1827). Brackenridge's *Modern Chivalry: Containing the Adventures of Captain John Farrago and Teague O'Regan, His Servant* (published in installments, 1792–1815), features an explicit Don Quixote-Sancho pair in Farrago and O'Regan. Tenney's *Female Quixotism, Exhibited in the Romantic Opinions and Extravagant Adventures of Dorcasina Sheldon* (3 vols., 1801) is the story of a young woman named Dorcas who poeticizes her name to Dorcasina, and who sees the world in terms of her favorite fictional romances, particularly those of Samuel Richardson.

Two of the greatest American novelists of the nineteenth century display, each in his own way, a strong Cervantine influence: Herman Melville (1819–91) and Mark Twain (1835–1910). Melville's admiration for *Don Quixote* was unlimited, and is clearly seen in nearly all of his works. His monumental *Moby Dick* (1851) tells the tale of Captain Ahab's single-minded and obsession with an ideal—the White Whale—that is larger than life, and the whalers and harpooners are compared with quixotic knights-errant. Melville's *The Confidence Man* (1857), written while the author was reading and annotating his copy of *Don Quixote,* reflects the metafictional self-consciousness of Cide Hamete Benengeli, a figure in whom Melville displayed a great interest (see Levin, *"Don Quixote* and *Moby-Dick"*). Nearly all of Mark Twain's fiction bears a direct and unmistakable resemblance to the work of Cervantes. *The Adventures of Tom Sawyer* (1876) features a classic boyish Don Quixote in the title character; *The Adventures of Huckleberry Finn* (1885) extends the theme of appearance and reality, on several levels, as Huck and Jim tilt at the windmill-giants of hypocrisy and slavery and the imaginative Tom makes a decisive return; while in *A Connecticut Yankee in King Arthur's Court* (1889) time-traveler Hank Morgan is literally relocated in a legendary chivalric past. Washington Irving, Kate Chopin, Stephen Crane, William Dean Howells, and Henry James are among other the writers of the nineteenth century whose work clearly recalls Cervantes.

The novel in Spain may have faded into near oblivion during the eighteenth century, but, likc in other countries, it rose to prominence again in the nineteenth century. The greatest of all Spanish novelists, after Cervantes, and one of the half dozen most distinguished novelists of the nineteenth century is Benito Pérez Galdós. Almost everything Galdós' wrote reflects *Don Quixote* in some way, and no other writer more thoroughly infused his work with a truly Cervantine spirit than Galdós. Among Galdós' most outstanding achievements, two of the most prominent will illustrate the point. *La desheredada* (1881; *The Disinherited Lady*) is the story of

Isidora Rufete, a young woman from La Mancha who has been led to believe that she is the unrecognized but legitimate heir to a wealthy family fortune and lives quixotically in search of proof of her claim. The novel is also populated by other quixotic characters: her lover from El Toboso, Agusto Miquis; her uncle, Don Santiago Quijano-Quijada, who encourages her fantasies; and José Relimpio, the quixotic defender of innocent virgins. *Misericordia* (1897; *Compassion*), Galdós' last major novel, is the story of the elderly servant named Benina (Benigna) who supports her quixotic mistress Doña Paca by begging and invents the figure of a benevolent protector—who seems actually to take on reality. Again, there are other quixotic characters: Almudena, the blind Muslim beggar who idealizes Benina, making her his Dulcinea and even doing a quixotic penance for her; and the absurdly quixotic Don Frasquito, who literally rides out on a Rocinante-like horse to rescue Benina. Sometimes one has the feeling when reading the novels of Galdós that this really is the work of a reincarnated Cervantes. Other important novelists of nineteenth-century Spain also reflect the influence of Cervantes and *Don Quixote:* Emilia Pardo Bazán, Leopoldo Alas (Clarín), Armando Palacio Valdés, and Jacinto Octavio Picón.

Throughout the rest of Europe, major novelists in every country continue the Cervantine tradition. In France, Gustave Flaubert (1821–80), who admired Cervantes above all other writers, is the author of what is generally considered the greatest quixotic heroine of the century, if not of all time: Emma Bovary, the protagonist of *Madame Bovary* (1856–57), the prototypical "Don Quixote in skirts." Emma, steeped in genre fiction— popular women's' romances, historical romances, women's' magazines, and contemporary sentimental novels—and disillusioned and bored by her marriage to the prosaic Charles Bovary, dreams of true love and adventure, but situations that promise to be exciting liaisons turn into tawdry affairs with lovers who are cynical and mediocre opportunists. Emma's grotesque suicide at the end of the novel puts an end to quixotic dreaming. Meanwhile, other major novelists of the century also show direct relationships to Cervantes: Stendhal, Honoré de Balzac, Théophile Gautier, Victor Hugo, Alphonse Daudet, Guy de Maupassant, and Emile Zola.

In the emerging literature of Russia, Fyodor Dostoevsky (1821–81) is probably the most Cervantine of writers and a person who considered *Don Quixote* to be among the greatest human achievements of all times. Prince Myshkin, protagonist of *Idiot* (1968–69; *The Idiot*) is modeled explicitly on Don Quixote and Jesus Christ, and there is no small amount of Don Quixote in the figure of Raskolnikov in *Prestuplenie i nakazanie* (1866; *Crime and Punishment*), whose defining idea, largely inspired by his reading about Napoleon, is that some people can impose their own will on the world. Also reflecting the presence of Cervantes in their work are some of the major Russian writers of the century: Nikolai Gogol, Nikolai Leskov, Aleksandr Pushkin, Ivan Turgenev, and Leo Tolstoy. Other writers of the nineteenth century, such as Jean Paul in Germany, Alessandro Manzoni in Italy, Joaquim Maria Machado de Assis in Brazil, José Joaquín Fernández de Lizardi in Mexico, and Camilo Castelo Branco in Portugal, can all be considered in the light of the work of Cervantes. The nineteenth century is the age of the triumph of the novel, and everywhere within it Cervantes and *Don Quixote* are the informing muses.

DON QUIXOTE IN THE TWENTIETH AND EARLY TWENTY-FIRST CENTURIES

The twentieth century has seen an even greater proliferation of quixotic novels, as nearly every writer can be associated with Cervantes and his novel. A few brief examples will have to suffice. In England, Joseph Conrad presents the sea itself as a source of quixotic illusion in *Lord Jim* (1900), and in *Zuleika Dobson* (1911), Max Beerbohm makes an extended comparison of his heroine with the singular Marcela from *Don Quixote*. G. K. Chesterton's *The Return of Don Quixote* (1927) describes a struggle with the mechanized giants of the twentieth century. The sex-changing hero/heroine of Virginia Woolf's *Orlando, A Biography* (1928) is a book-inspired quixotic character; Wyndham Lewis, in his best novel, *Self-Condemned* (1954), writes of a man who imposes a romantic penance upon himself, comparable to that of Don Quixote in Sierra Morena; and in the metafictional *The Comforters* (1957), by Muriel Spark, the protagonist, like Don Quixote and Sancho early in part 2, is aware that she is being written as a literary character. In John Fowles' novel *The French Lieutenant's Woman* (1969), the protagonist, Sara Woodruff, is a typical quixotic dreamer in a metafictional tale in which the author associates with his characters and ponders how to write the story; Robin Chapman takes characters from Cervantes' part 2 and continues their story in *The Duchess' Diary* (1980); Graham Greene tells the story of a modern descendent of Don Quixote in *Monsignor Quixote* (1982); and in *The Moor's Last Sigh* (1995), Indian/British Salman Rushdie, who considers Cervantes as one of his literary parents, writes of a remote village in Spain named Benengeli and alludes several times to Cervantes' novel. Finally, South African/British Julian Branston's *The Eternal Quest* (2003; aka *Tilting at Windmills*) is a historical novel about Cervantes' writing of *Don Quixote*.

In the literature of the United States, Sinclair Lewis' entire work is characterized by a "quixotic vision" made up of literature, adventure, and enchantment, as it is in *Main Street* (1920) where the protagonist attempts to remake her adopted Midwest town into a progressive and idyllic location. F. Scott Fitzgerald's *The Great Gatsby* (1925) is about a man who reinvents and renames himself and who loves an unattainable Dulcinea-like woman; William Faulkner, who reread *Don Quixote* once every year, populates all of his novels with quixotic characters, like Quentin Compson (whom Faulkner himself compared to Don Quixote) in *The Sound and the Fury* (1929); and although Vladimir Nabokov criticized what he perceived as the excessive cruelty of Cervantes' novel, he wrote a very quixotic novel of his own in *Lolita* (1955). In the first novel of Herbert Lobsenz, *Vangel Griffin* (1961), a young American goes to Spain and gets involved with modern avatars of Don Quixote and Sancho; Saul Bellow's *Herzog* (1964) is a self-proclaimed modern Jewish Quixote; Joyce Carol Oates converted life into literature in *them* (1969), a novel about a mother and her two children, all of whom read and dream about a better life; and Eudora Welty's *Losing Battles* (1970) is the story of a school teacher who tries quixotically to influence her students. John Kennedy Toole's posthumous novel, *A Confederacy of Dunces* (1980), is the story of an overweight self-proclaimed genius whose quixotic project is to reform the twentieth century; Paul Auster, who keeps going back to *Don Quixote* as the foundational novel that best addressed all the problems of narration, is the author of a brilliant metafiction in *City of Glass* (1985), in which, among other things, he speculates on the authorship of *Don Quixote;* and punk novelist Kathy Acker makes Don Quixote into a woman having an abortion in her novel titled simply *Don Quixote* (1986). John Barth, who has written of Cervantes as the true inventor of postmodernism, presents, in *Tidewater Tales* (1987), a meditation on story-writing through a rewriting of *Don Quixote;* Manuel Martinez is the author of *The Dreamer who Unlocked the Secrets of the Universe: The Adventures of Don Quixote in Miami* (2003), an oversize graphic novel (i.e., comic book) that tells the story of a psychiatrist who believes that he has been Don Quixote in the past and will someday be reincarnated as a cosmic knight. Cuban-American Roberto Arellano's *Don Dimaio of La Plata* (2004) is a wild romp about a drug- and pornography-obsessed mayor of a border town that is sprinkled throughout with obscene rewritings ("transfellations" is the author's term) of Cervantes' novel; and in Elisabeth Robinson's partly autobiographical *The True and Outstanding Adventures of the Hunt Sisters* (2004), a film producer attempts to make a movie based on *Don Quixote,* with John Cleese and Robin Williams in the lead roles, while dealing with her beloved sister's loosing bout with cancer. Mention here should be made also of Canadian novelist Ken Mitchell, whose *The Heroic Adventures of Donny Coyote* (2003) is a chapter-by-chapter rewriting of *Don Quixote;* it is a real *tour de force.*

This list could be extended indefinitely, but space forbids more than the briefest mention of other writers whose work is comparably related to that of Cervantes and his novel: in France, Andre Gide, Henri de Montherlant, Marcel Proust, Raymond de Queneau, and Jean-Paul Sartre; in Germany, Hermann Hesse, Franz Kafka, Thomas Mann, and Paul Schallück; in Russia, Mihail Bulgakov, Fyodor Sologub, and Alexandr Solzhenitsyn; in Spain, Francisco Arrabal, Azorín, Francisco Ayala, Juan Eslava Galán, Juan Goytisolo, Luis Landero, Segismundo Luengo, Carmen Martín Gaite, Carlos Rojas, Alfonso Mateo-Sagasta, Gonzalo Torrente Ballester, Andrés Trapiello, and Miguel de Unamuno; in Spanish America (whose literature, if read in ignorance of Cervantes, is read in ignorance), Juan José Arreola, Eduardo Barrios, Jorge Luis Borges, Alejo Carpentier, Mario Denevi, Carlos Fuentes, Jorge Ferretis, Heriberto Frías, Gabriel García Márquez, Juan Miguel de Mora, Angelina Muñiz-Huberman, Manuel Scorza, and Agustín Yañez; and countless others. It would seem that novelists everywhere have always written under the sign of Cervantes, and indeed that is the case.

THE QUIXOTIC NOVEL

A term used frequently in the previous paragraphs is "quixotic novel,"' and it now deserves clarification and discussion. Throughout this book the term is used to refer to any novel that bears some degree of intertextual relationship to *Don Quixote.* The quixotic novel most typically is one that involves a character who has some of those qualities we associate with Don Quixote or displays an innovative, postmodern, narrative self-awareness that places a work in juxtaposition to Cervantes. Often there is an element of satire in a quixotic novel, but by no means are all such novels mere satires or anti-romances.

The argument I want to make here is that all the novels previously discussed—and virtually all other novels written after 1605—are, by definition, quixotic novels. That is, they are novels grounded—directly or indirectly, consciously or unconsciously—in *Don Quixote.* And I am not the first to make such a claim. In a famous essay, Harry Levin coined the term "the quixotic principle" to refer to "the tragicomic irony of the conflict between real life and the romantic imagination;" it is "the rivalry between the real world and the representation that we make of it for ourselves" ("The Quixotic Principle" 58). For Levin, this principle is a constant in novels written at all times and in all places since *Don Quixote*. Like Levin, Lionel Trilling (previously cited in chapter 4) traces all literature back to the reality-appearance theme of *Don Quixote*. Similarly, Harold Bloom has written that "All novels since *Don Quixote* rewrite Cervantes' universal masterpiece, even when they are quite unaware of it" (*The Western Canon* 441). Spanish philosopher José Ortega y Gasset has written that we need "a book that would show in detail that every novel ever written bears *Don Quixote* within it like an inner filigree" (*Meditations on "Quixote"* 162). It would not be difficult to see how such a book might be structured around the figure of Don Quixote himself. In fact, one can identify five degrees of quixotic novels.

First, there are the literal sequels, the continuations of the story of Don Quixote and Sancho or their literal reincarnations. Sometimes in these sequels Don Quixote is only a secondary character, rather than the protagonist. The literal sequels to *Don Quixote* began during Cervantes' lifetime with the continuation published under the pseudonym of Alonso Fernández de Avellaneda in 1614. Throughout the centuries there have been dozens of (mostly Spanish and Spanish-American) novels in which Don Quixote and Sancho Panza are brought back to life and have new adventures in time and space, or the life and times of other characters from the novel are recounted. In general, these continuations are undistinguished works, often with a specific agenda of social, political, or literary satire. Literal sequels are the most obvious and least interesting kinds of novels related to Cervantes and *Don Quixote*.

Second, we have the namesakes of Don Quixote, novels in which the protagonist is explicitly identified, usually in the title, as a kind of Don Quixote. Several works previously mentioned are namesakes: the novels of Lennox, Graves, Tenney, Chesterton, Greene, Acker, Martinez, and Mitchell. And there are many more, bearing titles such as *The Amicable Quixote; The Infernal Quixote; The Philosophical Quixote; A Modern Quixote; The New Don Quixote; Don Quixote in Exile; El alma de Don Quijote; El Quijote del siglo XVIII; Don Quijote en América; Don Quixote, U.S.A.; The Don Quixote of America; Un don Chisciotte in America; Der Don Quijote von München; Don Quichotte de la démanche; Don Quixote de la Manchuela; El nuevo Quijote de Barcelona; Quixote de la Cantabria; Don Quichotte in Köln; Sir Quixote of the Moors; A Quixotic Woman; Donna Quixote; La Quijotita; My Lady Quixote; Don Chipote; Don Coyote; Don Quickshot; Don Quijancho; John Quixote.* While these namesakes can sometimes be interesting and original works of fiction, more often then not they are relatively weak and uninspired imitations.

The third category of quixotic novels includes those whose protagonist is explicitly (either within the text or in extratextual authorial statements) based or inspired, at least in part, on *Don Quixote.* Of the works mentioned previously, the following can be considered examples of the explicit quixotic novel: Fielding's *Joseph Andrews,* Sterne's *Tristram Shandy,* Wieland's *Don Sylvio von Rosalia,* Goethe's *Wilhelm Meister,* Scott's *Waverley,* Rushdie's *Moor's Last Sigh,* Melville's *Moby Dick,* Mark Twain's *Huckleberry Finn,* Pérez Galdós' *Desheredada,* Dostoevsky's *Idiot,* Bellow's *Herzog,* Auster's *City of Glass,* and Barth's *Tidewater Tales.* Many of these are great novels by any standard, and in general we can say that as novels tend to become less explicit (less slavish or derivative) in their relationship to *Don Quixote,* they have the potential to become better, more original, works of art.

The fourth category consists of those novels whose protagonist duplicates (or at least approximates) Don Quixote's basic premise of a fantasy or alternative reality inspired in books (or film, television, or other media), or who, like Don Quixote, consciously chooses to imitate ideal models from these media. Among the works previously mentioned, the following are all implicit quixotic novels: Austen's *Northanger Abbey,* Eliot's *Middlemarch,* Dickens' *Pickwick Papers,* Flaubert's *Madame Bovary,* Conrad's *Lord Jim,* Woolf's *Orlando,* Wyndham Lewis' *Self-Condemned,* Spark's *Comforters,* Fowles' *French Lieutenant's Woman,* Lewis' *Main Street,* Fitzgerald's *Great Gatsby,* Nabokov's *Lolita,* Oates' *them,* and Welty's *Losing Battles.* Again, the less obvious, direct, and explicitly imitative of *Don Quixote,* the greater the potential for originality and profundity. Categories three and four are the richest and most interesting groups.

And finally, in just a short extension of the previous category, the fifth and final category of quixotic novels includes all those novels in which the protagonist, like Don Quixote, is dissatisfied with his or her life and circumstances and attempts to change them in some way—in other words, just about every novel ever written. In a very real sense, to be a novel is to be a quixotic novel.

Linguist Noam Chomsky has proposed that, in a certain (deep) sense, there is only one human language—with very many (surface) variations. I suggest that in the same deep sense, there is only one novel—with very many surface variations. It is significant that virtually every kind of novel written throughout the world since the eighteenth century has been seen by its major practitioners as having its roots in *Don Quixote.* The great eighteenth-century comic novelists (Fielding, Sterne, Diderot) all hearken back to Cervantes for their inspiration. The great realists of the nineteenth century (Eliot, Mark Twain, Pérez Galdós) model their novels and their characters on those of Cervantes. The modern novelists of the early-to-mid-twentieth century (Unamuno, Bulgakov, Faulkner) specifically sought inspiration in Cervantes' novel. Contemporary authors of self-conscious, metafictional, postmodern novels (García Márquez, Rushdie, Auster) explicitly write in the tradition of Cervantes. Perhaps the novel, like language itself, is an example of a theme and variations: all novels are but variations on the theme(s) of *Don Quixote*.

The claim of universal quixotism in the novel would seem to lead inevitably to certain conclusions concerning the achievement of Cervantes. As M. M. Bakhtin has argued convincingly and at length, literary genres are divided into two groups—the novel and all the rest (*Dialogic Imagination,* especially 3–40 and 259–422). The other primary genres—lyric and epic poetry and drama—had their origins in the remote past, with no discernable beginning in historic time or place; there is no known first lyric or epic poet, no first dramatist. The romance—long prose fictions of adventure—had existed in the cultures of ancient Greece (Heliodorus' *Ethopian History*) and Rome (Apuleius' *Golden Ass*) and in various forms throughout the Middle Ages. But the novel (in the modern sense of the term, as used throughout this book) is the only genre to have come into being in modern times, in an era of historic awareness, after the invention of the printing press, in a specific time and place: Europe during the sixteenth and seventeenth centuries. Ever since Aristotle, Bakhtin reminds us, we have had a poetics of the lyric, the epic, and the dramatic, but this traditional poetics does not adequately describe the novel, a genre in which there is no specific form, structure, theme, character, language, or ideology. For Bakhtin, a novel is never characterized by a single voice, tone, point of view, ideology, or consciousness; rather, the novel is a place where unique human beings, all with their own consciousness, ideology, point of view, language, and voice, and all within their unique personal, historical, cultural, and geographic context, exist, meet, speak, and interact. More than any other, the novel is the genre of laughter, parody, double-voicedness, heteroglossia, dialogism, and polyphony. These, Bakhtin says, are also the characteristics of the modern world, so we can say that the novel is the quintessential modern genre; once the novel is on the scene, all other genres can be "novelized" to some degree or another. And in recent centuries all genres are novelized; that is, they are, like the novel, modern.

But even as literature in general has been novelized, literature has also been radically transformed—and marginalized—by the technologies of visual media. At the beginning of the twenty-first century, poetry—in the sense of the recited or written word of the poet—exists primarily in popular song, rap, and music videos. Traditional poetry is rarely read today except by students in classrooms and small groups of cultural elites (often poets themselves). The live theater exists primarily in small civic productions and large musical spectacles; for the most part, the stage has been marginalized by the cinema and television, and, increasingly, by the Internet and computer games. A far smaller percentage of today's literate population read books compared to the percentage of readers a century—or even half a century—ago. Those who do read actual literature—as opposed to nonfiction books and magazines—read primarily prose fiction. In effect, literature in the twenty-first century *is* the novel.

Taking all of the above into account, and *if* literature is the novel, and *if* the novel had a specific beginning, and *if* the first (or, at least, the first truly major) novelist was Cervantes, and *if Don Quixote* is the prototype of all novels ever written, *then* it is impossible not to conclude that Cervantes occupies a unique place at the very center of the western canon. Canon enthusiasts like Harold Bloom (*Western Canon* 45–75) place Shakespeare alone at the heart of the western canon, and English professors everywhere enthusiastically agree. But the one writer and the one book that are the first, best, most influential, and most admired examples of the most important literary genre ever created would logically seem to merit a (perhaps *the*) place of honor: Cervantes, even more than Shakespeare, is the central author, and *Don Quixote* is the central work, in the literary canon.

DON QUIXOTE BEYOND THE NOVEL

The influence of *Don Quixote* extends far beyond the novel (and the short story; a genre not considered in the previous sections for lack of space) itself. In the following sections, I would like to call attention briefly to the rich quixotic traditions in poetry, theater, film, music, art, and popular culture. As before, space allows only for the briefest of commentaries in these areas (and, as before, the interested reader is referred to my *Cervantes Encyclopedia* for further information).

Don Quixote in Poetry

Not surprisingly, many Spanish and Spanish American poets have found inspiration in Cervantes' novel or in his characters. In Spain, several of the best poets of the twentieth century have sought inspiration in, or paid poetic homage to, Cervantes. Two examples will suffice. León Felipe (1884–1968) consistently romanticized Don Quijote (Felipe's signature line traces a trajectory from barber's basin to helmet to halo) and used symbolically the knight's figure in his passionate poetry about the Spanish Civil war and his own subsequent exile. Felipe's posthumous book *Rocinante* (1969) brings together many lines of the poet's work throughout his career. Jorge Guillén (1893–1986), in his book *Aire nuestro* (1968; *Our Air*), has evoked in his poetry better than anyone since Cervantes himself two scenes from the novel: "Noche del caballero" ("The Knight's Night") about the dark night of the fulling mill (part 1, ch. 20) and "Dimisión de Sancho" ("Sancho's Resignation") on the end of Sancho's governorship of Barataria (part 2, ch. 53). In addition, Cervantes and his novel have been important in the work of poets such as Julia Castillo, Gabriel Celaya, Gerardo Diego, Jaime Ferrán, Ramón de Garciasol, Antonio Machado, Manuel Machado, Enrique de Mesa, Blas de Otero, Mario Serjan, and Miguel de Unamuno.

In Spanish America, two names stand out, beginning with the first truly important and internationally famous writer to come from Spanish-speaking America, the Nicaraguan Rubén Darío (1867–1916). Darío is the author of two of the most frequently cited poems ever written about Cervantes and Don Quixote, which he published in *Cantos de vida y esperanza* (1905; *Songs of Life and Hope*). The first is the gentle "Soneto a Cervantes" ("Sonnet to Cervantes"), an uncharacteristically pensive poem in which the poet reflects on his hours of sadness and solitude, but evokes his good friend Cervantes. The second is titled "Letanías de Nuestro Señor don Quijote" ("Litany for Our Lord Don Quixote"), and in it Darío invokes the spirit of Don Quixote as a sort of patron saint and liberator of the downtrodden, asking him to pray for troubled modern mankind. The Argentine, Jorge Luis Borges (1899–1986), is best known for his cerebral, paradoxical, metaliterary, postmodern short prose fictions (including several about Cervantes and Don Quixote), but he is also the author of half a dozen very straightforward, nostalgic, lyrical, personal evocations of Cervantes and his characters. For example, in "El testigo" (1972; "The Witness"), Don Quixote's attack on the windmill is seen by a boy who later goes off to the Spanish colonies in America.

Among the poets of the world whose work has been substantially influenced by Cervantes and his creations, the following deserve mention: the Sicilian Giovanni Meli; the Swedes Olof von Dalin, Carl Jonas Love Almqvist, Per Daniel Amadeus Atterbom, and Sigfrid Lindström; the English William Wordsworth; the Russians Aleksandr Pushkin and Fyodor Sologub; the

Rumanian Mihai Eminescu; the Greek Nikos Kazantzakis; the Brazilians Paulo Menotti del Picchia and Raul Pedroza; and the Finn Leena Krohn.

Don Quixote on Stage

As indicated above, it was in the seventeenth- and eighteenth-century theater of Spain, England, and France that *Don Quixote* first had its greatest impact. Since then, plays adapting, based on, or inspired by *Don Quixote* have abounded. Leaving until the later operas, *zarzuelas,* and ballets, and passing over some interesting works from the nineteenth and early twentieth centuries—by, for example, George Almar, Azorín, María Amparo Ruiz de Burton, Mabel Dearmer, Antonio Espiñeira, Jacinto Grau and Adrià Gual, Isabella Gregory, G. E. Morrison, Narciso Serra, and Royall Tyler—I will make brief mention of a dozen of the more interesting plays of the twentieth century. Note that none of these plays is an attempt to reproduce Cervantes' novel on stage; rather, they all use some aspect of the premise of *Don Quixote*—characters, themes, devices—in order to create original works of art.

First is the original and influential play *Dulcinée* (1938) by Gaston Baty (1892–1952), in which Aldonza is transformed by Don Quixote's love for her, comes to believe she really is Dulcinea, sets out to complete his mission, and dies a martyr. Several other plays, films, poems, short stories, and novels have been influenced by this largely forgotten but very interesting and original play (see Mancing, "Dulcinea del Toboso"). *Dulcinéa, ou a última aventura de D. Quixote* (1943; *Dulcinea, or Don Quixote's Last Adventure*), by Portuguese writer Carlos Selvagem (pseudonym of Alfonso dos Santos), has Don Quixote struggle unsuccessfully to free an oppressed people, but it is more interesting for its presentation of the prostitute Florinda who is recruited to play the role of Dulcinea and seduce the noble knight, but then when she is unsuccessful and begins to see herself as Dulcinea, is put to death. The influence of Baty's drama is evident. In a radically different sort of work, the Uruguyan Alvaro Fernández Suárez (pseudonym of Juan de Lara) wrote one of the most original dramas based on a scene from the novel: *El retablo de Maese Pedro* (1946; *Maese Pedro's Puppet Show*), in which actors interact with each other, some puppets, and the public in some brilliant and hilarious scenes of metafictional comedy. Alfonso Paso's *Una tal Dulcinea* (1961; *A Certain Dulcinea*), later also made into a film (1963), mixes fantasy and reality, legend and life, time-travel (or not), an elaborate-staged deceit, and a quixotic modern man who loves a woman from the past. Antonio Buero Vallejo's verse play *Mito* (1967; *Myth*) is about a fading opera star who has lost his role of Don Quixote to a younger actor, believes he can communicate with visitors from outer space by means of a special receiver (the prop for Mambrino's helmet), recruits his Sancho, and is ridiculed by other actors who play quixotic practical jokes on him. Dale Wasserman's musical drama *Man of La Mancha* (1965), in which an imprisoned Cervantes saves his manuscript of the novel by acting it out, is the most frequently performed version of Don Quixote, having been translated into dozens of languages, been staged in over a hundred countries, with many thousands of performances constantly for four decades, and made into a popular film (1972). It may be almost as well known as the original novel itself, and many people's image of Don Quixote is derived from this work.

In recent years there has been a series of highly original plays based on the novel. Alfonso Sastre's *El viaje infinito de Sancho Panza* (1984; *Sancho Panza's Infinite Voyage*) is about Sancho, confined to an asylum, who recounts to his psychiatrist how he inspired Don Quixote to become a knight-errant and how he, Sancho, was always the one who transformed reality, seeing windmills, and so forth. Federico Schroeder Inclán's *Don Quijote murió del corazón* (1985; *Don Quixote Died of a Heart Attack*) follows a twentieth-century Don Quixote, suffering from multiple-personality disorder, who is institutionalized and talking with his psychiatrist, and who in the end dies of a heart attack. In a radically different vein, Eric Overmyer's *Don Quixote de La Jolla* (1993) is pure burlesque, a madcap play about actors acting as actors acting out something more or less about Don Quixote, riding bicycles, dancing the lambada, leaving the stage, and talking about their performance. Carlos Ansó wrote *Don Quijote, o, el sueño de Cervantes* (*Don Quixote, or, Cervantes' Dream*) in Italian in 1995 and translated it into Spanish in 1998. The action takes place in Cervantes' home as he is writing his novel and features discussions with his wife and daughter, visits from Don Quixote and Sancho, Cervantes disguising himself as Cide Hamete Benengeli and spying on the knight and squire, and the death of Don Quixote. *Miguel Will* (1997), by José Carlos Somoza, is the story of how William Shakespeare wrote, directed, and acted in a play based on *Don Quixote* titled *Cardenio* (see the previous discussion of the historical basis for this play). Shakespeare's dilemma is how to bring the metafictional tale of a comic yet, at the same time, noble knight, to the more limited medium of the theater. In the end, after his failure, Shakespeare is visited by Cervantes who assures him that within 500 years the two of them will be considered the greatest of all writers. And, finally, *El Quijote de la Cancha* (1998; *Don Quixote of La Cancha*), by Adolfo Mier Rivas is a farce about a harried newspaper reporter named Miguel Cervantes and the photographer, named Sancho, who works with him. The two go undercover to expose corruption in La Cancha, the great open-air market in Cochabamba, Bolivia, where he gets involved with an attractive, uneducated vendor named Aldonsa, with whom he falls in love and whom he calls, of course, Dulcinea.

The steady stream of plays based on or inspired in *Don Quixote,* from Guillén de Castro's 1605 comedy to the present, is, among other things, a testament to the generative power of Cervantes' original idea and to the visual potential in the main characters. When theatrical versions of *Don Quixote* are added to modern films and television productions (along with book illustrations, paintings, drawings, sculptures, and so forth), the result may be that Don Quixote has more often been seen than imagined by solitary readers throughout the century.

Don Quixote in Music

Many of the earliest stage versions of *Don Quixote* were musicals, operas in many cases, and since then there has always been a close association between Cervantes' novel and music. Actually, the first music related to the novel dates from before the publication of Don Quixote. A previously-written poem by Cervantes, "Dulce esperanza mía" ("My sweet hope"), later incorporated into *Don Quixote* part 1, chapter 23, was set to music by royal musician Luis Salvador in 1591. Most of the early musical comedies and operas of the seventeenth and eighteenth centuries are not great works. Worthy of note, however, is the opera *Vida do Grande D. Quixote de La Mancha e do Gordo Sancho Pança* (1733; *Life of the Great Don Quixote de La Mancha and of the Fat Sancho Panza*) by the Portuguese *converso* António José da Silva (ca. 1707–1739), known as *o Judeu* (the Jew) who was executed by the Portuguese Inquisition. The plot is based mostly on the 1615 *Quixote* and features Sancho's governorship. But what is most noteworthy for modern readers is the work's metatheatrical features, such as when Sancho is asked where he is and he responds that he is in a theater in Lisbon; such literary self-consciousness, so characteristic of Cervantes, was not at all common in Silva's time. The best-known modern opera based on the novel is *Don Quichotte* (1910), adapted from Jacques Le Lorrain's heroic four-act drama *Le chevalier de la longe figure (Don Quichotte)* (1906; *The Knight of the Long Face [Don Quixote]*), with a libretto by Henri Cain and music by Jules Massenet. Massenet's music was largely composed for the great Russian singer

Fyodor Chaliapin, Jr., who starred in the title role and then translated the work into Russian (and then who went on to star in the first sound version of a *Don Quixote* film). The minimal plot mostly involves the retrieval of a necklace belonging to Dulcinea from bandits who have stolen it. There have been several other operas based on the novel and, in Spain, a number of *zarzuelas* (a popular minor genre of light comedy in which music and spoken parts alternate, usually based on folkloric or typical social characters) by some of the best practitioners of the genre: Luis Arnedo, Gustavo Adolfo Bécquer, Ruperto Chapí, Sinesio Delgado, Carlos Fernández Shaw, Francisco García Cuevas, Diego Giménez Prieto, Luis Mariano de Larra y Wetoret, Eduardo Montesinos López, and Antonio de Reparaz.

There are also two major ballets, both perennial favorites, based on *Don Quixote*. The first is *Don Kikhot* (ca. 1869), a short four-act ballet based on Camacho's wedding (the characters here are called Gamache, Kitri, and Basil), with libretto by Marius Petipa and music by Ludwig Minkus. This ballet was revised (and often retitled *Don Quichotte*) into a considerably longer five-act version (ca. 1871). The two versions of this ballet remain popular today and are the standard Russian dance versions of Cervantes' novel; they have been performed and filmed frequently in modern times. The second ballet is the modern *Don Quixote* (1965) written for the New York City Ballet by Nicolas Nabokov, with choreography by George Balanchine, who had previously danced in the Petipa/Minkus ballet and who initiated the new project. Broader in scope, this popular ballet includes scenes from several sections of the novel.

Some of the other outstanding examples of music inspired by the novel are Anton Rubenstein's orchestral version of *Don Quixote* (1871); Richard Strauss' symphonic poem *Don Quixote* (1898), featuring the solo cello to represent Don Quixote; Manuel de Falla's *El retablo de Maese Pedro* (1923; *The Puppet-Show of Maese Pedro*), an adaptation of *Don Quixote* part 2, chapter 26; Oscar Esplá's symphonic version of *Don Quijote velando las armas* (1929; *Don Quixote Standing Guard over His Arms*); Maurice Ravel's three songs that make up his *Don Quichotte à Dulcinée* (1932), originally commissioned for Feodor Chaliapin the film *Don Quichotte* directed by Georg Wilhelm Pabst; Jacques Ibert's *Don Quichotte* (1933), the music actually used in the Pabst film; Rodolfo Halffter's *Tres epitafios* (1952; *Three Epitaphs*); Joaquín Rodrigo's symphonic poem on the theme of *Ausencias de Dulcinea* (1948; *Absence of Dulcinea*), using the text of Don Quixote's poem in part 1, chapter 26; Eric Marchelie's *Don Quijote y Dulcinea* (1998), for guitar and cello; and Richard Carr's piano music for the album *An American Quixote* (1999). Overall, however, the

most popular Quixote-related music of all time is probably the songs composed by Mitch Leigh and Joe Darion for *Man of La Mancha,* especially
"The Quest," better known by its opening lines: "To dream the impossible
dream / to fight the unbeatable foe," phrases first coined in 1930 as part of
some advertising copy and then (re)invented by Dale Wasserman, author
of the play (see Wasserman, *The Impossible Musical* 193; for more on
Don Quixote in music in general, see Esquival-Heinemann, *Don Quijote's
Sally,* and López Navia, "Las recreaciones musicales").

Don Quixote on Screen

There have been almost as many films about Don Quixote as there have
been plays. In fact, *Don Quixote* has been adapted to film or has inspired
film more often than any other work of literature. Beginning with the short
black-and-white French efforts of 1898 and 1903, both of which are lost,
Don Quixote was one of the first subjects of early, primitive film productions (the first Shakespeare-based film dates from 1899). Since then, there
have been dozens of direct adaptations of the novel for film. Some of the
most interesting are *Don Quixote* (1915), directed by Edward Dillon, with
supervision by D. W. Griffith, the first Hollywood version of the novel; an
English *Don Quixote* (1923), directed by Maurice Elvey; *Don Quixote af
Mancha* (1923), a Danish film directed by Lau Lauritzen; *Don Quichotte*
(1933), a French-English production, the first *Quixote* with sound,
directed by Georg Wilhelm Pabst and featuring the great Russian tenor
Feodor Chaliapin, Jr., as Don Quixote, and with different casts for the
French and English versions; *Don Quijote de la Mancha* (1947), directed
by Rafael Gil, the first full-length Spanish version, considered by many
as the best and most faithful film of the novel, and by others as a reflection of the traditional values of Franco's Spain; *Don Kikhot* (1957), in
Russian, directed by Grigori Kozintsev, a Marxist Don Quixote who is a
hero defending the rights of the weak against the powerful nobles and the
Church, a work considered by many as the best, not the most faithful, film
version of the novel; *Man of La Mancha* (1972), directed by Arthur Hiller,
the popular film version of Dale Wasserman's play (described previously);
Don Quijote cabalga de nuevo (1973; *Don Quixote Rides Again*), directed
by Roberto Gavaldón and featuring the great Mexican comedian/actor
Cantinflás as Sancho Panza in one of his typical performances consisting
of nonstop verbal humor; *The Adventures of Don Quixote* (1973), directed
by Alvin Rakoff for the BBC and starring Rex Harrison as a very British
Don Quixote; *Monsignor Quixote* (1985), an adaptation of the Graham

Greene novel (discussed previously), directed by Rodney Bennett and starring Alec Guinness in one of his best roles; *El Quijote de Miguel de Cervantes* (1991), a five-hour, five-chapter mini series (of part 1 of the novel only!) for Spanish television, directed by Manuel Gutiérrez Aragón, from a script by Nobel-Prize laureate Camilo José Cela, and starring Fernando Rey and Alfredo Landa as Don Quixote and Sancho, the very incarnation of these characters for millions who watched this extraordinarily well done and extremely popular series; *Don Quixote* (2000), a film directed by Peter Yates and starring John Lithgow (who was the driving force behind the making of the film) as Don Quixote and made for Turner Network Television; and *El caballero don Quijote* (2002; English title: *Don Quixote, Knight Errant*), Manuel Gutiérrez Aragón's version of part 2, a two-hour film (not specifically made for TV), this time with Juan Luis Galiardo and Carlos Iglesias as Don Quixote and Sancho. In addition, there have been two films titled *Dulcinea* (1947 and 1963), both direct adaptations of Gaston Baty's famous play discussed previously, and a half a dozen other films specifically about Dulcinea. There have been numerous animated versions, beginning with *Garbancito de la Mancha* (the first full-length animated feature film) and continuing through *Donkey Xote* (currently in production as of this writing), a version of the story told by Sancho's ass and Rocinante. In addition to the many films made in Spain, the United States, France, Italy, and Germany, there have been versions, adaptations, documentaries, and spin-offs filmed in Argentina, Australia, Austria, Belgium, Brazil, Bulgaria, Chile, the Czech Republic, Denmark, Finland, Hungary, Israel, Japan, Mexico, Poland, Portugal, Russia, the Slovak Republic, South Korea, and Yugoslavia. There have been films with titles like *Don Quickshot of the Rio Grande* (1923), *Don Quijote del altillo* (1936; *Don Quixote in the Attic*), *Un Quijote sin Mancha* (1969; *A Spotless Quixote*), *Rocío de La Mancha* (1963), *Scandalous John* (1971; the Spanish title was *Don Quijote del Oeste*), *The Amorous Adventures of Don Quixote and Sancho Panza* (1976; aka *When Sex Was a Knightly Affair*), *Don Cipote de la Manga* (1983; a silly movie about a quixotic were wolf), *Rocinante* (1987), *Dean Quixote* (2000), and *The Gentleman Don La Mancha* (2004).

And then there are the films never made; there are several of them, the most famous of which is the Orson Welles' *Don Quixote*. From the mid-1950s until his death in 1985 Welles worked on the film, and during this period his actors died or grew up, he changed his concept of the film, footage was stored in various places and in the possession of different people, and yet Welles kept saying that he was on the verge of finishing the work. In 1992, Welles' associate Jesús Franco put together and released a version of the work *Don Quijote de Orson Welles,* which does not include some of the most valuable footage (not available to Franco) and which is certainly far from what Welles would have wanted. More recently, in 2000, Terry Gilliam began to make a film titled *The Man who Killed Don Quixote,* featuring Johnny Depp as a man who goes back in time and becomes Sancho Panza. But after only a few days of filming, with scenes ruined by U.S. military planes flying overhead, disastrous weather—a flood in La Mancha, of all places—and a major illness to Jean Rochefort (the French actor who was to play Don Quixote), work was halted and the project was abandoned; the story of the film's failure was chronicled in the 2002 film *Lost in La Mancha.*

Since the 1950s, television has competed with film as a medium for the presentation of visual versions of the novel (some of the films mentioned in the previous paragraphs were originally done for television). The first televised version was *Don Quixote* (1952), directed by Sidney Lumet and starring Boris Karloff as Don Quixote and Grace Kelly as Dulcinea. What a shame that performance was not recorded! The first version of Wasserman's *Man of La Mancha* was the (nonmusical) drama titled *I, Don Quixote,* directed by Karl Genus and broadcast live in 1959 starring Lee J. Cobb as Don Quixote. Again, it is too bad that it was not recorded, for it was a superb performance. By far the most successful televised version of the novel is the 39-part animated series *Don Quijote de la Mancha* (1979–81) directed by Palomo Cruz Delgado, with the voices of distinguished actors Fernando Fernán Gómez and Antonio Ferrandis as Don Quixote and Sancho. This was perhaps the most successful (and most expensive) animated version of a work of literature ever done for television. It was the most-often seen production in the history of Spanish television, and the series was dubbed into more than 30 different languages and eventually shown in over 100 countries. Between movie and television versions, Don Quixote (or variations on the concept of Don Quixote) has appeared on screen more than any other literary character. Shakespeare's plays have also inspired very many movies, although none of them can match the record of *Don Quixote* on film; one could go so far as to say that Cervantes and Shakespeare are the most prolific (if posthumous) screenwriters of all time.

All of these films and television programs are problematic, of course. It is possible to adapt a play to the screen and capture 100 percent of it in a way that very closely approximates a theatrical version; in fact, many theatrical performances have been filmed in their entirety. There have, for example, been a number of superb and very faithful film versions of Shakespeare plays. But you simply cannot "film" a novel, especially a long and complex novel like *Don Quixote.* The closest any film comes to presenting the novel as Cervantes wrote it is the five-hour *El Quijote de Miguel de Cervantes* previously discussed. But that film only presents the first half of the novel and, even then, fails to convey at least half of Cervantes' text. It would probably take at least 25 hours to film *Don Quixote* in a way that begins to approximate the way you can film, say, *Hamlet* in two or three hours, and no such effort has ever been made for any work of prose fiction. Film versions of Shakespeare plays *are* (or, at least, can be) Shakespeare's work. But film versions—even excellent ones, and there are several—of *Don Quixote* are *never* Cervantes' work, but interpretations, summaries, adaptations, re-creations, weak approximations, or variations on a theme. Shakespeare wrote for a visual medium, the theater, and can be understood very well in a sister visual medium, film. Cervantes wrote for the imaginative and creative reader and can only truly be understood by reading his novel (for more on film and television versions of *Don Quixote,* see Cervera and Iriarte, eds., *Don Quijote y el cine,* Payán, ed., *El "Quijote" en el cine,* and Rosa, González, and Medina, eds., *Cervantes en imágenes;* in this case, do *not* consult my *Cervantes Encyclopedia,* where the entry on "Cervantes in film" is inadequate and even incorrect at times).

Don Quixote in Art

The first known illustration of *Don Quixote* is a poor woodcut that serves as the frontispiece for a 1605 Lisbon pirated edition of the novel; it depicts a walking figure (Sancho) leading a knight (Don Quixote) mounted on a powerful horse (certainly no Rocinante), but the figures are so generic that it would be impossible to identify them by name if it were not for the context of the book. In 1614 a stylized Don Quixote and other characters from the novel are depicted as carnivalesque figures in a German publication (note that this is a date much earlier than the 1683 first translation of the novel into German). The next, and most interesting (in the sense of the first genuinely original), representation of Don Quixote and Sancho is the engraving that serves as the frontispiece of a 1618 Paris (and redrawn for a 1620 London) edition. It depicts Don Quixote, wearing Mambrino's helmet and riding Rocinante, followed by Sancho on his ass, and with a windmill in the background. Clearly, this is the first unmistakable graphic version of the characters, and it provides proof that the windmill and helmet were part of the quixotic iconography right from the very beginning (see Lo Ré, "More on the Sadness" and "A New First").

Because *Don Quixote* has been illustrated more often than any other lit-erary work, and its characters have often been depicted apart from editions of the novel, it is only appropriate to take note of some of the most impor-tant artists who have made artistic interpretations of its' characters and scenes. Much of our concept of Don Quixote (and Sancho and Dulcinea del Toboso) comes from these graphic interpretations; in fact, since the seventeenth century very few people have read the novel without first hav-ing some familiarity with the image of Don Quixote, a factor that inevita-bly influences the reader's understanding of the text.

The first important (not the actual first) illustrated version of the novel is the previously mentioned luxury edition prepared by Lord Carteret in 1738, with engravings by John Vanderbank. The most famous illustrations of all time are those of Gustave Doré, done for a 1863 French edition. Doré's romantic vision of Don Quixote has become the most popular and most frequently reprinted (and imitated) set of illustrations; for many people, Doré's Quixote *is* Don Quixote. One can find illustrated *Quixotes* in virtually every style imaginable: romantic, realistic, impressionist, surrealistic, cubist, abstract, cartoon, caricature, and more. Among the literally hundreds of artists who have illustrated the book or have other-wise made significant interpretations of Don Quixote, Cervantes, Sancho Panza, Dulcinea, Rocinante, the windmills, and much more are: Charles-Antoine Coypel, William Hogarth, Antonio Carnicero, Francisco de Goya, Jean-Honoré Fragonard, Robert Smirke, Eugene Delacroix, Tony Johannot, Honoré Daumier, Mariano Fortuny, G. Roux, Jean-Baptiste Camille Corot, Paul Cézanne, Odilon Redon, José Guadalupe Posada, Daniel Urrabieta Vierge, Edward Hopper, Antonio de la Gandara, Antonio Muñoz Degrain, Julio González, José María Sert, Leonardo Alenza, Jackson Pollock, Ignacio Zuloaga, Salvador Dalí, Elvira Gascón, José Segrelles, Pablo Picasso, Enrique Herreros, Mario Orozco Rivera, Marc Chagal, Pilar Coomonte, Gregorio Prieto, Walter Solón Romero, Joan Ponç, Andrés Salgó, Antonio Saura, and Antonio Mingote (for more on the iconography of Don Quixote, see Schmidt, *Critical Images;* Lenaghan et al, *Imágenes del "Quijote;"* and Allen and Finch, *Don Quijote en el arte*). The iconography that has grown up around Cervantes' novel has led to the establishment of a museum devoted to that one subject: the Museo Iconográfico del *Quijote* in Guanajuato, Mexico. Directed by Eulalio Ferrer, whose personal collection of over 600 works of art on the theme of Don Quixote is the basis for the collection, this is the only museum in the world devoted to a single literary character (see Rodríguez, *Museo iconográfico*).

Don Quixote in **Popular Culture**

From the very start, Don Quixote was a popular figure, appearing in parades and festivities, a figure immediately recognizable to everyone, even those who had not actually read the book. It is quite unique for a literary figure to be such a popular phenomenon beyond the text of the novel, to the degree of Don Quixote. Even today, the image of Don Quixote is more universally recognized than that of any other literary character ever created—far more than, for example, Sherlock Holmes, who probably comes in a distant second. Tall, thin Don Quixote; short, fat Sancho Panza; the skinny nag Rocinante; the windmills; and Mambrino's helmet—recall that all of these were present in the frontispiece of the 1618 French edition—have all been a constant part of popular culture from the early seventeenth century to today.

Don Quixote is far more than a literary character; he is a genuine myth. What all myths have in common—what makes them myths—is that they are easily recognized outside of their original context. Don Quixote is one of the few great modern literary myths (others, perhaps, are Hamlet, Don Juan, and Faust). A mythic figure lives in what Bakhtin calls "great time": "Works break through the boundaries of their own time, they live in centuries, that is, in *great time* and frequently (with great works, always) their lives there are more intense and fuller than are their lives within their own time" (*Speech Genres* 4). As such he joins the great figures of ancient mythology and literature (Mars, Venus, Cupid; Zeus, Helen of Troy, Odysseus) and the Old and New Testament (Eve, Noah, Moses; Jesus, Mary Magdalene, Judas). To them we can also add the great myths of modern popular culture (Mickey Mouse, King Kong, Barbie) and modern literature (Sherlock Holmes, Tarzan, Wizard of Oz). And, of course, there are also the near-mythic contemporary icons of popular film (Charlie Chaplin, John Wayne, Marilyn Monroe), sports (Babe Ruth, Knute Rockne, Michael Jordan), and music (Billie Holliday, Elvis Presley, Madonna).

Four centuries of editions, translations, retellings, adaptations, festivals, cartoons, jokes, advertisements, musical plays, movies, TV programs, graphic images, and commercial products (ranging from DQ Rum, Sancho Panza Cigars, Dulcinea nail polish, and Rocinante cheese; to ceramic tiles, tee shirts, key chains, and coffee mugs) have made it possible for people the world over to know what "quixotic" means, to catch the connotations of a windmill, or to recognize the gaunt figure on the old nag as Don Quixote. And, like all great myths, Don Quixote is a protean figure: he is equally recognizable as a deluded madman, a visionary, a comic bumbler, an eccentric do-gooder, a serious but failed reformer, a dreamy idealist, a fanatic true believer, a Christ-like moral symbol, or an imaginative escapist. We can all recognize a Don Quixote figure, whether the incarnation be in an aging man, a young woman, an imaginative youth, or a cartoon character. Even if all novels are quixotic novels, as has been suggested previously, it is probably more the mythic than the textual Don Quixote that has made Cervantes' novel the prototype of the eighteenth-century comic novel, the nineteenth-century realist novel, and the twentieth-century modernist and postmodern novel.

DON QUIXOTE AT 400

The year 2005 was the 400th anniversary of the publication of part 1 of *Don Quixote;* as such, it was a year of celebration throughout the world, but especially in Spain. Hundreds of scholarly conferences and special seminars, editions of the novel and scholarly studies, exhibitions of books and art, plays and musical performances, movies, and television programs throughout the year made Cervantes and *Don Quixote* a constant presence in Spanish life. In Spain, an edition that only cost 1€ went on sale; not to be outdone, populist President Hugo Chávez of Venezuela launched Project Dulcinea, a plan to distribute a million copies of the book for free. The commercialization of the "product" of *Don Quixote* and the attempts (often cynical and self-serving) of politicians to associate themselves with the novel evoked criticism and satire as the book and the character were used to sell and promote careers. Travel agencies offered special "Route of Don Quixote" excursions and tours; restaurants offered special Quixote menus; children's drawings were exhibited in the Madrid subway; classic videos and DVDs were (re-)released; the entire text of part 1 of the novel was reproduced on a single page consisting of a large hanging canvas displayed in the courtyard of a cultural center in Madrid; and (often unimaginative) plays, street performances, and dance reviews abounded. The face and figure of Don Quixote was ubiquitous on television, in newspapers, and on billboards; many Spaniards grew tired of the hoopla and began to long for the disappearance of the omnipresent knight and squire.

Yet, at the same time, there was a festive air in cities like Madrid, Alcalá de Henares, and nearly all towns and villages of La Mancha throughout the year. Cervantes and his novel were spoken of with a sense of pride and honor never seen before. The final chapters of this book were written in Madrid in the summer and fall of 2005 while the author was on sabbatical leave, an experience made richer by the constant Quixote-related activities available. It is hoped that the spirit of the celebratory year comes through in the book's pages.

WORKS CITED

Allen, John Jay, and Patricia S. Finch. *Don Quijote en el arte y pensamiento de Occidente.* Madrid: Cátedra, 2004.

Bakhtin, M. M. *The Dialogic Imagination: Four Essays.* Ed. Michael Holquist. Trans. Caryl Emerson and Michael Holquist. Austin: U of Texas P, 1981.

———. *Speech Genres and Other Late Essays.* Ed. Caryl Emerson and Michael Holquist. Trans. Vern W. McGee. Austin: U of Texas P, 1986.

Bloom, Harold. *The Western Canon: The Books and School of the Ages.* New York: Harcourt Brace, 1994.

Cervera, Elena, and Ana Cristina Iriarte, eds. *Don Quijote y el cine.* Madrid: Filmoteca Española, 2005.

Cox, Ralph Merritt. *The Rev. John Bowle: The Genesis of Cervantean Criticism.* Chapel Hill: U of North Carolina P, 1971.

Esquival-Heinemann, Bárbara. *Don Quijote's Sally into the World Opera. Libretti between 1680 and 1976.* New York: Lang, 1993.

Lenaghan, Patrick, Javier Blas, and José Manuel Matilla. *Imágenes del "Quijote": Modelos de representación en las ediciones de los siglos XVII a XIX.* Madrid: Calcografía Nacional, 2003.

Levin, Harry. *"Don Quixote* and *Moby-Dick."* In *Cervantes Across the Centuries: A Quadricentennial Volume.* Ed. Angel Flores and M. J. Benardete. New York: Gordian P, 1947. 227–36.

———. "The Quixotic Principle: Cervantes and Other Novelists." In *The Interpretation of Narrative: Theory and Practice.* Ed. Morton W. Bloomfield. Cambridge: Harvard UP, 1970. 45–66.

Lo Ré, Anthony G. "More on the Sadness of Don Quixote: The First Known Quixote Illustration, Paris, 1618." *Cervantes* 9.1 (1989): 75–83.

———. "A New First: An Illustration of Don Quixote as 'Le Capitaine de Carnaval', Leipsig, 1614." *Cervantes* 10.2 (1990): 95–100.

López Navia, Santiago Alfonso. "Las recreaciones musicales." In *Inspiración y pretexto: Estudios sobre las recreaciones del "Quijote."* Madrid: Iberoamericana, 2005.

Mancing, Howard. *The Cervantes Encyclopedia.* 2 vols. Westport, CT: Greenwood P, 2004.

———. "Dulcinea del Toboso—On the Occasion of Her 400th Birthday." *Hispania* 88.1 (2005): 53–63.

———. "Jacinto María Delgado and Cide Hamete Benengeli: A Semi-Classic Recovered and a Bibliographical Labyrinth Explored." *Cervantes* 7.1 (1987): 13–43.

Ortega y Gasset, José. *Meditations on "Quixote."* Trans. Evelyn Rugg and Diego Marín. New York: W. W. Norton, 1961.

Paulson, Ronald. *Don Quixote in England: The Aesthetics of Laughter.* Baltimore: Johns Hopkins UP, 1998.

Payán, Miguel Juan, ed. *El "Quijote" en el cine.* Madrid: Jaguar, 2005.

Rodríguez, Antonio. *Museo iconográfico del "Quijote."* Mexico: Fundación Cervantina Eulalio Ferrer, 1987.

Rosa, Emilio de la, Luis M. González, and Pedro Medina, eds. *Cervantes en imágenes: Donde se cuenta cómo el cine y la televisión evocaron su vida y su obra.* Enlarged ed. Alcalá de Henares: Festival de Cine de Alcalá de Henares, 2005.

Schmidt, Rachel. *Critical Images: The Canonization of "Don Quixote" Through Illustrated Editions of the Eighteenth Century.* Montreal: McGill-Queen's UP, 1999.

Shakespeare, William, and John Fletcher. *Cardenio, or The Second Maiden's Tragedy.* Ed. Charles Hamilton. Lakewood, CO: Glenbridge, 1994.

The Tragedy of John Bowle. Special issue of *Cervantes* 23.2 (2003).

Wasserman, Dale. *The Impossible Musical.* New York: Applause, 2003.

Chapter 8

BIBLIOGRAPHICAL ESSAY

The annual bibliography published by the Modern Language Association of America (MLA) is the most extensive and authoritative bibliography in the field of literary studies. The print version of the *MLA Bibliography* has in recent years been somewhat superceded by the online searchable version on the Internet. This version is available by subscription and can be accessed through most research libraries. For our purposes here, however, the print version is much more useful, as it reveals its organizing taxonomy very clearly in a way that the online version does not. Because of its comprehensiveness and recognized authority, the *MLA Bibliography* is arguably the single best indicator of a writer's status in the critical canon. Logically, the writers who receive most attention year after year, and thus more entries annually, would seem to be the ones most highly esteemed by literary scholars. In fact, and not surprisingly, William Shakespeare is in a class by himself as the object of over 500 scholarly studies per year in the final decade of the twentieth century (1991–2000). Joining him is a second (non-British) group, made up of those who are the subject of over 100 studies annually: Dante, Cervantes, and Goethe. These four writers—one medieval Italian, one Englishman and one Spaniard both from the Renaissance, and one German from the late eighteenth century—arguably form the essential minimal core of the western canon, those writers who are most legitimately considered as the defining figures of the western tradition.

In addition to the annual *MLA bibliography,* in both the print and the online versions, there are several very good bibliographies (as well as many that are now quite dated) that can be consulted by the student of *Don Quixote*. The most massive Cervantes bibliography is that of Jaime Fernández, *Bibliografía del "Quijote"* (1995) and the expanded version on line, *Cervantes International Bibliography Online* (CIBO) cited later in this chapter in the section on Cervantes and the Internet. Eduardo Urbina's nearly annual *Anuario Bibliográfico Cervantino* has appeared frequently since 1996, and the latest editions are of great value. There is also a very large and inclusive bibliography included in volume 2 of the *Don Quixote* edition by Francisco Rico et al, 2nd ed. (2004).

Given the enormous size of the critical and interpretive tradition that accompanies the works of Cervantes (and that involves all of his works, but *Don Quixote* is the subject of most of it), any descriptive bibliography will necessarily be selective. In previous chapters there are lists of works cited that can help orient interested readers to specific themes, characters, and scenes. In this chapter, I will make a brief, sweeping, selective review of the critical tradition that has been developed with regard to Cervantes' novel. As before, emphasis here is on works written in English since this book is written primarily as an introduction to the novel for English-speakers. Since much of the best scholarship on Cervantes is, of course, in Spanish, it will also be necessary to include mention of a number of works in Spanish, but there will be few citations of works written in other languages. Again, the selective nature of this survey is stressed.

GENERAL INTRODUCTIONS TO CERVANTES AND *DON QUIXOTE*

This book is not by any means the first to present itself as an introduction to the novel for students and nonspecialists. The ubiquitous commercial study guides should be avoided at all costs, as they are superficial, condescending, and misleading, generally prepared by non-Spanish-speaking generalists who simply do not understand the novel in any meaningful way. There was, however one exception: the superb Cervantes scholar John J. Allen wrote a *Monarch Notes* guide titled *Cervantes' "Don Quixote"* (1975) that, while brief, was at least very well-informed and capable of actually fulfilling the supposed role of these notes. Unfortunately, this work has long been out of print and is very difficult to locate.

Probably the classic short introductory volume written in Spanish to present Don Quixote in a concise way to students, first-time readers, and other nonspecialists is Martín de Riquer's *Cervantes y el "Quijote"* (1960), better known in subsequent editions titled *Aproximación al "Quixote"*

(1967) and *Nueva aproximación al "Quijote"* (1989) and most recently included in his *Para leer a Cervantes* (2003). The book is a minor classic and probably the best of its kind in Spanish. More recently, the *Invitación al Qvijote* (2004), by Jaime Fernández, provides another good introduction to the novel in Spanish.

Manuel Durán's *Cervantes* (1974) is the introductory book on Cervantes for the Twayne World Author Series, one of the first editorial efforts of its kind. Books in this series are terribly uneven, but Durán's balanced presentation of Cervantes' life and works is quite good, if now somewhat dated. P. E. Russell's *Cervantes* (1985) is, like Durán's book, a general introduction to Cervantes and his works, with emphasis on *Don Quixote*. Consistent with the position he has taken for years, Russell argues for the "hard" reading (explained later in this chapter) of the novel. Edward C. Riley's *Don Quixote* (1986) is a careful, measured presentation of the novel by one of the truly great Cervantes scholars of the twentieth century. Luis A. Murillo's very nice *Critical Introduction to "Don Quixote"* (1988) analyzes the plot in some detail, and traces themes such as myth and chivalry throughout the novel.

Carroll B. Johnson's more recent *Don Quixote: The Quest for Modern Fiction* (1990) is by all standards an excellent contemporary introduction to the novel. Plot summary only occupies about a third of the book, as Cervantes and his work are placed in historical and critical context, and then Johnson offers a reading of the novel grounded primarily in psychoanalytic theory and dealing with reader response. In his *Miguel de Cervantes: "Don Quixote"* (1990), Anthony J. Close, like Russell, emphasizes his strong reading of *Don Quixote* as a comic novel.

All of these books have the same purpose: to introduce *Don Quixote* to nonspecialist readers, contextualizing and offering a critical understanding of both the author and his work. Every one of these authors is a distinguished Cervantes specialist whose critical work will again be cited later in this chapter. Because they are single-authored books, each book presents a coherent view of Cervantes and his novel. But because these authors have also written on *Don Quixote* for a long time, they have developed their unique understanding of the work. Therefore, the reader who takes, for example, Carroll Johnson as his or her introductory guide to the novel approaches *Don Quixote* with a mind-set different from one who has used Anthony Close to introduce the novel.

This reference guide is intended to fit within the critical genre described in this section. It, too, aims to present a coherent, contextualized view of Cervantes and *Don Quixote*. The emphases here on Don Quixote's concept of chivalry, aspects of style and narrative technique in the novel, Bakhtin's concept of the novel as a literary genre, and the influence of *Don Quixote* throughout the centuries are all reflections of the author's own interests and previous work on Cervantes.

ANTHOLOGIES OF CERVANTES CRITICISM

Another way to begin to acquaint oneself with Cervantes criticism is by reading, or, at least, sampling, one of the many anthologies consisting of essays by different critics and scholars on a variety of subjects. The classic volume of this type is *Cervantes Across the Centuries,* ed. Angel Flores and M. J. Benardete (1947, the 400th anniversary of Cervantes' birth). With essays by important mid-century critics and a series of (still very useful and informative) reviews of Cervantes' reception and influence in various countries, this was at the time a major contribution to the criticism. Lowry Nelson, Jr., also edited *Cervantes, a Collection of Critical Essays* (1969), a popular and influential anthology that includes some classic studies.

Probably the most important of all anthologies of Cervantes scholarship is *Suma Cervantina,* ed. Juan Bautista Avalle-Arce and Edward C. Riley (1973). Two of the great Cervantes scholars of the twentieth century collaborated on a systematic introduction to Cervantes, with what was then state-of-the-art (if traditional and conservative) essays by some of the finest scholars on all of his works and on several general themes.

Another very good anthology, consisting mostly of standard essays in Spanish, is *El "Quijote" de Cervantes,* ed. George Haley (1980). A very good collection of essays is *Cervantes and the Renaissance,* ed. Michael D. McGaha (1980). Richard Bjornson edited a volume titled *Approaches to Teaching Cervantes's "Don Quixote"* (1984) as a contribution to the MLA series on how specialists and generalists teach important works of literature. Because it has an emphasis on teaching techniques, this volume is unique among the anthologies discussed in this section. Ruth El Saffar edited *Critical Essays on Cervantes* (1986), another good selection of criticism. Harold Bloom has a prolific publishing program, which includes a series of anthologies on major authors, and one of them is *Cervantes* (1987). Bloom's more recent collection, *Miguel de Cervantes* (2004), is a broader anthology and occupies a slot in another of his lengthy series of such books. An excellent collection of essays, in Spanish, is *Cervantes,* ed. Anthony J. Close (1995). Anne J. Cruz and Carroll B. Johnson collaborated on an interesting anthology oriented toward the concept of postmodernism, titled *Cervantes and His Postmodern Constituencies* (1999). The collection of essays edited by Francisco La Rubia Prado, titled *Cervantes For the 21st Century* (2000) features some excellent recent work. However, the two most recent works in this genre, and they are good ones, are *The Cambridge Companion to Cervantes,* ed. Anthony J. Cascardi (2002), and *Cervantes' "Don Quixote": A Casebook* (2005), ed. Roberto González Echevarría.

Not all of these anthologies of criticism are devoted exclusively to *Don Quixote,* but of course it is the novel that receives special attention in all of them. The advantage of consulting works such as these is that even if they are uneven, as they are, they provide a showcase of some of the best writings of some of the best scholars in the field. Also included within the category of anthologies are all the proceedings of special symposia or congresses devoted to Cervantes and *Don Quixote.* These books, often very large or in multiple volumes, tend to be even more uneven in quality than the works cited in the text. The celebration year of 2005, the 400th anniversary of the publication of Cervantes' novel, is already spawning a record number of such proceedings.

ENCYCLOPEDIAS

The first efforts to organize information about Cervantes and his works into encyclopedic form have occurred in recent years. The pioneering effort along these lines is Juan Bautista Avalle-Arce's *Enciclopedia cervantina* (1997), a comprehensive work that includes entries for almost all of Cervantes' works, characters, place names, historical figures, important concepts, some subsequent writers inspired by Cervantes, and much more, with an extensive system of cross references. It is particularly valuable for its' entries on earlier Cervantes scholarship (especially the historical and textual), works attributed to Cervantes, and all original poems and foreign phrases included within the prose works. This was complemented two years later by César Vidal's *Enciclopedia del "Quijote"* (1999), a work that includes a chapter-by-chapter summary of the plot, several introductory chapters, the alphabetized list of entries (including many for specific vocabulary words), a valuable list of the proverbs from *Don Quixote,* a very detailed chronology, and indices. Antonio Rodríguez Vicéns' recent *Diccionario de "El Quijote"* (2003) is yet another valuable and extensive encyclopedia-like compendium.

The Cervantes Encyclopedia, 2 vols., by the author (2004), is the first work of its kind designed to be totally accessible to readers of English, with complete cross-references for readers of Spanish. It is relatively comprehensive, including entries on all known works written by Cervantes, with a detailed plot summary of each one; virtually all the characters in Cervantes' works; historical personages of importance in the life and times of Cervantes; places and items of interest in the author's life and works; names from history, myth, and literary works cited or alluded to in Cervantes' works; concepts and terms important to understanding the life, times, and works of Cervantes; most of the important episodes in *Don Quixote* and selected episodes from his other works; authors and works of literature cited or alluded to in the works of Cervantes; important theories and theorists of the novel; hundreds of modern novelists and other writers inspired or influenced by Cervantes, especially by *Don Quixote;* some artists and musicians similarly inspired or influenced by Cervantes, especially by *Don Quixote;* and several of the more salient aspects of contemporary Cervantes scholarship and criticism. The comprehensiveness of the work makes a valuable point of departure for readers coming to *Don Quixote* for the first time.

Finally, the Centro de Estudios Cervantinos, under the direction of Carlos Alvar, has begun to publish a 10-volume *Gran Enciclopedia Cervantina (Great Cervantes Encyclopedia)*. The entire work was originally projected to be available in 2005, but only late in that year, as this book was in preparation, was Vol. I: A published.

JOURNALS

All major Hispanic journals, as well as nearly all journals with a comparative orientation, have published and continue to publish important shorter scholarly studies on Cervantes. The first modern scholarly journal devoted specifically to Cervantes and his works was *Anales Cervantinos,* published, under the auspices of the Cervantes section of the Consejo Superior de Investigaciones Científicas, from 1951 to 1959, when publication was suspended. Restarted in 1971, it continued publication until 2000, when it was again suspended, but it was revived yet once again in 2004. It is fondly hoped that there will be no further interruptions in the publication schedule of this important source of current Cervantes scholarship. In spite of its sometimes very uneven quality, the journal remains a valuable source for much excellent scholarship in the field.

The Cervantes Society of America (CSA), a professional organization dedicated to the study and promotion of the works of Cervantes, was founded by a group of Hispanic scholars at a meeting at Fordham University in the winter of 1977. The first president was Juan Bautista Avalle-Arce, and he has been succeeded by some of the best and most influential scholars in the field (as of this writing the president is Edward H. Friedman, author of a major book on Cervantes' theater and a number of important shorter essays on his works). The first editor of the society's journal was John J. Allen, and he, too, has been succeeded by comparably outstanding and dedicated scholars. The primary activity of the CSA is to publish *Cervantes: Bulletin of the Cervantes Society of America,* the single most important source for the latest and best scholarship on Cervantes. Readers who want to focus on the most up-to-date critical writing on *Don Quixote* and other works by Cervantes would be best advised to start with the most recent issues of this journal.

CERVANTES ON THE INTERNET

There are dozens, if not hundreds, of Web sites devoted to, or substantially involving, Cervantes and *Don Quixote* on the Internet. Many of them are superficial, sometimes filled with errors and ephemera. Perhaps the worst way to begin one's study of *Don Quixote* is to start reading Web pages that could present a distorted or factually incorrect impression of the novel. Therefore, no effort to include a lengthy or detailed list or bibliography of such sites will be included here. But, since the amount of "information" received by means of the Internet is greater every day, a few of the more substantial sites, with good probabilities of long-term availability, are found at the following URLs:

1. Biblioteca Virtual Miguel de Cervantes: http://cervantesvirtual.com, texts of many Spanish and Spanish American writers, including an extensive page on Cervantes; this is supposedly the most-visited of all Spanish Web sites;

2. Cervantes: Bulletin of the Cervantes Society of America: http://www2.h-net.msu.edu/červantes/bcsalist.htm, which contains the full text of all issues of the journal;

3. H-Cervantes: http://www.h-net.org/červantes, an online scholarly discussion about Cervantes and his works;

4. Instituto Cervantes: http://www.cervantes.es, an organization that promotes Spain and things Spanish in general, as well as matters relating to Cervantes;

5. Miguel de Cervantes Saavedra: http://cervantes.uah.es, which has a great deal on Cervantes including his complete works (UAH stands for Universidad de Alcalá de Henares);

6. The Cervantes Project; C.I.B.O: Cervantes International Bibliography Online: http://www.csdl.tamu.edu/cervantes/english/biblio. html, a large site with the most complete Cervantes biography on the Web, texts, bibliography, images, links, and more;

7. Works of Miguel de Cervantes: http://users.ipfw.edu/jehle/cervante. htm, which contains old- and modernized-spelling versions of 10 volumes of the edition of Cervantes' Obras Completas by Schevill and Bonilla;

8. "Cervantes" entry in Wikipedia, the free encyclopedia: http:// en.wikipedia.org/wiki/Miguel_de_Cervantes, which presents a useful introductory overview of Cervantes and his works and contains some useful links to other pages;

9. Comunidad Quijote: http://www.elquijote.com, a large and popular site dedicated to the novel, with many links and discussion pages;

10. *The History of Don Quixote, Vol. I, Complete:* http://www.gutenberg. org/files/5921/5921-h/5921-h.htm, a reproduction of the Ormsby translation and Doré illustrations from one of the most beautiful of all Quixote volumes ever printed in English; a link to volume 2 is also included;

11. Museo Iconográfico del Quijote: http://www.guanajuato.gob.mx/ museo, the home page of this museum, with a link to images of 50 works of art by different artists from the collection.

CERVANTES SCHOLARSHIP IN THE EARLY TWENTIETH CENTURY

Eighteenth- and nineteenth-century scholarship on Cervantes and his works—with the exception of some important historical discoveries and textual work—was often little more than personal diatribes or esoteric theories about the meaning of *Don Quixote.* Literary scholarship in the modern sense of the term is a twentieth-century phenomenon. Spanish historian Américo Castro is arguably the most influential Cervantes scholar of all time. His groundbreaking book *El pensamiento de Cervantes* (1925) placed Cervantes within major Renaissance intellectual currents and controversies. The book has been reedited and reprinted several times, most importantly in a revised edition by Julio Rodríguez Puértolas (1972). Castro continued his study of Cervantes, often specifically emphasizing his *converso* background, in a series of later books, particularly *Hacia Cervantes* (1957) and *Cervantes y los casticismos españoles* (1966).

Second only to the work of Castro in lasting influence is Salvador de Madariaga's *Guía del lector del "Quijote"* (1926), translated by the author himself as *"Don Quixote": An Introductory Essay in Psychology* (1935). In addition to chapters devoted to characters such as Cardenio and Dorotea, this book introduces the concepts of the "quixotization" of Sancho and the "sanchification" of Don Quixote, the mutual influence of the two characters on each other during the course of the novel. Madariaga's book still reads easily in the twentieth-first century and continues to influence readers.

Two other important works that contemporary readers continue to find valuable were written early in the twentieth century by philosophers who were members of the so-called Generation of 1898. The first is Miguel de Unamuno, whose *Vida de Don Quijote and Sancho* (1905), written to celebrate the 300th anniversary of the first publication of *Don Quixote,* is a very idiosyncratic, romantic, and personal, chapter-by-chapter rewriting and interpretation of Cervantes' novel. It still makes for interesting and provocative reading today. It was translated into English by Anthony Kerrigan as *Our Lord Don Quixote* (1976). The second is José Ortega y Gasset's *Meditaciones del "Quijote"* (1914), translated by Evelyn Rugg and Diego Marín, with introduction and notes by Julián Marías, as *Meditations on "Quixote"* (1961). This is both a meditation on the novel in general and *Don Quixote* in particular and an early exercise in perspectivist criticism (see more on this concept later in this chapter).

HARD AND SOFT (AND PERSPECTIVIST) READINGS OF *DON QUIXOTE*

In recent decades literary scholarship has largely become divided into competing (and often confusing) factions based on specific theoretical approaches. One way to review the contemporary scholarly context surrounding *Don Quixote* would be to proceed by grouping studies of the novel according to their conceptual, methodological, or theoretical approach. Such a method would involve, at a minimum, consideration of work grounded in the following theories: chaos theory, cognitive theory, comparative studies, cultural materialism, deconstruction, feminism, formalism, Marxism, media studies, narratology, new historicism, phenomology, post-colonialism, poststructuralism, psychoanalysis (there are several versions: Freudian, Jungian, and Lacanian), queer theory, semiotics, stylistics, and others. But it would take almost as long to sort out, define or describe, and make distinctions among sometimes similar or overlapping approaches as it would to discuss the importance of the specific studies. Rather, the following sections will simply single out a number of important contemporary scholars and their work, which obviously often includes important work in all of these theoretical areas. But in this section, it seems appropriate to introduce a readily accessible (for its lack of jargon) interpretive framework that should prove useful to nonspecialist readers: "hard" versus "soft" readings of *Don Quixote*.

The distinction between hard and soft readings of *Don Quixote* had its origins in an essay titled "The Function of the Norm in *Don Quixote*" (1958) by Oscar Mandel (the only essay ever published on Cervantes by this scholar of comparative literature). According to Mandel's thesis, the prototypical hard critic is one who refuses to sympathize or identify with Don Quixote. The hard critic reads *Don Quixote* as a satire, a funny book, and nothing else; he or she considers that this is the only right way to understand the novel, and disdains those soft-headed and soft-hearted readers who mistakenly understand the novel in terms of nobility or even tragedy. In contrast, the soft critic is one who very much sympathizes and identifies with Don Quixote. The soft critic reads *Don Quixote* as a serious psychological study and a profound philosophical statement of human nature, asserts his or her right to react sympathetically to the text, and pities those hard-headed and hard-hearted readers who cannot see beyond the superficial comedy.

Erich Auerbach can be taken as a prototypical hard critic when he writes: "The whole book is a comedy in which well-founded reality holds madness up to ridicule" (*Mimesis* 347). Probably the two major hard critics in contemporary scholarship are the British scholars Anthony J. Close and P. E. Russell. Close's *The Romantic Approach to "Don Quixote"* (1978) is both an excellent survey of the reception history of Cervantes' novel and a powerful argument for the hard school. He continues this emphasis in the previously mentioned, *Miguel de Cervantes: "Don Quixote."* Most recently, Close has meticulously examined Cervantes' poetics and practices of comic fiction in *Cervantes and the Comic Mind of his Age* (2000). Russell's influential article that is also a major contribution to the subject is "Don Quixote as a Funny Book" (1969), which he also continues in his book *Cervantes,* also cited earlier.

The softer approach to *Don Quixote* has its origins in the eighteenth century, especially with the great German romantic writers (see chapter 7). The English Hispanophile Gerald Brenan can serve as a prototype of the soft position: "the significant thing about this novel—its claim to be twice over a tragedy—is that it is not only shows us the defeat of the man of noble feelings by the second-rate and vulgar, but that it convinces us that that defeat was right" (*The Literature of the Spanish People* 194). When the soft position is taken to its logical conclusion, Don Quixote's nobility and idealism make him into a Christ-like hero. Miguel de Unamuno, in his previously-cited *Vida de Don Quijote y Sancho,* is perhaps the ultimate soft reader of *Don Quixote,* with his references to "Our Lord Don Quixote" and "Saint Quixote de la Mancha." Few critics today would argue seriously for an Unamuno-like position, yet almost everyone demonstrates at least a degree of softness in his or her work.

John J. Allen was particularly perplexed by the fact that some readers saw Don Quixote as nothing but the butt of the joke, a comic character from beginning to end, while others saw him as a sublime and noble human being. How could it be, he wondered, that two readers could read the same text and reach such diametrically opposed conclusions? It was in large part in order to answer this question that he wrote *Don Quixote, Hero or Fool?* (1969), a short but intense book which also makes a major contribution to the understanding of Cervantes' narrative technique. In brief, Allen's answer is that the comic dominates in part 1 of the novel but that there is a shift in reader reaction to Don Quixote in part 2. Ten years later, Allen published his own sequel, *Don Quixote, Hero or Fool? (Part II)* (1979), which furthers his earlier work and adds an important consideration of the role of irony in the novel.

At Allen's suggestion, the barber's shaving basin/Mambrino's helmet comes to represent this critical debate. The hard critics, of course, insist that is—and only can be—a shaving basin, and anyone who says anything else is simply wrong. For them, this is a perfect symbol of how Don Quixote is out of touch with reality, demonstrably wrong in his assertions, and therefore funny. The soft critics agree with Don Quixote that it is a helmet, or, at least, that it can be one, for him. They tend to endorse Don Quixote's comment to Sancho in part 1, chapter 25: "and so, what seems to you like a barber's basin, seems like Mambrino's helmet to me, and it may seem like something else to another person."

But both this quote by Don Quixote and Sancho's later introduction of another possibility when he calls the item a *baciyelmo* (basin-helmet) at the end of part 1, chapter 44, seem to point to some sort of middle-of-the-road, or relativist, position. The idea is that the item can be a basin and a helmet at the same time, or it can be either, depending on your perspective. And here is where Leo Spitzer's idea of "perspectivism" gets introduced into the hard-soft debate. Perspectivism—the idea that everything depends on your point of view—becomes the term sometimes used to designate the middle ground between the hard and soft positions. In short, then, the hard critics are defenders of the basin, soft critics are defenders of the helmet, and perspectivists (who want to eat their cake and have it, too) are defenders of the basin-helmet. This critical framework thus provides a broad spectrum along which all critical understandings of *Don Quixote* can be located.

It is worth noting, too, that it is very difficult to find a student today (at least in most classrooms in North American universities) who enlists under the banner of the basin and call themselves hard critics of *Don Quixote.* Perhaps influenced by romantic plays like *Man of La Mancha* or other aspects of the myth of Don Quixote, today's students tend to want to feel empathy for the poor, noble, misunderstood knight-errant right from the beginning of the novel, even when they acknowledge that the first chapters are among the most comic parts of the novel. There are, however, plenty of students who rush to align themselves with the perspectivist position. Here, most probably, a major influence is postmodernist theory, which holds that everything is ideology and discourse, any one of which is as valid as any other. Extreme relativist thinking, together with not having to take a position, is one of the least intellectually-demanding paths available to students of the humanities today, and the siren-call of the basin-helmet is difficult for many to resist.

CLASSIC ESSAYS

Before undertaking a chronological review of scholarship dealing with Cervantes' novel in the last half century, I would like to consider a series of shorter articles and essays from mid-century. The influence of these essays on Cervantes scholarship and on readers' understanding of *Don Quixote* extends far beyond their relatively brief length. Clearly, a selection has been made here; many more important shorter works could have been considered, but there is simply not room to be comprehensive.

The great German philologist and literary historian Erich Auerbach (mentioned previously as a classic hard critic) wrote one of the most important and influential books on the theory and history of literature, especially the novel: *Mimesis,* trans. Willard Trask (1953; original German ed. 1946; Spanish trans. 1950), an extended study of the techniques for representing degrees of reality in fiction, with one chapter devoted to each of a series of authors and works from the Middle Ages to the twentieth century. There was nothing on Cervantes in the German work, but this was remedied in the Spanish translation and in the English version with the inclusion of a chapter titled "The Enchanted Dulcinea" (334–58), dealing with the scene in part 2, chapter 10, when Sancho deceives Don Quixote. Auerbach's method is to analyze a specific passage, then expand his reading to the entire chapter and ultimately the whole work. His overall interpretation of the novel, as discussed previously, is that the book is a great comedy.

Jaime Oliver Asín's "La hija de Agí Morato en la obra de Cervantes" (1947) was a groundbreaking historical study, showing that the character of Zoraida in the captive's tale (part 1, chs. 39–41) was based on a historical character, identifying her father and other historical figures whom Cervantes must have known during his years of captivity in Algiers. The relationships among history, personal experience, and artistic creation in this episode are still matters of interest and research in contemporary scholarship.

Another of the great German philologists, Leo Spitzer, included a chapter titled "Linguistic Perspectivism in the *Don Quijote*" in his *Linguistics and Literary History* (1948). In the book he describes and exemplifies what he calls the "philological circle," the hermeneutic process by which he goes from word to whole work and back again in order to continually refine his understanding. This essay is the classic expression of perspectivism in Cervantes criticism.

Bruce W. Wardropper, a scholar whose series of short but profound essays on Golden Age Spanish works have become classics, wrote two important essays on *Don Quixote:* "The Pertinence of 'El curioso impertinente' " (1957), the first truly major attempt to relate the embedded story of part 1, chapters 33–35, to the rest of the novel; and "*Don Quixote:* Story or History?" (1965), a subtle philological, stylistic, and historical study that is still a point of departure for studies of genre and narrative technique in *Don Quixote.*

E. C. Riley is the author of what may be the most important and influential mid-century book on Cervantes' novel. He anticipated this book with the essay titled "Don Quixote and the Imitation of Models" (1954), an insightful presentation of the subject of *imitatio* in *Don Quixote,* a subject discussed in chapter 5.

Finally, George Haley's essay "The Narrator in *Don Quijote:* Maese Pedro's Puppet Show" (1965) is a brilliant examination of both the scene of the puppet show in part 2, chapter 26, and the narrative structure of the novel in general (see the discussion of this subject in chapter 5). Later, Haley followed this up with a related essay titled "The Narrator in Don Quixote: A Discarded Voice" (1984). The latter work is not as well known or as influential as his earlier, classic article, but should be considered an important complement to it.

SOME MAJOR CERVANTES SCHOLARS AND THEIR WORK

The following sections are intended to be understood as a brief, selective, and superficial introduction to some of the major Cervantes scholars of the final decades of the twentieth century and the beginning of the twenty-first. Given the intended audience for this book, emphasis is placed heavily on those who write primarily in English, but with the inclusion of a number of major scholars whose work is mostly or exclusively in Spanish. This survey is by no means comprehensive, as many who are worthy are omitted simply for lack of space, and, by the same token, several who are cited either previously or in earlier chapters are not included here. One aim is to include as wide as possible a selection of approaches and understandings of the novel. The reader who is interested in a more detailed review of contemporary Cervantes scholarship should consult José Montero Reguera's *El "Quijote" y la crítica contemporánea* (1997), an excellent thematic and chronological survey.

The 1960s

No survey of this sort could fail to begin with the book that might rival the work of Américo Castro's *Pensamiento de Cervantes* as the most influential book in the history of Cervantes studies: E. C. Riley's *Cervantes's Theory of the Novel* (1962). Probably no scholarly work has had as much direct influence on a subsequent generation of Cervantes scholars as this one. Riley's laborious stitching together the fabric of a literary theory from Cervantes' many works is a stunning critical achievement. Not long before his death, Riley also published a collection of many of his important essays published individually over the years in a volume titled *La rara invención: Estudios sobre Cervantes y su posteridad literaria* (2001).

Three other important contributions date from the decade of the 1960s. The first is Manuel Durán's *La ambigüedad en el "Quixote"* (1960), a careful study of ambiguity and perspectivism in the novel. Richard Predmore's modest book titled *The World of "Don Quixote"* (1967) offers insights into numerous cultural and historical values important to Cervantes. Particularly interesting are his explorations of the worlds of being and of seeming and the role of enchantment in the novel. Predmore's later very nice illustrated biography *Cervantes* (1973), was the first in a series of modern biographies of Cervantes in English (see chapter 2 for more on biographies of Cervantes). Also very important was the publication of Helmut Hatzfeld's 2nd ed., revised and expanded edition, of *El "Quijote" como obra de arte del lenguaje* (1966; first Spanish ed. 1949; original German ed. 1927). A detailed labor of philological investigation and description of stylistic elements in the novel, Hatzfeld's still valuable work is too often ignored today.

Another major Cervantes scholar who came to the fore in the 1960s is Juan Bautista Avalle-Arce, who had been an active Renaissance scholar for over a decade, and whose *Enciclopedia cervantina* (1997) is discussed previously. The prolific Avalle-Arce's first book on Cervantes was a collection of essays titled *Deslindes cervantinos* (1961), later expanded and retitled *Nuevos deslindes cervantinos* (1975) and which includes his reading of Don Quixote's life as a living "work of art." In addition to many short studies published independently and excellent editions of many of Cervantes' works, Avalle-Arce's major work of interpretation is *Don Quijote como forma de vida* (1976), in which his chapters on Don Quixote's "gratuitous act" during his penance in part 1, chapter 25, and on the death of Don Quixote are essential reading. Alberto Navarro's survey of the early reception history of the novel, *El Quijote español del siglo XVII* (1964) also merits recognition.

The 1970s

The decade of the 1970s begins with a worthy successor to Riley's work on Cervantes' literary theory: Alban K. Forcione's *Cervantes, Aristotle, and the Persiles* (1970). Forcione, who simultaneously published an important book of Cervantes' *Persiles* and who has since written two major books of the *Novelas ejemplares,* specifically related Cervantes' practice to the literary theory of his day, especially as derived from Aristotle. The next year, 1971, saw the publication of an important—and certainly unique—book, Arthur Efron's *Don Quixote and the Dulcineated World* (1971). Efron understands Don Quixote as the unwitting personification of reactionary cultural forces, the forces that "dulcineate" (make sweet, palatable) the world for the easily manipulated masses. Efron also makes an important contribution in the book to the hard and soft debate in his discussion of the cautionary versus idealist readings of the novel. Angel Rosenblat's *La lengua del "Quijote"* (1971) is an outstanding complement to Hatzfeld's work on language and style in *Don Quixote,* and a work that deserves more attention in contemporary criticism than it generally receives.

After already establishing her credentials as a Cervantes scholar with an important book on the *Novelas ejemplares,* Ruth El Saffar turned to *Don Quixote* with her groundbreaking study of narrative technique: *Distance and Control in "Don Quixote": A Study in Narrative Technique* (1975). El Saffar went on to become the greatest Cervantes scholar of her generation with a series of short studies and her work as a Jungian theorist and therapist. Her *Beyond Fiction: The Recovery of the Feminine in the Novels of Cervantes* (1984) is perhaps the single most important feminist (and Jungian) study of Cervantes' works, and as such is a landmark of criticism. Also worth mentioning here is the anthology of psychoanalytic criticism El Saffar edited with Diana de Armas Wilson, *Quixotic Desire* (1993). With her NEH seminars and other mentoring efforts, El Saffar exercised an enormous influence in Cervantes studies, and her premature death from cancer deprived the profession of one of its brightest stars. Luis Andrés Murillo's *The Golden Dial* (1975) is a subtle, lyrical exploration of the function of time in the novel, the eternal 'summer of myth.'

Two other major Spanish Cervantes specialists emerged in the 1970s. The first was Francisco Márquez Villanueva, who has carved out a major name for himself in the field with the following books: *Fuentes literarias cervantinas* (1973); *Personajes y temas del "Quijote"* (1975); and *Trabajos y días cervantinos* (1995), a collection of some of the best independently-published shorter studies. No one surpasses Márquez Villanueva in painstakingly researched and argued interpretations of themes and characters in Cervantes' works.

The second was the elegant Helena Percas de Ponseti, whose huge *Cervantes y su concepto del arte* (2 vols., 1975) is a painstaking and sensitive examination of several aspects of the novel, notably including a seminal study of the Cave of Montesinos episode. Percas' subsequent *Cervantes the Writer and Painter of "Don Quijote"* (1988) is a very thorough examination of Cervantes' ability to evoke images by means of narrative art. These two books are essential works for any student of Cervantes' novel.

Two other writers deserve mention from this period. The first is novelist Gonzalo Torrente Ballester, whose *El "Quijote" como juego* (1975) reads the novel not as the story of a madman, but as a tale about someone who treats the world as if it were a child's game, falling into and out of roles as context permits. With the mention of Torrente's book, it is necessary to make a brief digression in order to acknowledge that there is a minor but fascinating critical camp that insists that Don Quixote is not mad, but acting or playing at being a knight-errant. The first work in this tradition was Mark Van Doren's short book *Don Quixote's Profession* (1958), in which the author maintains that Don Quixote is at heart an actor who literally takes the world as his stage for a play about chivalry. Along with Torrente, Arturo Serrano Plaja, in *"Magic" Realism in Cervantes* (1970; Spanish original, 1967), understands Don Quixote in terms of play. More recently, prolific playwright Dale Wasserman, author of *Man of La Mancha,* has described both Cervantes and his novel in terms of theatricality in *The Impossible Musical* (2003).

Also of interest is the work of José Antonio Maravall, whose series of books on Spanish society and culture have profoundly influenced a generation of scholars interested in materialist approaches to history. His *Utopia and Counterutopia in the "Quixote"* (1991; original Spanish in 1976) is a fundamental work for many scholars, while others tend to relegate it to the sociological margins of literary study.

The 1980s

The 1980s saw an explosion of first-rate criticism on *Don Quixote.* Alexander Welsh's *Reflections on the Hero as Quixote* (1981) is an attempt to clarify what a quixotic novel consists of and provides a series of exemplary comparative readings. Maureen Ihrie's *Skepticism in Cervantes* (1982) is a penetrating inquiry into Cervantes' religious and moral skepticism. *The Chivalric World of "Don Quijote"* (Mancing, 1982) focuses on Don Quixote's image of himself as a knight-errant and the implications of this concept for the style and narration of the novel. Carroll B. Johnson's *Madness and Lust* (1983) takes a Freudian approach and considers Alonso Quijano as a man experiencing a mid-life crisis and dealing with his deep feelings toward the women in his life. Johnson's more recent *Cervantes and the Material World* (2000) is a brilliant series of materialist- (Marxist) oriented studies of *Don Quixote* and other works of Cervantes.

Edwin Williamson's *The Half-way House of Fiction* (1984) is a significant inquiry into the relationship between *Don Quixote* and medieval chivalric romance. John G. Weiger is the author of two major books of Cervantes criticism: *The Substance of Cervantes* (1985), and *In the Margins of Cervantes* (1988); his intelligent presentation of a Cervantes more aware of his accomplishments than most of his contemporaries, and his subtle arguments concerning aspects of narration in the novel, are exemplary work. Daniel Eisenberg made major contributions with a masterful edition of Diego Ortúñez de Calahorra's romance of chivalry titled *Espejo de príncipes y caballeros,* 6 vols. (1975), a fundamental bibliography of the romances of chivalry titled *Castilian Romances of Chivalry in the Sixteenth Century*

(1979)—now superceded by his collaboration with Mari Carmen Marín Pina on *Bibliografía de los libros de caballerías castellanos* (2000)—and a major study of the same romances, *Romances of Chivalry in the Spanish Golden Age* (1982), He also published a collection of essays titled *A Study of "Don Quixote"* (1987), and, more recently, *Estudios Cervantinos* (1991), a collection of some previously published essays. As of this writing, Eisenberg is editor of *Cervantes: Bulletin of the Cervantes Society of America* and, as such, one of the most influential figures in Cervantes scholarship at the beginning of the twenty-first century.

James A. Parr's *"Don Quixote": An Anatomy of Subversive Discourse* (1988) is the major narratological study of the novel. This book, plus Parr's large number of shorter pieces on aspects of narration, together with his new book titled *Don Quixote, Don Juan, and Related Subjects* (2004), have established him as the premier structuralist student of the novel. Two more recent books in the same semiotic-structuralist-narratological tradition are José María Paz Gago's *Semiótica del "Quijote"* (1995) and María Stoopen's *Los autores, el texto, los lectores en el "Quijote" de 1605* (2002). While both books extend Parr's work, neither surpasses his book. Finally, Stephen Gilman, disciple of Américo Castro and long-time scholar of Spanish Golden Age literature, especially Fernando de Rojas' *La Celestina,* wrote a general overview of Cervantes' work shortly before his death: *The Novel According to Cervantes* (1989).

The 1990s

There was no diminution of important criticism on *Don Quixote* in the 1990s. Eric J. Ziolkowski's *The Sanctification of Don Quixote* (1991) traces the tradition of romantic readings of Don Quixote as a Christ figure. Steven Hutchinson's *Cervantine Journeys* (1992), as its point of departure, takes the fact that throughout Cervantes' works characters travel constantly from one place to another and contemplates the implications of such frequent journeying. Hutchenson's more recent book *Economía ética en Cervantes* (2001) is an important contribution to materialist studies of the works of Cervantes. Félix Martínez-Bonati's *"Don Quixote" and the Poetics of the Novel* (1992) argues that *Don Quixote* is not, as has often been claimed, a prototype of the realist novel. Dominick Finello's *Pastoral Themes and Forms in Cervantes's Fiction* (1994) is the most comprehensive study of various manifestations of the pastoral in Cervantes' works, specifically including *Don Quixote,* where the pastoral is almost as omnipresent as the chivalric. Finello's more recent *Cervantes: Essays on Social and Literary Polemics* (1998) is a collection of essays on social and literary themes. Santiago Alfonso López Navia's *La ficción autorial en el "Quijote"* (1996) is a valuable and wide ranging study of metafictional narration, literary history, and sequels and imitations of Cervantes' novel; his very recent *Inspiración y pretexto* (2005) continues his work in the same area. E. Michael Gerli's *Refiguring Authority* (1995) consists of a nuanced series of essays on themes that include Cervantes' art of literary creation.

Henry Sullivan established his reputation as a major scholar in the field of Golden Age theater in the 1970s and only turned his attention to Cervantes in the final decade of the century. In his controversial *Grotesque Purgatory* (1996) Sullivan meticulously and forcefully argues for a Lacanian reading of the novel. Edward Dudley's *The Endless Text* (1997) again reconsiders the links between *Don Quixote* and medieval chivalric romance. Augustin Redondo is a prolific scholar whose careful and precise essays on Cervantes, particularly on the comic and carnivalesque aspects of his work, first appeared in the late 1970s. Many of them were collected in the important *Otra manera de leer el "Quijote": historia, tradiciones culturales y literatura* (1997) in which he consistently argues for a comic, carnivalesque, reading of Cervantes' novel. Frederick A. de Armas, who has long been the premier student of the relationships between Italian culture, especially painting, and Spanish literature, published a book specifically relating these themes to Cervantes in *Cervantes, Raphael and the Classics* (1998). James Iffland's *De fiestas y aguafiestas* (1999) is a controversial reading of *Don Quixote* in light of the apocryphal continuation. Hans-Görg Neuschäfer's short book *La ética del "Quijote": Función de las novelas intercaladas* (1999) presents a provocative thesis about the relationship between the primary text of *Don Quixote* and the several embedded narratives, particularly those of part 1.

CERVANTES SCHOLARSHIP AT THE BEGINNING OF THE TWENTY-FIRST CENTURY

Diana de Armas Wilson, who earlier established her credentials as a major *Persiles* scholar, might claim the honor of writing the first major book on Cervantes in the new century. Her stunningly original *Cervantes, the Novel, and the New World* (2000) examines Cervantes' novel in light of his undoubted (if not previously recognized in any substantial way) interest in the New World.

Jean Canavaggio, longtime Cervantes scholar whose major contributions have been in the areas of Cervantes' theater and who is the author of the most highly esteemed contemporary biography of Cervantes (see chapter 1), published a collection of his essays under the title of *Cervantes, entre vida y creación* (2000). Charles D. Presberg's *Adventures in Paradox* (2001) examines paradox and narrative technique in *Don Quixote*. Carolyn A. Nadeau's *Women of the Prologue* (2002) features a surprisingly revealing examination of a brief mention of the names of three women in the prologue to part 1 of *Don Quixote* and expands this close reading into an important feminist study of the novel. Barbara Fuchs' *Passing for Spain* (2003) is an innovative study of aspects of gender and sexuality in Cervantes' work. Robert ter Horst's *The Fortunes of the Novel* (2003) is a reassessment of the role of Cervantes and *Don Quixote* in the history of the novel. Juan Carlos Rodríguez, one of the major Marxist scholars of his generation, is the author of the prize-winning *El escritor que compró su propio libro* (2003), a long and detailed study of the novel with emphasis on Cervantes' originality, the metafiction of *Don Quixote,* and the reality of book publication in the Spanish Golden Age.

Martín de Riquer, whose editions of *Don Quixote* are among the most read of all time and who is a distinguished authority on matters of chivalry, published a large collection of his work on Cervantes, including his previously-mentioned introduction to Cervantes' novel and his theory about the identity of Avellaneda, in *Para leer a Cervantes* (2003). David Quint, best known as an authority on Renaissance epic poetry, has examined structural and thematic threads in *Don Quixote* in his recent book *Cervantes's Novel of Modern Times* (2003), a thorough and subtle examination of certain episodes and themes in the novel, but a book that is far less radically original than the promotional material surrounding it claims. José Manuel Lucía Megías has exhaustively studied the Spanish romances of chivalry, and especially the surprisingly large number of such books that were written but never published in the Renaissance, and has related this work to Cervantes in *De los libros de caballerías manuscritos al "Quijote"* (2004).

Undoubtedly, the 2005 celebration of the 400th anniversary of the publication of part 1 of *Don Quixote* will produce an explosion of scholarly and popular publications on Cervantes' novel. Interested readers are advised to check for the most recent and most promising of these publications—and also be warned that much of what sees print will not be of the highest quality or of greatest originality. But the opportunity to approach, perhaps for the first time, the greatest of all novels at a time of celebration and recognition is to be celebrated and enjoyed.

WORKS CITED

Allen, John J. *Cervantes' "Don Quixote."* New York: Monarch, 1975.

———. *Don Quixote, Hero or Fool? A Study in Narrative Technique.* Gainesville: U of Florida P, 1969.

———. *Don Quixote, Hero or Fool? A Study in Narrative Technique. (Part II).* Gainesville: U of Florida P, 1979.

Alvar, Carlos, ed. *Gran Enciclopedia Cervantina.* Vol. I: A. Madrid: Castalia, 2005.

Anales Cervantinos, 1–9 (1951–59), 10–35 (1971–2000), 36– (2004).

Auerbach, Erich. "The Enchanted Dulcinea." In *Mimesis: The Representation of Reality in Western Literature.* Trans. Willard Trask. Princeton: Princeton UP, 1953. 334–58.

Avalle-Arce, Juan Bautista. *Deslindes cervantinos.* Madrid: Edhigar, 1961.

———. *Don Quijote como forma de vida.* Madrid: Fundación Juan March/Castalia, 1976.

———. *Enciclopedia cervantina.* Alcalá de Henares: Centro de Estudios Cervantinos, 1997.

———. *Nuevos deslindes cervantinos.* Barcelona: Ariel, 1975.

Avalle-Arce, Juan Bautista, and Edward C. Riley, eds. *Suma Cervantina.* London: Tamesis, 1973.

Bjornson, Richard, ed. *Approaches to Teaching Cervantes's "Don Quixote."* New York: MLA, 1984.

Bloom, Harold, ed. *Cervantes.* New York: Chelsea House, 1987.

———, ed. *Miguel de Cervantes.* New York: Chelsea House, 2004.

Brenan, Gerald. *The Literature of the Spanish People: From Roman Times to the Present Day.* Cambridge: Cambridge UP, 1953.

Canavaggio, Jean. *Cervantes, entre vida y creación.* Alcalá de Henares: Centro de Estudios Cervantinos, 2000.

Cascardi, Anthony J., ed. *The Cambridge Companion to Cervantes.* Cambridge: Cambridge UP, 2002.

Castro, Américo. *Cervantes y los casticismos españoles.* Madrid: Alfaguara, 1966.

———. *Hacia Cervantes.* Madrid: Taurus, 1957.

———. *El pensamiento de Cervantes.* Madrid: Revista de Filología Española, 1925.

———. *El pensamiento de Cervantes.* Ed. Julio Rodríguez Puértolas. Barcelona: Noguer, 1972.

Cervantes: Bulletin of the Cervantes Society of America, 1– (1981–).

Close, Anthony J., ed. *Cervantes.* Alcalá de Henares: Centro de Estudios Cervantinos, 1995.

———. *Cervantes and the Comic Mind of his Age.* Oxford: Oxford UP, 2000.

———. *Miguel de Cervantes: "Don Quixote."* Cambridge: Cambridge UP, 1990.

———. *The Romantic Approach to "Don Quixote." A Critical History of the Romantic Tradition in "Quixote" Criticism.* Cambridge: Cambridge UP, 1978.

Cruz, Anne J., and Carroll B. Johnson, eds. *Cervantes and His Postmodern Constituencies.* New York: Garland, 1999.

de Armas, Frederick A. *Cervantes, Raphael and the Classics.* Cambridge: Cambridge UP, 1998.

Dudley, Edward. *The Endless Text: "Don Quixote" and the Hermeneutics of Romance.* Albany: State U of New York P, 1997.

Durán, Manuel. *La ambigüedad en el "Quixote."* Xalapa: Universidad Veracruzana, 1960.

———. *Cervantes.* New York: Twayne, 1974.

Efron, Arthur. *Don Quixote and the Dulcineated World.* Austin: U of Texas P, 1971.

Eisenberg, Daniel. *Castilian Romances of Chivalry in the Sixteenth Century: A Bibliography.* London: Grant & Cutler, 1979.

———. *Estudios Cervantinos.* Barcelona: Sirmio, 1991.

———. *Romances of Chivalry in the Spanish Golden Age.* Newark, DE: Juan de la Cuesta, 1982.

———. *A Study of "Don Quixote."* Newark, DE: Juan de la Cuesta, 1987.

Eisenberg, Daniel, and Mari Carmen Marín Pina. *Bibliografía de los libros de caballerías castellanos.* Zaragoza: Prensas Universitarias de Zaragoza, 2000.

El Saffar, Ruth. *Beyond Fiction: The Recovery of the Feminine in the Novels of Cervantes.* Berkeley: U of California P, 1984.

———, ed. *Critical Essays on Cervantes.* Boston: G.K. Hall, 1986.

———. *Distance and Control in "Don Quixote": A Study in Narrative Technique.* Chapel Hill: U of North Carolina P, 1975.

El Saffar, Ruth, and Diana de Armas Wilson, *Quixotic Desire: Psychoanalytic Perspectives in Cervantes.* Ithaca: Cornell UP, 1993.

Fernández, Jaime. *Bibliografía del "Quijote," por unidades narrativas y materiales de la novela.* Alcalá de Henares: Centro de Estudios Cervantinos, 1995.

———. *Invitación al Qvijote.* Barcelona: Lunwerg, 2004.

Finello, Dominick. *Cervantes: Essays on Social and Literary Polemics.* Rochester, NY: Tamesis, 1998.

———. *Pastoral Themes and Forms in Cervantes's Fiction.* Lewisburg: Bucknell UP, 1994.

Flores, Angel, and M. J. Benardete, eds. *Cervantes Across the Centuries: A Quadricentennial Volume.* New York: Dryden P, 1947.

Forcione, Alban K. *Cervantes, Aristotle, and the Persiles.* Princeton: Princeton UP, 1970.

Fuchs, Barbara. *Passing for Spain: Cervantes and the Fictions of Identity.* Urbana: U of Illinois P, 2003.

Gerli, E. Michael. *Refiguring Authority: Reading, Writing, and Rewriting in Cervantes.* Lexington: UP of Kentucky, 1995.

Gilman, Stephen. *The Novel According to Cervantes.* Berkeley: U of California P, 1989.

González Echevarría, Roberto, ed. *Cervantes' "Don Quixote": A Casebook.* New York: Oxford UP, 2005.

Haley, George. "The Narrator in Don Quixote: A Discarded Voice." In *Estudios en Honor a Ricardo Guillón.* Ed. Luis T. González-del-Valle and Darío Villanueva. Lincoln, NE: Society of Spanish and Spanish-American Studies, 1984. 173–83.

———. "The Narrator in *Don Quijote:* Maese Pedro's Puppet Show." *MLN* 80 (1965): 146–65.

———, ed. *El "Quijote" de Cervantes.* Madrid: Taurus, 1980.

Hatzfeld, Helmut. *El "Quijote" como obra de arte del lenguaje.* 2nd ed., revised and expanded. Madrid: C.S.I.C., 1966 (first Spanish ed. 1949; original German ed. 1927).

Hutchinson, Steven. *Cervantine Journeys.* Madison: U of Wisconsin P, 1992.

———. *Economía ética en Cervantes.* Alcalá de Henares: Centro de Estudios Cervantinos, 2001.

Iffland, James. *De fiestas y aguafiestas: risa, locura e ideología en Cervantes y Avellaneda.* Madrid: Iberoamericana, 1999.

Ihrie, Maureen. *Skepticism in Cervantes.* London: Tamesis Books, 1982.

Johnson, Carroll B. *Cervantes and the Material World.* Urbana: U of Illinois P, 2000.

———. *Don Quixote: The Quest for Modern Fiction.* Boston: Twayne, 1990.

———. *Madness and Lust: A Psychoanalytical Approach to "Don Quixote."* Berkeley: U of California P, 1983.

La Rubia Prado, Francisco, ed. *Cervantes For the 21st Century/Cervantes para el siglo XXI: Studies in Honor of Edward Dudley.* Newark, DE: Juan de la Cuesta, 2000.

López Navia, Santiago Alfonso. *La ficción autorial en el "Quijote" y en sus continuaciones e imitaciones.* Madrid: U Europea de Madrid-CEES, 1996.

———. *Inspiración y pretexto: Estudios sobre las recreaciones del "Quijote."* Madrid: Iberoamericana, 2005.

Lucía Megías, José Manuel. *De los libros de caballerías manuscritos al "Quijote."* Madrid: Ensayo, 2004.

Madariaga, Salvador de. *"Don Quixote": An Introductory Essay in Psychology.* Oxford: Clarendon P, 1935.

———. *Guía del lector del "Quijote."* Madrid: Espasa-Calpe, 1926.

Mancing, Howard. *The Cervantes Encyclopedia,* 2 vols. Westport, CT: Greenwood P, 2004.

———. *The Chivalric World of "Don Quijote": Style, Structure and Narrative Technique.* Columbia: U of Missouri P, 1982.

Mandel, Oscar. "The Function of the Norm in *Don Quixote." Modern Philology* 55 (1958): 154–63.

Maravall, José Antonio. *Utopia and Counterutopia in the "Quixote."* Trans. Robert W. Felkel. Detroit: Wayne State UP, 1991.

Márquez Villanueva, Francisco. *Fuentes literarias cervantinas.* Madrid: Gredos, 1973).

———. *Personajes y temas del "Quijote."* Madrid: Taurus, 1975.

———. *Trabajos y días cervantinos.* Alcalá de Henares: Centro de Estudios Cervantinos, 1995.

Martínez-Bonati, Félix. *"Don Quixote" and the Poetics of the Novel.* Trans. by Dian Fox in collaboration with the author. Ithaca: Cornell UP, 1992.

McGaha, Michael D., ed. *Cervantes and the Renaissance.* Newark, DE: Juan de la Cuesta, 1980.

Montero Reguera, José. *El "Quijote" y la crítica contemporánea.* Alcalá de Henares: Centro de Estudios Cervantinos, 1997.

Murillo, Luis A. *Critical Introduction to "Don Quixote."* New York: Peter Lang, 1988.

———. *The Golden Dial. Temporal Configurations in "Don Quixote."* Oxford: Dolphin, 1975.

Nadeau, Carolyn A. *Women of the Prologue: Imitation , Myth, and Magic in "Don Quixote I."* Lewiston, PA: Bucknell UP, 2002.

Navarro, Alberto. *El Quijote español del siglo XVII.* Madrid: Ediciones Rialp, 1964.

Nelson, Lowry, Jr. ed. *Cervantes, a Collection of Critical Essays.* Englewood Cliffs, NJ: Prentice-Hall, 1969.

Neuschäfer, Hans-Görg. *La ética del "Quijote": Función de las novelas intercaladas.* Madrid: Gredos, 1999.

Oliver Asín, Jaime. "La hija de Agí Morato en la obra de Cervantes." *Boletín de la Real Academia Española* 27 (1947): 245–339.

Ortega y Gasset, José. *Meditaciones del "Quijote."* Madrid: Imprenta Clásica Española, 1914.

———. *Meditations on "Quixote."* Ed. Evelyn Rugg and Diego Marín. Intro. Julián Marías. New York: W. W. Norton, 1961.

Ortúñez de Calahorra, Diego. *Espejo de príncipes y caballeros,* 6 vols. Ed. Daniel Eisenberg. Madrid: Espasa-Calpe, 1975.

Parr, James A. *"Don Quixote": An Anatomy of Subversive Discourse.* Newark, DE: Juan de la Cuesta, 1988.

———. *Don Quixote, Don Juan, and Related Subjects.* Cranbury, NJ: Susquehana UP, 2004.

Paz Gago, JoSc María. *Semiótica del "Quijote": Teoría y práctica de la ficción narrativa.* Amsterdam: Rodopi, 1995.

Percas de Ponseti, Helena. *Cervantes the Writer and Painter of "Don Quijote."* Columbia: U of Missouri P, 1988.

———. *Cervantes y su concepto del arte: Estudio crítico de algunos aspectos del "Quijote,"* 2 vols. Madrid: Gredos, 1975.

Predmore, Richard. *Cervantes.* New York: Dodd, 1973.

———. *The World of "Don Quixote."* Cambridge: Harvard UP, 1967.

Presberg, Charles D. *Adventures in Paradox: "Don Quijote" and the Western Tradition.* University Park: Pennsylvania State UP, 2001.

Quint, David. *Cervantes's Novel of Modern Times: A New Reading of "Don Quixote."* Princeton: Princeton UP, 2003.

Redondo, Augustin. *Otra manera de leer el "Quijote": historia, tradiciones culturales y literatura.* Madrid: Castalia, 1997.

Rico, Francisco et al. "Bibliografía y abreviaturas." In *Don Quijote. Vol. II: Volumen complementario.* Ed. Francisco Rico *et al.* Barcelona: Galaxia Gutenberg/Círculo de Lectores/Centro para la Edición de los Clásicos Españoles, 2004. 1121–1367.

Riley, Edward C. *Cervantes's Theory of the Novel.* Oxford: Clarendon P, 1962.

———. *Don Quixote.* London: Allen and Unwin, 1986.

———. "Don Quixote and the Imitation of Models." *Bulletin of Hispanic Studies* 31 (1954): 3–16.

———. *La rara invención: estudios sobre Cervantes y su posteridad literaria.* Barcelona: Crítica, 2001.

Riquer, Martín de. *Aproximación al "Quijote."* Barcelona: Teide, 1967.

———. *Cervantes y el "Quijote."* Barcelona: Teide, 1960.

———. *Nueva aproximación al "Quijote."* Barcelona: Teide, 1989.

———. *Para leer a Cervantes.* Barcelona: El Acantilado, 2003.

Rodríguez Vicéns, Antonio. *Diccionario de "El Quijote."* Ecuador: np, 2003.

Rodríguez, Juan Carlos. *El escritor que compró su propio libro: Para leer el "Quijote."* Barcelona: Debate, 2003.

Rosenblat, Angel. *La lengua del "Quijote."* Madrid: Gredos, 1971.

Russell, P. E. *Cervantes.* New York: Oxford UP, 1985.

———. "Don Quixote as a Funny Book." *Modern Language Review* 64 (1969): 312–26.

Serrano Plaja, Arturo. *"Magic" Realism in Cervantes: Don Quixote as Seen Through "Tom Sawyer" and "The Idiot."* Trans. Robert S. Rudder. Berkeley, U of California P, 1970 (Spanish original, 1967).

Spitzer, Leo. "Linguistic Perspectivism in the *Don Quijote.*" In *Linguistics and Literary History: Essays in Stylistics.* Princeton: Princeton UP, 1948. 41–85.

Stoopen, María. *Los autores, el texto, los lectores en el "Quijote" de 1605.* Mexico City: Facultad de Filosofía y Letras, UNAM, 2002.

Sullivan, Henry. *Grotesque Purgatory: A Study of Cervantes's "Don Quixote," Part II.* University Park: Pennsylvania State UP, 1996.

ter Horst, Robert. *The Fortunes of the Novel: A Study in the Transposition of a Genre.* New York: Peter Lang, 2003.

Torrente Ballester, Gonzalo. *El "Quijote" como juego.* Madrid: Guadarrama, 1975.

Unamuno, Miguel de. *Our Lord Don Quixote: The Life of Don Quixote and Sancho, with Related Essays.* Ed. Anthony Kerrigan. Princeton: Princeton UP, 1976.

————. *Vida de Don Quijote and Sancho.* Madrid: Fernando Fe, 1905.

Urbina, Eduardo. *Anuario Bibliográfico Cervantino.* Multiple vols. Vol. I: *Cervantes,* special issue (1996). Subsequent vols.: Alcalá de Henares: Centro de Estudios Cervantinos, 1997–.

Van Doren, Mark. *Don Quixote's Profession.* New York: Columbia UP, 1958.

Vidal, César. *Enciclopedia del "Quijote".* Barcelona: Planeta, 1999.

Wardropper, Bruce W. *"Don Quixote:* Story or History?" *Modern Philology* 63 (1965): 1–11.

————. "The Pertinence of 'El curioso impertinente.' " *PMLA* 72 (1957): 587–600.

Wasserman, Dale. *The Impossible Musical.* New York: Applause, 2003.

Weiger, John G. *In the Margins of Cervantes.* Hanover, NH: UP of New England, 1988.

————. *The Substance of Cervantes.* New York: Cambridge UP, 1985.

Welsh, Alexander. *Reflections on the Hero as Quixote.* Princeton: Princeton UP, 1981.

Williamson, Edwin. *The Half-way House of Fiction; "Don Quixote" and Arthurian Romance.* Oxford: Clarendon P, 1984.

Wilson, Diana de Armas. *Cervantes, the Novel, and the New World.* Oxford: Oxford UP, 2000.

Ziolkowski, Eric J. *The Sanctification of Don Quixote: From Hidalgo to Priest.* University Park: Pennsylvania State UP, 1991.

BIBLIOGRAPHY

Note: There is extensive documentation throughout the previous chapters, so this final bibliography need not be very extensive. It consists of exactly 25 books published (with two exceptions) within the last quarter of a century, in English, which are relatively accessible to a student or general reader.

Allen, John J. *Don Quixote, Hero or Fool? A Study in Narrative Technique.* Gainesville: U of Florida P, 1969.

Bloom, Harold, ed. *Miguel de Cervantes.* New York: Chelsea House, 2004.

Canavaggio, Jean. *Cervantes.* Trans. J. R. Jones. New York: W. W. Norton, 1990.

Cascardi, Anthony J., ed. *The Cambridge Companion to Cervantes.* Cambridge: Cambridge UP, 2002.

Close, Anthony J., ed. *Cervantes and the Comic Mind of his Age.* Oxford: Oxford UP, 2000.

Dudley, Edward. *The Endless Text: "Don Quixote" and the Hermeneutics of Romance.* Albany: State U of New York P, 1997.

El Saffar, Ruth. *Beyond Fiction: The Recovery of the Feminine in the Novels of Cervantes.* Berkeley: U of California P, 1984.

Finello, Dominick. *Pastoral Themes and Forms in Cervantes's Fiction.* Lewisburg: Bucknell UP, 1994.

Garcés, María Antonia. *Cervantes in Algiers: A Captive's Tale.* Nashville: Vanderbilt UP, 2002.

Gilman, Stephen. *The Novel According to Cervantes.* Berkeley: U of California P, 1989.

González Echevarría, Roberto, ed. *Cervantes' "Don Quixote": A Casebook.* New York: Oxford UP, 2005.

Johnson, Carroll B. *Don Quixote: The Quest for Modern Fiction.* Boston: Twayne, 1990.

Mancing, Howard. *The Cervantes Encyclopedia,* 2 vols. Westport, CT: Greenwood P, 2004.

Martínez-Bonati, Félix. *"Don Quixote" and the Poetics of the Novel.* Trans. by Dian Fox in collaboration with the author. Ithaca: Cornell UP, 1992.

Parr, James A. *"Don Quixote": An Anatomy of Subversive Discourse.* Newark, DE: Juan de la Cuesta, 1988.

Paulson, Ronald. *Don Quixote in England: The Aesthetics of Laughter.* Baltimore: Johns Hopkins UP, 1998.

Percas de Ponseti, Helena. *Cervantes the Writer and Painter of "Don Quijote."* Columbia: U of Missouri P, 1988.

Quint, David. *Cervantes's Novel of Modern Times: A New Reading of "Don Quixote."* Princeton: Princeton UP, 2003.

Riley, Edward C. *Cervantes's Theory of the Novel.* Oxford: Clarendon P, 1962.

Russell, P. E. *Cervantes.* New York: Oxford UP, 1985.

Weiger, John G. *The Substance of Cervantes.* New York: Cambridge UP, 1985.

Welsh, Alexander. *Reflections on the Hero as Quixote.* Princeton: Princeton UP, 1981.

Williamson, Edwin. *The Half-way House of Fiction; "Don Quixote" and Arthurian Romance.* Oxford: Clarendon P, 1984.

Wilson, Diana de Armas. *Cervantes, the Novel, and the New World.* Oxford: Oxford UP, 2000.

Ziolkowski, Eric J. *The Sanctification of Don Quixote: From Hidalgo to Priest.* University Park: Pennsylvania State UP, 1991.

INDEX

Abencerraje y la hermosa Jarifa, El
(Anonymous), 89
Abindarráez, 89
Abraham, 58
Academy of Argamasilla del Alba, 111
Achilles, 99
Acker, Kathy, 165, 167
Acquaviva, Giulio (cardinal), 3
acting troupe, 31, 89
actor theory, 200–201
Adjunta del Parnaso (*Appendix to Parnassus*), 14
adventure romance, 80
Adventures of Augie March, The (S. Bellow), 84
Adventures of Don Quixote, The (A. Rakoff), 176
Adventures of Don Sylvio of Rosalva, The (C. M. Wieland), 160, 168
Adventures of Felix Krull, Confidence Man, The (T. Mann), 84
Adventures of Huckleberry Finn, The (M. Twain), 84, 162, 168
Adventures of Sir Launcelot Greaves, The (T. Smollett), 156
Adventures of Tom Sawyer, The (M. Twain), 162
Aeneas, 107
affectation, 106
Africa, 54, 56
Aire nuestro (J. Guillén), 171
Alas, Leopoldo (Clarín), 163
Alcalá de Henares, 1–2, 182

Alcalá de Henares, University of, 73, 191
Alcalde de Zalamea, El (P. Calderón de la Barca), 66
Alcazarquivir, battle of, 56
Alemán, Mateo, 45, 83, 85, 106, 112, 114–15
Alenza, Leonardo, 180
Alexander VI (pope), 52
Alfonso X, 67
Algiers, 4–6, 28, 37–38, 41–42, 55, 116, 127, 197
Ali Pasha, 55
Allen, John J., 6, 46, 146, 180, 186, 191, 195
Almar, George, 172
Almqvist, Carl Jonas Love, 171
Alonso, Pedro, 22, 101, 138
Altisidora, 35–39, 114, 122, 132
Alvar, Carlos, 190
Amadís de Gaula (G. R. de Montalvo), 79, 82, 85, 88, 90, 98, 109, 119, 127
Amadís de Gaula, 26, 93, 107, 110
Amadís series, 79
Amante liberal, El (*The Generous Lover*), 12
American Quixote, An (R. Carr), 175
Amicable Quixote (Anonymous), 156
Amorous Desperation (Anonymous), 159
Anales Cervantinos, 190
Andalusia, 8, 52, 92
Angelica, 26, 90

Anselmo (*El curioso impertinente*), 27, 67–70, 95, 132, 144
Ansó, Carlos, 173
anthologies of Cervantes criticism, 188–89
Antonio, Don (*La señora Cornelia*), 13
Antonio, Marco (*Las dos doncellas*), 13
Apollo, 14, 88
Appendix to Parnassus. See *Adjunta del Parnaso*
Apuleius, 88, 169
Arabs as liars, 111–12
Aragon, 52
Arcadia, La (J. Sannazaro), 80
Arcadia, the feigned, 88
Archives of La Mancha, 110–11, 115–16
Arellano, Roberto, 165
Aretino, Pietro, 73
Argamasilla del Alba, 41, 93
Argensola, Bartolomé, 89
Argensola, Lupercio, 89
Arias Montano, Benito, 73
Ariosto, Ludovico, 73, 90, 108
Aristotelianism, 73
Aristotelian literary theory (poetics), 105
Aristotle, 105, 169, 199
Armada, the Invincible, 8, 10, 57
armies (flocks) of sheep, 24, 95, 122, 141
arms and letters, theme of, 28–29, 99–100.
    See also Don Quixote: arms and letters speech of
Arne, Thomas Augustine, 155
Arnedo, Luis, 175
Arrabal, Fernando, 3, 166
Arreola, Juan José, 166
Arthur, King, 91
Arthurian chivalric tradition, 91
Asensio, Eugenio, 15
ass, Sancho's, 30, 44, 113, 135, 147, 152
Asturias, 51
Atterbom, Per Daniel Amadeus, 171
Auerbach, Erich, 194, 196–97
Ausencias de Dulcinea (J. Rodrigo), 175
Austen, Jane, 161, 168
Auster, Paul, 165, 168–69
auto-da-fe (*auto de fe*), 61
autos sacramentales, 78
Avalle-Arce, Juan Bautista, 46, 188–90, 199
Avellaneda, Alonso Fernández de, 16, 30, 37, 43, 89, 114–15, 142, 158, 167, 204
Avila, Francisco de, 152
Ayala, Francisco, 166
Aylward, Edward T., 16

Ayres, James, 155
Azorín, 166, 172
Aztec empire, 54, 79

baciyelmo (basin-helmet), 28, 134, 195.
    See also Mambrino
bagnio (*baño*), 4
Bagnios of Algiers, The. See *Baños de Argel, Los*
Bakhtin, Mikhail M., 72, 81, 90, 109, 115, 129–30, 134, 139, 169, 181, 188
Balanchine, George, 175
ballad, 42, 75–76, 81, 89
Ballet de Don Quichot (Anonymous)
Balzac, Honoré de, 163
Bandello, Matteo, 73, 79, 91
Baños de Argel, Los (*Bagnios of Algiers, The*), 14
Barataria (island), 121, 141, 146
barber. *See* Nicolás, Maese
barber's basin. *See* Mambrino
barber with the basin, 25, 28
Barbie, 181
Barcelona, 37–38, 62, 114
Barrick, Mac E., 90
Barrios, Eduardo, 166
Barth, John, 165, 168
Basilio, 32, 101, 131–32, 147
basin-helmet (*baciyelmo*), 28, 134, 195.
    See also Mambrino
Basque squire (squire of lady in coach), 23, 110, 127
Bataillon, Marcel, 2
Baty, Gaston, 172, 177
Bazán, Alvaro de, Marqués of Santa Cruz, 57
Beaumont, Francis, 153
Bécquer, Gustavo Adolfo, 175
Beerbohm, Max, 164
Behn, Aphra, 155
Being There (J. Kozinski), 97
Béjar, Duke of, 22
Belerma, 32, 91
Belgium, 53
Belianís de Grecia (J. Fernández), 79, 88, 94
Belianís de Grecia, 93, 107
Bellow, Saul, 84, 97, 165, 168
Bembo, Pietro, 73
Benardete, M. J., 188
Benedictine friars, 23, 65, 144–45

Benengeli, Cide Hamete, 23, 40, 41, 90, 108, 110–14, 121–22, 139, 147, 154, 162

Bennett, Rodney, 176–77

Bentibolli, Cornelia (*La señora Cornelia*), 13

Berenjena, Cide Hamete, 112

Berganza (*Coloquio de los perros*), 13, 103

Bernardo del Carpio, 91

bestsellers, 85

Bible, 88, 103

bibliographies of Cervantes and *Don Quixote*, 185–86

Biblioteca Virtual Miguel de Cervantes, 191

Bjornson, Richard, 83, 188

Black Legend, 70–72

Bloom, Harold, 167, 170, 188

Boccaccio, Giovanni, 73, 79, 91, 117

bodily humors, theory of, 90

Bodleian Library, 11

Boiardo, Matteo Maria, 73, 90

Bonilla, Adolfo, 45, 192

book-burning scene. *See* library, Don Quixote's

Bordelon, Laurent, 158

Borges, Jorge Luis, 112, 125, 171

Boscán, Juan, 75

Bourbon royal family, 53

Bourgeant, Guillaume Hyacînthe, 158

Bourgeois Romance, The (A. Furetière), 154

Bowle, John, 45, 157–58

Brackenridge, Hugh Henry, 162

Branston, Julian, 164

braying aldermen, 33, 122

Brenan, Gerald, 194

bronze head (talking head), 38, 62

Brooke, Henry, 156

Brunelo, 90

Buero Vallejo, Antonio, 172

Buezo, Catalina, 11

Bulgakov, Mihail, 166, 169

bulls that trample Don Quixote, 37

Burgess, Anthony, 11

Burkhardt, Jakob, 70

Burlador de Sevilla, El (Tirso de Molina), 78

Burton, María Amparo Ruiz de, 172

Byron, Lord, 1, 93

Byron, William, 1

Byzantine romance, 80

caballero, 63

Caballero don Quijote, El (M. Gutiérrez Aragón), 177

Caballero puntual, El (A. J. de Salas Barbadillo), 152

Cádiz, 9–10, 12

Cain, Henri, 174

Calaínos, 91

Calderón de la Barca, Pedro, 66, 74, 78, 105, 152

Calle: de Cantarranas, 17; de Cervantes, 17; de la Cruz, 6; de los Francos, 17; de los Leones, 17; de Lope de Vega, 17; del Príncipe, 6; del Rastro, 10;

Camacho the Rich, 32, 66, 132. *See also* wedding of Camacho

Camila (*El curioso impertinente*), 27, 67–70, 89, 92, 132, 144

Camilote, 137–38

Campo de Criptana, 142

Canavaggio, Jean, 1, 10, 204

canon, literary, 157, 170, 185

canon of Toledo, 29, 65, 89, 92, 95, 101, 108, 127, 132, 144

Canterbury Tales (G. Chaucer), 117

Cantinflas, 176

Cantos de vida y esperanza (R. Darío), 171

captain, captive. *See* Pérez de Viedma, Ruy; captive's tale

captive's tale, 27–28, 91–92, 99, 116, 118

Caraculiambro, 137

Cárcel de amor (D. de San Pedro), 80, 85, 112

Cardenio, 25–27, 63, 119, 126, 131, 143–44, 193. *See also* Cardenio-Dorotea-Fernando-Luscinda story

Cardenio-Dorotea-Fernando-Luscinda story, 25–27, 65, 91, 118–19, 152–53

Carlos I. *See* Carlos V

Carlos II, 53

Carlos V (Carlos I), 52–55, 57, 62, 74, 80

Carlos the Jackal, 97

Carnicero, Antonio, 180

carnival, 24, 90, 139, 145, 203

Carolingian chivalric tradition, 91

Carpentier, Alejo, 166

Carr, Richard, 175

Carrasco, Sansón, 30, 40, 93, 112, 127, 131, 142, 144, 147. *See also* Knight of the Forest (Mirrors); Knight of the White Moon

Carrizales (*El celoso extremeño*), 12

Carroll, Lewis, 161

Carteret, Lord, 45, 157–58, 180

Casa de los celos y selva de Ardenia, La (*House of Jealousy and Forest of Ardennes, The*), 14

Casamiento engañoso, El (*Deceitful Marriage, The*), 13
Cascardi, Anthony J., 189
Casildea de Vandalia, 31, 122, 140
Castelo Branco, Camilo, 164
Castiglione, Baldassar, 73
Castile, 52
Castillo, Julia, 171
Castro, Américo, 44, 192–93, 198, 202
Castro, Guillén de, 152, 174
Castro del Río, 8, 41–42
Catholic Monarchs (*Reyes Católicos*), 2, 53–55, 60, 80
cats that scratch Don Quixote, 35, 135
Cave of Montesinos. *See* Montesinos, Cave of
Caxton, William, 84
Ceballos, María de, 10
Cecial, Tomé, 131–32
Cela, Camilo José, 177
Celaya, Gabriel, 171
Celestina, La (F. de Rojas), 82, 85, 95, 129
Celoso extremeño, El (*The Jealous Old Man from Extremadura*), 12
censorship, 73, 105, 151
Centro de Estudios Cervantinos, 190
Cervantas, Las, 10
Cervantes, Andrea (sister of Cervantes), 1, 10, 104
Cervantes, Juan de (brother of Cervantes), 2
Cervantes, Juan de (grandfather of Cervantes), 10
Cervantes, Luisa (sister of Cervantes), 2
Cervantes, Magdalena (sister of Cervantes), 2, 10, 104
Cervantes, Miguel de, 1–17, 102; as author, 108; biographies of, 1, 157, 199, 204; as a classical author, 152–53, 157–60; as dramatist, 5–7, 14–16; education of, 87; as a humanist, 74; literary influences on, 87–91; literary theory of, 105–9, 198–99; narrative theory of, 109–22; as narrator of *Don Quixote*, 110–11, 115–16; as novelist, 7, 11–14, 16–17, 41–43; as poet, 8–9, 14, 76; as screenwriter, 178; as soldier, 3–5, 55; and religion, 103–5
Cervantes, Rodrigo de (brother of Cervantes), 2–4
Cervantes, Rodrigo de (father of Cervantes), 1–2
Cervantes: Bulletin of the Cervantes Society of America, 191, 202
Cervantes encyclopedias, 189–90
Cervantes family, 1–2, 9–11

Cervantes journals, 190–91
Cervantes on the Internet, 191–92
Cervantes Project, 192
Cervantes Society of America, 190–91
Cézanne, Paul, 180
Chagal, Marc, 180
Chaliapin, Fyodor, Jr., 175–76
Challes, Robert, 158
Chapí, Ruperto, 175
Chaplin, Charlie, 181
Chapman, Mark David, 97
Chapman, Robin, 164
characters in *Don Quixote*, 142–48. *See also* women characters in *Don Quixote*
Charlemagne, 91
Chaucer, Geoffrey, 117
Chávez, President Hugo, 182
Chejne, Anwar G., 103
Chesterton, G. K., 164
chivalric romance. *See* romance of chivalry
chivalry, concept of, 88, 93–95
Chomsky, Noam, 168
Chopin, Kate, 162
Christianity, 56, 58, 61, 103–4
Christian saints, carved figures of, 37
Cipión (*Coloquio de los perros*), 13, 103
City of Glass (P. Auster), 165, 168
Clamurro, William H., 14
Clara, Doña, 1, 28, 132, 144
Clarisas (Poor Claires), 104
Clarissa (S. Richardson), 157
Clavileño the Swift, 35, 122
Cleese, John, 166
Clemencín, Diego, 45
Clemens, Samuel L. *See* Twain, Mark
clergy, 64–65
Close, Anthony J., 143, 147, 187–88, 194
Cobb, Lee J., 178
Cohen, J. M., 46, 47
Colman, George, 155
Coloquio de los perros, El (*The Dialogue of the Dogs*), 13, 82, 106
Columbus, Christopher, 53
Comedia (Tragicomedia) de Calisto y Melibea. *See Celestina, La*
Comforters, The (M. Spark), 164, 168
Comical History of Don Quixote, The (T. D'Urfey), 154
Comical Romance, The (P. Scarron), 154
Comic History of Francion, The (C. Sorel), 154
commercial study guides, 185

Comunidad Quijote, 192
Conde Lucanor, El (Juan Manuel), 117
Confederacy of Dunces, A (J. K. Toole), 165
Confidence Man, The (H. Melville), 162
Connecticut Yankee in King Arthur's Court, A (M. Twain), 162
Conrad, Joseph, 164, 168
Consejo Superior de Investigaciones Científicas, 190
Constantinople, 4, 12
Constitutions of the Great Governor Sancho Panza, The, 36
Consuegra, 142
Continuation of the History of the Admirable Don Quixote of La Mancha (R. Challes), 158
conversos. See New Christians
Coomonte, Pilar, 180
Córdoba, 2, 52, 58
Corneille, Pierre, 78
Corot, Jean-Baptiste Camille, 180
corral, 5–6, 77
Corral: de la Cruz, 6; del Príncipe, 6
Cortés, Hernán, 54
Cortinas, Leonor de (mother of Cervantes), 1, 6
Coruña, La, 57
Costa Fontes, Manuel da, 61
Costanza (*La ilustre fregona*), 13
Council of Trent, 72
Counter Reformation, 72, 103
cousin, humanist scholar, 74, 132
Cox, Ralph Merritt, 157
Coypel, Charles-Antoine, 158, 180
Crane, Stephen, 162
Crime and Punishment (F. Dostoevsky), 97, 163–64
cristianos nuevos. See New Christians
cristianos viejos. See Old Christians
Cristina (*La guarda cuidadosa*), 99
Crowne, John, 155
Cruz, Anne J., 188–89
Cruz Delgado, Palomo, 178
crypto-Jews, 59–60
Cuesta, Juan de la, 45, 151
Cueva de Salamanca, La (*Magic Cave of Salamanca, The*), 16
Cupid, 88, 181
Curioso impertinente, El, 27, 67–70, 91, 99, 117–18, 121–22, 126, 153, 156, 197
Cuvelier de Trye, Jean Guillaume Antoine, 158

Dalí, Salvador, 180
Dalin, Olof von, 171
Dancourt, Florent Carton, 158
Dante Alighieri, 72–73, 141, 185
Darío, Rubén, 171
Darion, Joe, 176
date of composition of *Don Quixote*: part 1, 42–43; part 2, 43
Daudet, Alphonse, 163
daughter of Doña Rodríguez, 36, 100
daughter of Juan Palomeque, 24, 28, 131, 134
Daumier, Honoré, 180
Davenant, William, 153
dead body, 25, 65
de Armas, Frederick A., 203
Dearmer, Mabel, 172
De Nero, Robert, 98
Deceitful Marriage, The. See Casamiento engañoso, El
Defoe, Daniel, 84, 156
Delacroix, Eugene, 180
Delgado, Jacinto María, 160
Delgado, Sinesio, 175
Delicado, Francisco, 61, 112
Della Casa, Giovanni, 73
Denevi, Mario, 166
Depp, Johnny, 178
descriptions in *Don Quixote*, 130–32
Desheredada, La (B. Pérez Galdós), 162–63, 168
Destouches, Philippe Néricault, 158
dialogism, 169
dialogued fictions, 82
dialogue in *Don Quixote*, 129–30
Dialogue of the Dogs, The. See Coloquio de los perros, El
Diana, La (J. de Montemayor), 7, 80, 85, 88, 98
Díaz del Castillo, Bernal, 79
Dickens, Charles, 133, 161, 168
Diderot, Denis, 72, 158, 168
Diego (*La ilustre fregona*), 13
Diego, Gerardo, 171
digressions, 106
Dillon, Edward, 176
Disputa de Elena y María (Anonymous), 99
Divorce Court Judge, The. See Juez de los divorcios, El
Don, honorific title of, 64
Don Dimaio of La Plata (R. Arrellano), 165
Donkey Xote (film), 177

Don Kikhot (G. Kozintsev), 176
Don Kikhot (M. Petipa and L. Minkus), 175
Don Quichotte à Dulcinée (M. Ravel), 175
Don Quichotte (G. W. Pabst), 175
Don Quichotte (H. Cain and J. Massenet), 174–75
Don Quichotte (J. Ibert), 175
Don Quichotte (N. Nabokov and G. Balanchine), 175
Don Quijote, o, el sueño de Cervantes (C. Ansó), 173
Don Quijote cabalga de nuevo (R. Gavaldón), 176
Don Quijote de la Mancha (G. de Castro), 152
Don Quijote de la Mancha (P. Calderón de la Barca), 78
Don Quijote de la Mancha (P. Cruz Delgado), 178
Don Quijote de la Mancha (R. Gil), 176
Don Quijote de Orson Welles (J. Franco), 178
Don Quijote murió del corazón (F. Schroeder Inclán), 173
Don Quijote velando las armas (O. Esplá), 175
Don Quijote y Dulcinea (E. Marchelie), 175
Don Quixote (M. Cervantes): as anthology of Renaissance literature, 87; in art, 179–80; in music, 154, 174–76; as novel, 81–82; as parody, 81; in poetry, 152, 170–72; in popular culture, 152, 181–83; as prototype of the novel, 95, 170; as realist novel, 202; on screen, 176–79; on stage, 152–55, 158, 172–74; in Brazil, 172; in England, 153–57, 161, 164, 176; in France, 154–55, 158–59, 163, 166, 172, 176; in Germany, 159–60, 166, 179; in Portugal, 172, 174; in Russia, 163–64, 166, 171, 176; in Spanish America, 165–66, 171–74, 176, 180; in Sweden, 171; in the United States, 161–62, 165, 173, 176–78; in the seventeenth century, 151–55, 179; in the eighteenth century, 155–60, 168–69, 174; in the nineteenth century, 160–64, 169; in the twentieth century, 164–66, 169, 171–78; in the twenty-first century, 165–66, 182–83; after 400 years, 182, 189, 204. *See also* characters in; date of composition of; descriptions in; dialogue in; folklore in; genesis of; hard vs. soft readings of; humorous names in; illustrations of; levels of style in; neologisms in; plot of; prologues to; reception history of; romantic

readings of; social criticism in; spelling of; textual problems in; theatrical episodes in; translations of; women characters in
Don Quixote, 21–40; arms and letters speech of, 28, 92, 99; as a Christ figure, 195, 202; description of, 130; as "the Don", 64; figure of, 152, 181–82; Golden Age speech of, 88, 99, 126; image of, 130, 142, 180–81; as Knight of the Lions, 32; as Knight of the Sad Face, 25; as myth, 181–82, 196; name of, 137
Don Quixote af Mancha (L. Lauritzen), 176
Don Quixote (A. Rubenstein), 175
Don Quixote de La Jolla (E. Overmyer), 173
Don Quixote (E. Dillon), 176
Don Quixote (K. Acker), 165
Don Quixote (M. Elvey), 176
Don Quixote (O. Welles), 177–78
Don Quixote (P. Yates), 177
Don Quixote (R. Strauss), 175
Don Quixote (S. Lumet), 178
Doré, Gustave, 130, 180, 192
Dorotea (Princess Micomicona), 26–27, 65, 92, 119, 122, 126, 130–32, 137, 140, 143–44, 147, 193
Dos doncellas, Las (*The Two Damsels*), 13
Dostoevsky, Fyodor, 97, 133, 163–64, 168
double-voiced discourse, 134, 169
Douglas, Kenneth, 47
DQ Rum, 181
Drake, Sir Francis, 9, 57
Dreamer who Unlocked the Secrets of the Universe, The (M. Martinez), 165
Duardos, Don (G. Vicente), 138
duchess, 34–37, 100, 105, 132, 145
Duchess' Diary (R. Chapman), 164
Dudley, Edward, 203
dueñas, bearded, 34
Dufresny, Charles, Sieur de la Rivière, 154
duke, 34–37, 39, 66, 100–1, 132, 146
duke and duchess, 34–37, 63, 100–101, 122, 142, 147
Dulcinea (films), 177
Dulcinea, or Don Quixote's Last Adventure (C. Selvagem), 172
Dulcinea del Toboso, 22, 25, 27, 39, 105, 122, 128, 140, 146–47, 151–52; description of, 132; in Avellaneda's *Quixote*, 16; name of, 139. *See also* Lorenzo, Aldonza; enchantment of Dulcinea; Maritornes-Aldonza-Dulcinea fusion
Dulcinea nail polish, 181
Dulcinée (G. Baty), 172

Dulcineo, 139
Dunn, Peter N., 82, 84
Durán, Manuel, 187, 198
Durandarte, 32, 91
D'Urfey, Thomas, 154
Dutch colonies, 54, 71
Ebro River, 33
Eccles, John, 154
Ecija, 8
Efron, Arthur, 199
Eight Plays and Eight Interludes, Never Performed. See *Ocho comedias y ocho entremeses, nunca representados*
Eisenberg, Daniel, 46, 79, 89, 201–2
ekphrasis, 106
Elección de los alcaldes de Daganzo, La (The Election of Magistrates of Daganzo), 15
Election of Magistrates of Daganzo, The. See *Elección de los alcaldes de Daganzo, La*
Eliot, George, 95, 126, 161, 168–69
Elizabeth, Queen of England, 10
El Saffar, Ruth, 140, 188, 200
Elvey, Maurice, 176
embedded narrative, 83, 117–22, 203. *See also* captive's tale; Cardenio-Dorotea-Fernando-Luscinda story; *Curioso impertinente, El*; Eugenio's tale; Sancho's story
emergence of the novel, 157
Eminescu, Mihai, 172
enchanted boat, 33, 144–45
enchanters, enchantment, 22–23, 32–34, 89, 110, 126, 141. *See also* enchantment of Dulcinea; enchantment of Don Quixote; Frestón
enchantment of Don Quixote, 29, 89, 122, 143
enchantment of Dulcinea, 31, 34, 37, 39, 122, 141, 147, 197
Enciclopédie, 72, 159
Enciso Zárate, Francisco, 79
Engaños deste siglo (F. Loubayssin de Lamarca), 152
England, 8, 54, 59, 70
English colonies, 54, 71
English Spanish Girl, The. See *Española inglesa, La*
Entertaining Story, The. See *Entretenida, La*
entremés (interlude), 14–16
Entremés de los romances (Anonymous), 42
Entremés famoso de los invencibles hechos de Don Quijote de la Mancha (F. de Avila), 152

Entretenida, La (The Entertaining Story), 15
Entry of Don Quixote de la Mancha into France, The (Anonymous), 154
epistolary novel, 80, 156
Erasmian thought, 60, 105
Erasmus, Desiderius, 61, 73, 89, 105
erotic and obscene language and imagery, 134, 139–40
Esclavo llamado Cervantes, Un (F. Arrabal), 3
Escorial (San Lorenzo de El Escorial), 55
escudos, 200 gold, 37
Esgueva River, 10
Eslava Galán, Juan, 166
Españas, Las, 52
Española inglesa, La (The English Spanish Girl), 12
Espejo de príncpes y caballeros (D. de Ordóñez de Calahorra), 79, 201
Espiñeira, Antonio, 172
Espinel, Vicente, 159
Esplá, Oscar, 175
Esquival-Heinemann, Bárbara, 176
Esquivias, 7–8, 42, 92–93, 137
Estebanillo González (Anonymous), 84
Eternal Quest, The (J. Branston), 164
Ethiopian History (Heliodorus), 80, 117, 169
Eugenio's tale, 29, 118. *See also* Leandra
European Renaissance, 70, 75, 80
Examen de ingenios para las ciencias (J. Huarte de San Juan), 90
Exemplary Novels. See *Novelas ejemplares*
Ezpeleta, Don Gaspar de, 10

fabla, 127–29, 134
Falla, Manuel de, 175
False Clélie, The (A.-T.-P. de Subligny), 154
Farnesio, Alejandro, Duke of Parma, 57
Farquhar, George, 155
Faulkner, William, 97, 165, 169
Faust, 181
Favart, Charles-Simon, 158
Felipe, León, 171
Felipe II, 4–5, 9–10, 53, 55–57, 74, 102
Felipe III, 53, 102, 142
Felipe IV, 53, 75
Félix, Ana (Ricota), 37–38
female assistant hermit, 33, 104
female characters in *Don Quixote*. *See* women characters in *Don Quixote*
Female Quixote, The (C. Lennox), 156
Female Quixotism (T. Tenney), 162
Fernández, Jaime, 186–87

Fernández, Jerónimo, 79, 88
Fernández de Avellaneda, Alonso. *See* Avellaneda, Alonso Fernández de
Fernández de la Torre, José Luis, 5
Fernández de Lizardi, José Joaquín, 164
Fernández Shaw, Carlos, 175
Fernández Suárez, Alvaro (Juan de Lara), 172
Fernando, Don, 26–28, 62, 119
Fernando of Aragon, 52, 60, 63
Fernán Gómez, Fernando, 178
Ferrán, Jaime, 171
Ferrandis, Antonio, 178
Ferrara, Duke of (*La señora Cornelia*), 13
Ferrer, Eulalio, 180
Ferretis, Jorge, 166
Ficino, Marsilio, 73
fictive personality, 97
Fielding, Henry, 155, 160, 168
Fierabrás, balm of, 23–24, 104
Filleau de Saint-Martin, François, 154, 158–59
Finch, Patricia S., 180
Finello, Dominick, 88, 202
first innkeeper, 22, 143
Fitzgerald, F. Scott, 165, 168
Flanders, 53
Flaubert, Gustave, 95, 132–33, 163, 168
Fletcher, John, 153
flocks (armies) of sheep, 24, 95, 122, 141
Flores, Angel, 188
Flores, R. M., 44
folklore in *Don Quixote*, 90, 120–21, 145
Fool of Quality, The (H. Brooke), 156
Forcione, Alban K., 17, 92, 199
Fortunas de amor, Las (A. de Lofrasso), 139
Fortunate Ruffian, The. See Rufián dichoso, El
Fortuny, Mariano, 180
Fourcroy, Bonaventure, 154
Fowles, John, 164, 168
Fragonard, Jean-Honoré, 180
Franca de Rojas, Ana (Ana de Villafranca), 7, 10
France, 36, 54, 57, 59–60, 70, 76, 80
Franciosini, Lorenzo, 153
Francis I, King of France, 55
Franco, Jesús, 178
freedom, theme of, 37, 91–92; religious, 36
French colonies, 54, 71
French Lieutenant's Woman, The (J. Fowles), 164, 168
Frestón, 23, 137. *See also* enchanters, enchantment
Frías, Heriberto, 166
Friedman, Edward H., 14, 191

friend of the prologue, 94, 107–8, 122
Fuchs, Barbara, 140, 204
Fuentes, Carlos, 166
Fuerza de la sangre, La (*The Power of Blood*), 12
fulling mill, 25, 171
Furetière, Antoine, 154
Gaiferos, Don, 33, 91
Galatea, La, 7, 80, 88, 98, 116
Galiardo, Juan Luis, 177
Gallardo español, El (*The Valiant Spaniard*), 14
galley slaves, 25, 141
Gandara, Antonio de la, 180
Gaos, Vicente, 46
Garbancito de la Mancha (film), 177
Garcés, María Antonia, 5
García Cuevas, Francisco, 175
García Márquez, Gabriel, 47, 166, 169
Garciasol, Ramón de, 171
Garcilaso de la Vega, 74, 76, 80, 89, 98–99
Gascón, Elvira, 180
Gaskell, Elizabeth, 161
Gatell, Pedro, 160
Gautier, Théophile, 163
Gavaldón, Roberto, 176
Generous Lover, The. See Amante liberal, El
genesis of *Don Quixote*, 41–42
Genus, Karl, 178
Gerli, E. Michael, 203
Germany, 36, 59
Gerrig, Richard J., 108, 133
Gide, Andre, 166
Gil, Fray Juan, 5
Gil, Rafael, 176
Gil Blas (A. R. Lesage), 158
Gilliam, Terry, 178
Gilman, Stephen, 202
Giménez Prieto, Diego, 175
Giraldi Cinzio, Giambattista, 73, 79, 91
Gitanilla, La (*The Little Gypsy Girl*), 1, 11, 106
Glass Graduate, The. See Licenciado Vidriera, El
goatherd in Sierra Morena, 25–26, 119
goatherds, 23, 99, 101
Goethe, Johann Wolfgang von, 159–60, 168, 185
Gogol, Nikolai, 164
Golden Age, myth of the, 23, 98–99. *See also* Don Quixote: Golden Age speech of
Golden Age, Spanish, 72–85
Golden Ass, The (Apuleius), 169
Góngora, Luis de, 77, 89, 98, 105
González, Julio, 180
González Echevarría, Roberto, 189

Goths (Visigoths), 59
Goya, Francisco de, 157, 180
Goytisolo, Juan, 166
Graffigny, Françoise d'Issembourg
 d'Happoncourt, Madame de, 158
Granada, 52–53, 55
Granada, Fray Luis de, 61, 74, 76–77
Gran capitán. See Hernández de Córdoba,
 Gonzalo
grandee (*grande*), 62–63
Grand Inquisitor. *See* Inquisitor General
Gran Sultana doña Catalina de Oviedo, La
 (*Wife of the Great Sultan, Doña Catalina de
 Oviedo, The*), 15
Grau, Jacinto, 172
Graves, Richard, 156, 167
Great Gatsby, The (F. S. Fitzgerald), 165, 168
great time, 181
Greco, El, 74
Greece, 55, 56, 169
Greek literature, history, mythology, and culture
 of, 74, 87–88
Green, Otis H., 90
Greene, Graham, 164, 168, 176
Gregorian calendar, 17
Gregorio, Don Gaspar, 38
Gregory, Isabella, 172
Griffith, D. W., 176
Grimmelshausen, Johann Jakob Chrisstoffel
 von, 84
Grisóstomo, 23, 63, 88, 119–20
Grossman, Edith, 47, 126, 128–29
Guadiana River, 32
Gual, Adrià, 172
Guarda cuidadosa, La (*The Vigilant Guard*),
 15, 99
Guarini, Giambattista, 73
Guérin de Bouscal, Guyon, 154
Guillén, Claudio, 89
Guillén, Jorge, 171
Guilmartin, John Francis, 56
Guinart, Roque, 37–38, 101, 104, 132, 147–48
Guinness, Alec, 177
Gutiérrez, Mari, 93
Gutiérrez Aragón, Manuel, 177
Guzmán de Alfarache (M. Alemán), 45, 83, 85,
 88, 106, 112, 114, 118

Haldudo the Rich, Juan, 66
Halevi-Wise, Yael, 120
Haley, George, 188, 197–98
Halffter, Rodolfo, 175

Hamilton, Charles, 153
Hamlet (W. Shakespeare), 179
Hamlet, 181
Hapsburg Spain, 52–53
hard critics. *See* hard vs. soft readings of *Don
 Quixote*
hard vs. soft readings of *Don Quixote*, 143,
 187–88, 193–96, 199
Harrison, Rex, 176
Hart, Thomas R, 14, 90
Hartzenbusch, Juan Eugenio, 41
Hassan Pasha, king of Algiers, 4–5
Hatzfeld, Helmut, 199
Hayes, Francis, 78
H-Cervantes, 191
Hebreo, León, 73
Helen of Troy, 181
Heliodorus, 80–81, 88, 117, 169
helmet of Mambrino. *See* Mambrino
Henderson the Rain King (S. Bellow), 97
hermit (absent), 33, 104
Hernández de Córdoba, Gonzalo, 55
Heroic Adventures of Donny Coyote, The
 (K. Mitchell), 166–67
Herrera, Fernando de, 74, 89, 105
Herrera, Juan de, 55
Herrero, Javier, 147
Herreros, Enrique, 180
Herzog (S. Bellow), 165, 168
Hesiod, 98
Hess, Andrew, 56
Hesse, Hermann, 166
heteroglossia, 129, 134, 169
hidalgo, 22, 63–64
Hiller, Arthur, 176
Hinckley, John W., Jr., 97–98
History of Cardenio, The (W. Shakespeare and
 J. Fletcher?), 153–54
*History of Don Quixote of La Mancha.
 Written by Cide Hamete Benengeli, an Arab
 Historian*, 110
History of Sancho Panza, Mayor of Blandanda
 (Anonymous), 159
*History of the Admirable Don Quixote de La
 Mancha* (F. Filleau de Saint-Martin), 154
*History of the Adventures of Joseph Andrews,
 The* (H. Fielding), 155, 168
*History of the Extravagant Imaginations of
 Monsieur Oufle, The* (L. Bordelon), 158
History of Tom Jones, a Foundling, The (H.
 Fielding), 156
Hogarth, William, 157, 180

Holliday, Billie, 181
Holmes, Sherlock, 181
Holy Brotherhood, 24, 28
Holy League, 55–56
Holy Roman and Universal Inquisition (Holy
    Office). *See* Inquisition
Holy Roman Empire, 53
Homer, 88, 95, 107
homoeroticism, 140
honor, 62, 67–70
Hopper, Edward, 180
Horace, 106
housekeeper, 22, 30, 62, 132, 137
House of Jealousy and Forest of Ardennes, The.
    See *Casa de los celos y selva de Ardenia, La*
house priest, 34, 65
Howard, Lord Charles, Earl of Nottingham,
    10–11, 57
Howells, William Dean, 161
Huarte de San Juan, Juan, 74, 89
Hugo, Victor, 163
humanism, 70, 73. *See also* Cervantes, Miguel
    de: as a humanist; Spanish humanism
humanist cousin, 32
humorous names in *Don Quixote*, 134, 136–39
Humphry Clinker (T. Smollett), 157
Hutchinson, Steven, 202
hybrid genre, 82
hybridization, 129
Hypochondriac Knight, The (G. S. du Verdier),
    154

I, Don Quixote (K. Genus), 178
Iberian Peninsula, 51, 53, 56, 58
Ibert, Jacques, 175
Idiot, The (F. Dostoevsky), 163, 168
Iffland, James, 203
Iglesias, Carlos, 177
Ihrie, Maureen, 201
illustrations of *Don Quixote*, 141, 130, 141, 157,
    179–80
Illustrious Kitchen-Maid, The. See *Ilustre
    fregona, La*
Ilustre fregona, La (*The Illustrious Kitchen-
    Maid*), 13, 83
imitation of models (*imitatio*), 98, 105, 107, 197
Inca empire, 54
Index of Forbidden Books, 61
Indies (*Las Indias*), 54
Inferno (Dante), 141
influence in literature, 87. *See also* Cervantes:
    literary influences on

inn of Juan Palomeque, 24, 26–28, 65–66,
    99, 117, 140, 155. *See also* inn scenes
inn scenes, 22, 33, 37, 39, 66–67, 92, 141.
    See also inn of Juan Palomeque
inns in Spain, 66
Inquisition (Holy Roman and Universal
    Inquisition, Holy Office), 60–62, 64,
    70–71, 103–5. *See also* Portuguese
    Inquisition
Inquisitor General (Grand Inquisitor), 60
Instituto Cervantes, 191
ínsula (island), 23, 36, 146. *See also* Barataria
interlude (*entremés*), 14–16
introductions to Cervantes and *Don Quixote*,
    186–88
Irving, Washington, 162
Isabel (*La española inglesa*), 12
Isabel of Castile, 52, 63
-*ísimo* ending, 135–36
Isla, José Francisco de, 160
island (*ínsula*), 23, 36, 146. *See also* Barataria
Italian literature, 89–90
Italian Renaissance, 72, 79
Italy, 3, 36, 53, 60, 70, 73–74, 80, 155

Jacques the Fatalist and His Master (D.
    Diderot), 158
James, Henry, 162
Jarvis, Charles, 46
Jealous Old Man, The. See *Viejo celoso, El*
Jealous Old Man from Extremadura, The. See
    Celoso extremeño, El
Jean Paul, 164
Jerónima, Claudia, 38, 122
Jerónimo, Don, 142
Jesus Christ, 58, 97–98, 110, 181
Jewish quarter (*judería*), 58–59
Jews, 53, 58–60, 70–71, 103
Jiménez-Fajardo, Salvador, 46
Johannot, Tony, 180
Johnson, Carroll B., 187–89, 201
Jones, Joseph R., 47, 146
Jordan, Michael, 181
Juan, Don (*La señora Cornelia*), 13
Juan, Don, 142
Juan de la Cruz, San, 76–77
Juan Manuel, Don, 117
Juan of Austria, Don, 4, 56
Judas, 181
judería (Jewish quarter), 58–59
Juez de los divorcios, El (*The Divorce Court
    Judge*), 15

Julián, Count, 51
Julian calendar, 17

Kafka, Franz, 166
Karloff, Boris, 178
Kazantzakis, Nikos, 172
Keller, John Easten, 16
Kelly, Grace, 178
Kent, Clark (Superman), 138
King Kong, 181
Knight of the Forest (Mirrors) (Sansón
    Carrasco), 31, 131, 140
Knight of the Lake, 29, 122
Knight of the Lions. *See* Don Quixote: as
    Knight of the Lions
Knight of the Long Face (Don Quixote), The
    (J. Le Lorrain), 174
Knight of the Mirrors (Forest) (Sansón
    Carrasco), 31, 131, 140
Knight of the Sad Face. *See* Don Quixote: as
    Knight of the Sad Face
Knight of the White Moon (Sansón Carrasco),
    38
Knights Templar, 63
Kozinski, Jerzy, 97
Kozintsev, Grigori, 176
Krohn, Leena, 172

Laberinto de amor, El (*The Labyrinth of Love*), 15
labrador. See peasants
Labyrinth of Love, The. See *Laberinto de amor, El*
Laclos, Pierre Choderlos de, 158
Lady Cornelia. See *Señora Cornelia, La*
La Mancha, 92–93, 138, 178, 182
Lancelot of the Lake (Lanzarote), 91, 137–38
Landa, Alfredo, 177
Landero, Luis, 166
Lanzarote (Lancelot of the Lake), 91, 137–38
Lara, Juan de. *See* Fernández Suárez, Alvaro
Larra y Wetoret, Luis Mariano de, 175
La Rubia Prado, Francisco, 189
Las Casas, Fray Bartolomé de, 71, 74
Lathrop, Tom, 46
Laura, 75
Lauritzen, Lau, 176
Lazarillo castigado, 83
Lazarillo de Tormes, 61, 64, 82–83, 85, 88, 95
Leandra, 29, 88, 91, 118. *See also* Eugenio's
    tale
Leigh, Mitch, 176
Le Lorrain, Jacques, 174
Lemos, Count of, 30

Lenaghan, Patrick, 180
Lennox, Charlotte, 156, 167
Leocadia (*La fuerza de la sangre*), 12
Leocadia (*Las dos doncellas*), 13
León, Fray Luis de, 74, 76
Leonisa (*El amante liberal*), 12
Leonora (*El celoso extremeño*), 12, 70
Lepanto, battle of, 3, 55, 57
Lerma, Duke of, 53
Lesage, Alain-René, 158–59
Leskov, Nikolai, 164
levels of style in *Don Quixote*, 125–29,
    133–40, 199
Levin, Harry, 99, 162, 166–67
Lewis, Sinclair, 165, 168
Lewis, Wyndham, 164, 168
library, Don Quixote's (book-burning scene),
    22, 42, 62, 65, 92, 94, 104, 108, 116, 141
Licenciado Vidriera, El (*Glass Graduate, The*),
    12, 74
Life and Opinions of Tristram Shandy, The
    (L. Sterne), 156, 168
Life in Algiers. See *Tratos de Argel, Los*
*Life of the Great Don Quixote de La Mancha
    and of the Fat Sancho Panza* (A. J. da Silva),
    174
limpieza de sangre (purity of blood), 2,
    59–60, 62
Lindström, Sigfrid, 171
lion, 32, 113, 141
Lisbon, 5, 57
literary theory, classical and Italian, 105, 107.
    See also Cervantes, Miguel de: literary
    theory of
literature and life, theme of, 96–98
literature as the novel, 169–70
Lithgow, John, 177
Little Gypsy Girl, The. See *Gitanilla, La*
Lobsenz, Herbert, 165
locus amoenus, 132
Lofrasso, Antonio de, 139
Lokos, Ellen D., 2–3, 14
Lolita (V. Nabokov), 165, 168
López Alonso, Antonio, 3
López de Hoyos, Juan, 2, 74, 105
López de Ubeda, Francisco, 112
López Navia, Santiago Alfonso, 176, 203
López Navío, José, 44
López Pinciano, Alonso de (El Pinciano), 74,
    90, 105
Lord Jim (J. Conrad), 164, 168
Lo Ré, Anthony G., 179

Lorenzo, Aldonza, 22, 26, 139, 146. *See also* Dulcinea del Toboso; Maritornes-Aldonza-Dulcinea fusion
Losing Battles (E. Welty), 165, 168
Lost in La Mancha (film), 178
Lotario (*El curioso impertinente*), 27, 67–70, 132
Loubayssin de Lamarca, Francisco, 152
Loyola, Ignacio de, 80
Lozana andaluza, La (F. Delicado), 112
Lucía Megías, José Manuel, 128, 204
Luengo, Segismundo, 166
Luis, Don, 28, 63, 144
Luis (*La fuerza de la sangre*), 12
Lumet, Sidney, 178
Luna, Juan de, 83
Luscinda, 26–27, 119, 132
Luxembourg, 53

Mabbe, James, 83
Machado, Antonio, 171
Machado, Manuel, 171
Machado de Assis, Joaquim Maria, 164
Machiavelli, Niccolò, 73
Mackey, Mary, 126
Madame Bovary (G. Flaubert), 95, 163, 168
Madariaga, Salvador de, 193
Madness of Orlando (L. Ariosto), 90
Madonna, 181
Madrazo, Santos, 66
Madrid, 2, 5–6, 11, 66, 182
Magic Cave of Salamanca, The. See *Cueva de Salamanca, La*
Main Street (S. Lewis), 165, 168
majordomo, duke's, 37, 132, 135
Malambruno, 34–35
Mal Lara, Juan de, 73
Malory, Sir Thomas, 117
Mambrino (helmet of Mambrino, barber's basin), 25, 90, 95, 137, 141, 179, 181, 195. *See also* basin-helmet
Mancha alta, La, 93
Mancing, Howard, 14, 81, 83–84, 106, 114, 116, 120, 128, 133, 141, 144, 147, 160, 172, 179, 189–90, 201
Mandel, Oscar, 194
Mann, Thomas, 84, 166
Man of La Mancha (A. Hiller), 176
Man of La Mancha (D. Wasserman), 173, 176, 178, 196
Man who Killed Don Quixote, The (T. Gilliam), 178

Man who Pretended to be from Biscay, The. See *Vizcaíno fingido, El*
Manzoni, Alessandro, 164
Maravall, José Antonio, 201
Marcela, 23–24, 88, 92, 95, 119–20, 126, 132, 147
Marchelie, Eric, 175
Marcos de Obregón (V. Espinel), 159
Marín Pina, Mari Carmen, 202
Maritornes, 24, 28, 131, 134, 147
Maritornes-Aldonza-Dulcinea fusion, 152
Marivaux, Pierre Carlet de Chamblain de, 158
Marlowe, Stephen, 42
Márquez Villanueva, Francisco, 139, 200
marranos. *See* New Christians
Mars, 181
Martín, Adrienne Laskier, 9
Martin, Jay, 97–98
Martinez, Manuel, 165, 167
Martínez-Bonati, Félix, 133, 202
Martín Gaite, Carmen, 166
Martín Morán, José Manuel, 44
Mártir, Pedro, 73
Marvelous Puppet Show, The. See *Retablo de las maravillas, El*
Marxist criticism (materialist-oriented studies), 201–2, 204
Mary Magdalene, 181
Massenet, Jules, 174
Masson de Morvilliers, Nicholas, 71–72
Mateo-Sagasta, Alfonso, 166
materialist-oriented studies (Marxist criticism), 201–2, 204
Maupassant, Guy de, 163
Mayáns y Síscar, Gregorio, 157
McCrory, Donald P., 1
McGaha, Michael D., 188
McGrady, Donald, 115
McKendrick, Melveena, 1, 14, 78
Mediterranean Sea, 4, 55–56
Meli, Giovanni, 171
Melisendra, 33, 91
Melville, Herman, 133, 148, 162, 168
Meninas, Las (D. de Velázquez), 75
Menotti del Picchia, Paulo, 172
merchants, Don Quixote's encounter with, 22
Mercury, 88
Merlin, 34, 91
Mesa, Enrique de, 171
metafiction, 75, 109–17, 164, 203–4
Mexía, Pero, 73
Mexico (New Spain), 7–8, 14

Mickey Mouse, 181
Micomicón, kingdom of, 27
Micomicona, Princess. *See* Dorotea
Middle East, 54, 56
Middlemarch (G. Eliot), 161, 168
Middleton, John, 153
Mier Rivas, Adolfo, 174
Miguel Will (J. C. Somoza), 173
military/religious orders. *See* Order of
  Alcántara; Order of Calatrava; Order of Malta
  (Saint John); Order of Santiago
Mill on the Floss, The (G. Eliot), 95, 161
mimesis, 105, 107
Mingote, Antonio, 180
Minkus, Ludwig, 175
Miranda, Don Diego de, 31, 93, 101, 106, 113,
  131, 147
Misericordia (B. Pérez Galdós), 163
Mitchell, Ken, 166–67
Mito (A. Buero Vallejo), 172–73
MLA Bibliography, 185
Moby Dick (H. Melville), 162, 168
Modern Chivalry (H. H. Brackenridge), 162
Modern Language Association of America, 185
Molho, Maurice, 139
Molière, 78
Moll Flanders (D. Defoe), 84, 156
Monipodio (*Rinconete y Cortadillo*), 12
Monroe, Marilyn, 181
Monroy, Juan Antonio, 88
Monsignor Quixote (G. Greene), 164, 168, 176–77
Monsignor Quixote (R. Bennett), 176–77
Montalvo, Garci Rodríguez de, 79, 80, 85,
  112, 127
Montemayor, Jorge de, 7, 80, 85, 98
Montero Reguera, José, 8, 198
Montesinos, Cave of, 32–33, 35, 74, 91, 113,
  122, 131, 141, 200
Montesinos López, Eduardo, 175
Montesquieu, Charles de Secondat,
  Baron de, 158
Montherlant, Henri de, 166
Moor's Last Sigh, The (S. Rushdie), 164, 168
Mora, Juan Miguel de, 166
Moraes, Francisco de, 79
Moreno, Don Antonio, 38, 62–63, 101, 132, 142
Morgante the Great (L. Pulci), 91
moriscos, 36, 60, 102, 139
morisco translator, 106, 110, 113
Morrison, G. E., 172
Morte Darthur, Le (T. Malory), 117
Moses, 181

Mota del Cuervo, 142
Motteux, Peter, 46
Müeller, Johann Gottwerth, 160
muleteer in inn of Juan Palomeque, 24, 111
muleteers (mule drivers), 22, 66
Muñatones de la Sierra, 137
Muñiz-Huberman, Angelina, 166
Muñoz Degrain, Antonio, 180
Murillo, Bartolomé Esteban, 74
Murillo, Luis Andrés, 46, 187, 200
Musäus, Johann Karl August, 160
Museo Iconográfico del *Quijote*, 180, 192
Muslim Spain, 51–53, 58, 71, 89
myth of the Golden Age, 23, 98–99. *See also*
  Don Quixote: Golden Age speech of

Nabokov, Nicolas, 175
Nabokov, Vladimir, 165, 168
Nadeau, Carolyn A., 204
Naples, 4, 90
Napoleon, 97, 164
narrative technique, 195, 200, 204
native Americans, 54, 56, 71
Navaggiero, Andrea, 73
Navarro, Alberto, 199
Nebrija, Antonio de, 73
Nelson, Lowry, Jr., 188
neologisms in *Don Quixote*, 134–36
Netherlands, 8, 52–53, 70
Neuschäfer, Hans-Jörg, 203
New Adventures of the Admirable Don Quixote
  (A.-R. Lesage), 158
*New and Truthful Sequel to the History and
  Adventures of the Incomparable Don Quixote
  de la Mancha* (Anonymous), 159
New Christians (*conversos, cristianos nuevos,
  marranos*), 2–3, 59–60, 73, 192
New Spain (Mexico), 7–8, 14
New World, 53–54, 57, 71, 79–80, 102, 203.
  See also Spanish colonies in America
Nicolás, Maese (barber), 22, 26, 29–30, 92,
  116, 122, 132, 140, 143, 147
niece, Don Quixote's (Quijana, Antonia), 22,
  30, 132, 137
Noah, 181
nobility, 62–67
Northanger Abbey (J. Austen), 161, 168
novel, as genre, 129, 134, 160–61, 169. *See
  also* dialogued fictions; *Don Quixote*: as
  novel; emergence of the novel; epistolary
  novel; literature as the novel; novelization;
  picaresque novel; poetics of the novel;

polyphonic novel; quixotic novel; romance novel; romance versus novel
novela (short fiction), 81
Novelas ejemplares (*Exemplary Novels*), 12–14, 81, 85, 91, 153, 155
novelization, 169
Numancia, La, 6–7

Oates, Joyce Carol, 165, 168
Ocho comedias y ocho entremeses, nunca representados (*Eight Plays and Eight Interludes, Never Performed*), 14
O'Connor, John H., 79
Odysseus, 99, 181
Odyssey (Homer), 95
Old Christians (*cristianos viejos*), 59
Oliver Asín, Jaime, 197
Orán, 5, 14
Order of Alcántara, 63
Order of Calatrava, 63
Order of Malta (Order of Saint John), 63
Order of Merced, 4
Order of Saint Francis, 104. *See also* Poor Claires
Order of Saint John (Order of Malta), 63
Order of Santiago, 63
Ordóñez de Calahorra, Diego de, 79
Oriel, Charles, 7
Orlando (V. Woolf), 164, 168
Orlando, 26, 90
Ormsby, John, 46–47, 192
Orozco Rivera, Mario, 180
Ortega y Gasset, José, 167, 193
Ortúñez de Calahorra, Diego, 201
Otero, Blas de, 171
Oudin, César, 153, 159
Ovando, Constanza de (niece of Cervantes), 1, 10, 62
Overmyer, Eric, 173
Ovid, 88, 98
Pabst, Georg Wilhelm, 175–76
palace of the duke and duchess, 34, 63, 89, 113–14, 121
Palacios, Catalina de (wife of Cervantes), 7, 10, 17, 92, 104, 137
Palacio Valdés, Armando, 163
Palmart, Lambert, 84
Palmerín cycle, 79
Palmerín de Inglaterra (F. de Moraes), 79
Palomeque, Juan, 24, 101
Pamela (S. Richardson), 85, 157
Pancino, 39

Panza, Sancho, 23–40, 43, 90, 101, 127–28, 132, 134, 136, 141, 144–46, 152, 179, 181; in Avellaneda's *Quixote*, 16; blanketing of, 24, 141; description of, 130–31; name of, 138–39; as reality instructor, 23, 145. *See also* ass, Sancho's; Sancho's story; Zancas, Sancho
Panza, Teresa, 30, 36, 39, 132
Pardo Bazán, Emilia, 163
Parker, Alexander A., 127
parody, literary, 81, 94, 169
Parr, James A., 46, 115–16, 202
Pasamonte, Ginés de, 25–26, 30, 44, 83, 88–89, 127, 131, 147. *See also* Pedro, Maese
Paso, Alfonso, 172
pastoral romance, 7, 80, 88, 94, 108, 117
pastoral themes, 202–3
Pastor de Iberia, El (B. de la Vega), 43
Patton, George S., 97
Paul, Saint (Saul of Tarsis), 138
Paulson, Ronald, 157
Pavia, battle of, 55
Paz Gago, José María, 115, 202
Peace of the Pyrenees, 57
peasants, peasantry (*labrador, villano, vulgo*), 63, 65–66, 92
peasant woman Sancho identifies as Dulcinea, 127, 131, 147
Pedro (goatherd), 119, 127
Pedro, Maese (puppet show), 33, 106, 108, 131, 141, 197. *See also* Pasamonte, Ginés de
Pedro de Urdemalas, 15
Pedroza, Raul, 172
Pelayo, King Don, 52
Pellicer, Juan, 45, 158
pen, Cide Hamete's, 40, 114
penance, Don Quixote's, 107, 140, 199
Percas de Ponseti, Helena, 200
Peregrine Pickle (T. Smollett), 157
Peregrino en su patria, El (L. de Vega), 81
Pérez, Pero (the priest), 22, 26, 29–30, 65, 89, 92–93, 104, 108, 116, 122, 128, 132, 140, 143, 147
Pérez de Guzmán, Alonso, Duke of Medina Sidonia, 57
Pérez de Oliva, Fernán, 74
Pérez de Viedma, Juan, 28, 99
Pérez de Viedma, Ruy (captain, captive), 27–28, 116, 118, 127, 131, 144. *See also* captive's tale
Pérez Galdós, Benito, 117, 126, 133, 162–63, 168–69
Peribáñez (Lope de Vega), 66
Perlerina, Clara, 35, 132

perspectivism, 193, 195–97
Petipa, Marius, 175
Petrarca, Francesco (Petrarch), 73, 75–76, 91
Pharsamon (P. Marivaux), 158
Philidor, 158
Philosophia antigua poética (A. López
 Pinciano), 105
Philosophical Quixote (Anonymous), 156
Pícara Justina, La (F. López de Ubeda), 112
picaresque novel, 83–83, 88, 108, 156, 158–59
pícaro, 9, 65–66, 83–84
Picasso, Pablo, 130, 180
Pichou, Le Sieur, 154
Picón, Jacinto Octavio, 163
Pierce, Frank, 79
pigs, that trample Don Quixote, 135
Pilon, Frederick, 155
Pizarro, Francisco, 54
Platonism, 73
plot of *Don Quixote*, 21–40; part 1, 21–29,
 143–44; part 2, 30–40, 144
poetics of the novel, 169
poetry, theme of, 106
Pollock, Jackson, 180
polyphonic novel, 130
polyphony, 129–30, 169
Ponç, Joan, 180
Poor Claires (*Clarisas*), 104
Portugal, 5, 56
Portuguese colonies, 71
Portuguese Inquisition, 104, 174
Posada, José Guadalupe, 180
Posthumous Papers of the Pickwick Club, The
 (C. Dickens), 161, 168
postmodernism, 188–89, 196
Power of Blood, The. See *Fuerza de la sangre, La*
Preciosa (*La gitanilla*), 1, 11
Predmore, Richard, 198–99
preliminaries, 21–22, 30
Presberg, Charles D., 204
Presley, Elvis, 181
Prévost, Antoin-François, Abbé, 158
priest. *See* Pérez, Pero
Prieto, Gregorio, 180
Primaleón (F. Enciso Zárate), 79, 138
Princess Micomicona. See Dorotea
printing in Spain, 84–85
Project Dulcinea, 182
prologues to *Don Quixote*: part 1, 22, 107–8;
 part 2, 30
Protestantism, Protestants, 8, 54, 56–57, 60,
 70, 72

Proust, Marcel, 166
proverbs, 127, 145
psychoanalytic criticism, 187, 200–202, 204
Pulci, Luigi, 91
puppet show. *See* Pedro, Maese
Purcell, Henry, 154
purity of blood (*limpieza de sangre*), 2,
 59–60, 62
Pushkin, Aleksandr, 164, 171
Putnam, Samuel, 46

queer theory, 140
Queneau, Raymond de, 166
Quevedo, Francisco de, 43, 77, 84, 152
Quijada, family surname in Esquivias, 93
Quijada, Gutierre, 138
Quijada de Salazar, Gabriel, 93
Quijana, Antonia (Don Quixote's niece), 22, 30,
 132, 137
Quijano, Alonso, 65, 138, 144
quijote, piece of leg armor, 138, 157
Quijote de la Cancha, El (A. Mier Rivas),
 173–74
Quijote de Miguel de Cervantes, El (M.
 Gutiérrez Aragón), 177, 179
Quijotiz, 39
Quint, David, 204
Quintañona, 91
Quiteria, 32, 101, 131–32
quixotic, meaning of, 143
quixotic adventure, structure of, 141
quixotic novel, 166–69, 201
quixotic principle, 166–67
quixotic syndrome, 97
quixotization, 145, 193

Racine, Jean, 78
Raffel, Burton, 47
Rakoff, Alvin, 176
Ravel, Maurice, 175
ráwi, Arabic storytellers, 41–42, 90
reader-response theory, 108, 187
reading, 108–9, 132–33, 170, 179
Real Academia Española (Royal Spanish
 Academy), 45, 46, 157–58
realism in literature, 107, 132–33, 148
reality and appearance, theme of, 70, 95–98, 167
reception history of *Don Quixote*, 142–43,
 151–83, 188, 199
Recio de Agüero, Pedro, 35
Reconquest, 52, 63
Red and the Black, The (Stendhal), 97

Redon, Odilon, 180
Redondo, Augustin, 203
Reed, Cory, 15
Reinaldos, 90
religious tolerance and intolerance, 58–61, 70–71
Renaissance, 70, 72. *See also* European
　Renaissance; Italian Renaissance; Spanish
　Renaissance
Reparaz, Antonio de, 175
*Retablo de las maravillas, El (The Marvelous
　Puppet Show)*, 15–16
Retablo de Maese Pedro, El (A. Fernández
　Suárez), 172
Retablo de Maese Pedro, El (M. de Falla), 175
Return of Don Quixote, The (G. K. Chesterton),
　164, 167
Rey, Fernando, 177
Reyes Católicos. See Catholic Monarchs
Rey Hazas, Antonio, 46
Ribera, José de, 74
Ricapito, Joseph V., 14
Ricardo (*El amante liberal*), 12
Ricaredo (*La española inglesa*), 12
Richardson, Samuel, 80, 85, 156–58, 162
Rico, Francisco, 46, 186
Ricota (Félix, Ana), 37–38
Ricote, 36–38, 93, 102–3, 127
Riewald, J. G., 94
Riley, Edward C., 82, 107–8, 130, 187–88, 197–98
Rinconete y Cortadillo, 12, 117
Ríos, Vicente de los, 45, 157
Riquer, Martín de, 186–87, 204
Rivers, Elias L., 89
Robinson, Elisabeth, 165–66
Robinson Crusoe (D. Defoe), 156
Robles, Blas de, 45
Robles, Francisco de, 45, 147
Rochefort, Jean, 178
Rocinante (L. Felipe), 171
Rocinante, 22, 24–25, 28, 31, 113, 138, 144,
　147, 152, 156, 179, 181
Rocinante cheese, 181
Rockne, Knute, 181
Rocroi, battle of, 55, 57
Roderick Random (T. Smollett), 157
Rodolfo (*La fuerza de la sangre*), 12
Rodrigo, Joaquín, 175
Rodrigo, King, 51
Rodríguez, Antonio, 180
Rodríguez, Doña, 35–37, 92, 100–101, 113, 147
Rodríguez, Juan Carlos, 204
Rodríguez-Luis, Julio, 125

Rodríguez Marín, Francisco, 46
Rodríguez Moñino, Antonio R., 43
Rodríguez Puértolas, Julio, 192
Rodríguez Vicéns, Antonio, 189
Rojas, Carlos, 166
Rojas, Fernando de, 61, 82, 85, 129
Roland, 91
romance. See ballad
romance, as a genre, 81. *See also* pastoral
　romance; romance novel; romance of
　adventure; romance of chivalry; romance
　versus novel; sentimental romance
romance novel, 154, 156
romance of adventure (Byzantine romance), 80
romance of chivalry, 22, 29, 42, 45, 79–80, 88,
　94–95, 108–10, 117, 127, 137, 146, 201–4
romance versus novel, 14, 81–82, 84, 148, 158,
　169
Roman literature, history, mythology, and
　culture, 74, 87–88
romantic readings of *Don Quixote*, 143, 193–95
Romantic writers and philosophers, 159–60
Rome, 3, 17, 56, 64, 169
Rosenblat, Angel, 199
Rosset, François, 153, 159
Rousseau, Jean-Jacques, 158
Roux, G., 180
Rowe, Nicholas, 155
Royal Spanish Academy (Real Academia
　Española), 45, 46, 157–58
Rubenstein, Anton, 175
Rufián dichoso, El (The Fortunate Ruffian), 14
*Rufián viudo llamado Trampagos, El (The
　Widowed Pimp Named Trampagos)*, 15
Ruidera, Lagoons of, 32
Rushdie, Salman, 164, 168–69
Russell, P. E., 187, 194
Ruth, Babe, 181
Rutherford, John, 47

Saavedra (*Los tratos de Argel*), 5–6
Saavedra, Isabel de (daughter of Cervantes),
　7, 10
Saavedra, Juan de, 6
Saavedra as surname, 6, 116
Sacripante, 90
Sade, Marquis de, 158
Salamanca, University of, 30, 73, 139
Salas Barbadillo, Alonso Jerónimo de, 152
Salgó, Andrés, 180
Salvador, Luis, 174
Sánchez Saus, Rafael, 6

sanchification, 193
Sancho Panza Cigars, 181
Sancho's story, 25, 120–21
San Lorenzo de El Escorial, 55
Sannazaro, Jacopo, 73, 80
San Pedro, Diego de, 80, 85, 112
San Quintín, battle of, 55
Santos, Alfonso dos. *See* Selvagem, Carlos
Sarbin, Theodore, 97
Sartre, Jean-Paul, 97, 166
Sastre, Alfonso, 173
Saul of Tarsis (Paul, Saint), 138
Saura, Antonio, 180
Saussurean linguistics, 109
Scarron, Paul, 154
Schallück, Paul, 166
Scheherazade, 117
Schevill, Rudolfo, 45, 192
Schiller, Friedrich, 159
Schlegel, August Wilhelm von, 159
Schlegel, Friedrich von, 159
Schmidt, Rachel, 7, 180
Schroeder Inclán, Federico, 173
Scorza, Manuel, 166
Scott, Sir Walter, 161, 168
Sears, Theresa Ann, 14
Sebastião, King of Portugal, 56
Second Maiden's Tragedy, The
    (W. Shakespeare and J. Fletcher?),
    153–54
Segrelles, José, 180
Segunda parte de la vida de Lazarillo
    de Tormes (J. de Luna), 83
Segunda parte del ingenioso hidalgo Don
    Quijote de la Mancha (A. F. de Avellaneda),
    16, 30, 37, 43, 89, 114, 158, 203
Self-Condemned (W. Lewis), 164, 168
Selvagem, Carlos (Alfonso dos Santos), 172
semidoncellas, 134
Señora Cornelia, La (*Lady Cornelia*), 13
sentimental romance, 80
Sergas de Esplandián, Las (G. R. de Montalvo),
    80, 112
Serjan, Mario, 171
Serra, Narciso, 172
Serrano Plaja, Arturo, 201
Sert, José María, 180
Server, Alberta Wilson, 16
Sessa, Duke of, 4
Sevilla Arroyo, Florencio, 46
Seville, 9, 12, 14, 41–42, 54, 58, 66–67
Shahryar, King, 117

Shakespeare, William, 1, 11, 17, 78, 125–26,
    153–54, 159, 170, 173, 176, 178–79, 185
Shelley, Mary, 161
Shelton, Thomas, 11, 46, 153
Shipley, George, 120
Sierra Morena, 25, 44
Siete Partidas, Las (Alfonso X), 67
Sigura, Antonio de, 2–3
Silva, António José da, 174
Simplicissimus (J.J.C. von Grimmelshausen), 84
Smirke, Robert, 180
Smith, Dawn L., 16
Smollett, Tobias, 46, 156–57
social criticism in *Don Quixote*, 100–103
soft critics. *See* hard vs. soft readings of *Don*
    Quixote
Sol (galley), 4
Soledades, Las (L. de Góngora), 98
Sologub, Fyodor, 166, 171
Solón Romero, Walter, 180
Solzhenitsyn, Alexandr, 166
Somoza, José Carlos, 173
sonnet about the raid on Cádiz, 9
sonnet about the tomb of Felipe II, 9
sonnet form, 75
Sorel, Charles, 154
Sorrows of Young Werther, The (J. W. von
    Goethe), 160
Sound and the Fury, The (W. Faulkner), 165
Spain, 51–70, 155, 160, 162, 166, 171. *See*
    also Golden Age, Spanish; Hapsburg Spain;
    inns in Spain; Muslim Spain; New Spain;
    printing in Spain; Spanish army; Spanish as
    the language of Cervantes; Spanish colonies
    in America; Spanish empire; Spanish
    humanism; Spanish Renaissance; Spanish
    theater
Spanish America, 71, 166, 171
Spanish army, 3, 55
Spanish as the language of Cervantes, 125
Spanish colonies in America, 7, 11, 54, 56, 71.
    See also New World
Spanish empire, 53–58, 70
Spanish Golden Age, 72–85
Spanish humanism, 70, 72–74. *See also*
    humanism
Spanish Renaissance, 70–75
Spanish theater, 5, 29, 77–78, 94
Spark, Muriel, 164, 168
Spencer, William, 4
Spiritual Quixote, The (R. Graves), 156
Spitzer, Leo, 195, 197

squire of lady in coach (Basque squire), 23, 110, 127
Stagg, Geoffrey L., 42, 44
Starkie, Walter, 46
Steele, Richard, 155
Stendhal, 97, 163
Sterne, Laurence, 148, 155–56, 160, 168
Stoopen, María, 115, 202
Strauss, Leo, 61
Strauss, Richard, 175
Subligny, Adrien-Thomas-Perdou de, 154
Sullivan, Henry, 203
Sultan of the Ottoman Empire, 15
Superman (Clark Kent), 138
Supreme Council of the Inquisition, 60
Syverson-Stork, Jill, 89

talking head (bronze head), 38, 62
tapestry, as seen from the reverse side, 38, 129, 134, 136
Tarfe, Alvaro, 39, 114, 132
Tarzan, 181
Tasso, Torquato, 73, 107
Tave, Stuart, 143
Téllez, Gabriel. See Tirso de Molina
Tenney, Tabitha, 162, 167
Tenorio, Don Juan, 69, 78, 181
Teodosia (Las dos doncellas), 13
Teresa de Avila (Teresa de Jesús), Santa, 77, 80, 97
ter Horst, Robert, 204
textual problems in Don Quixote, 44
Thackeray, William Makepeace, 161
theatrical episodes in Don Quixote, 89
them (J. C. Oates), 165, 168
Theobald, Lewis, 155
theoretical approaches, 193–94
theoreticism, 115
Thousand and One Nights, 117
Tidewater Tales (J. Barth), 165, 168
Tieck, Ludwig, 159–60
tilting at windmills, 141, 143
Timonel de Carcajona, 137
Tirso de Molina (Gabriel Téllez), 78, 105
titled nobles (títulos), 62
Toboso, El, 30, 105, 139
Toledo, 23, 58, 92
Tolstoy, Leo, 164
Tomás (La ilustre fregona), 13
Toole, John Kennedy, 165
Torquemada, Tomás de, 60
Torrente Ballester, Gonzalo, 166, 200–201

Tosilos, 36–39, 88, 100
Trabajos de Persiles y Sigismunda, Los (The Trials of Persiles and Sigismunda), 9, 16–17, 81, 85, 103–4
Trampagos (El rufián viudo), 15
transformation of reality, 22, 27, 88, 139, 141, 144
translations of Don Quixote, 133–36, 153
translator (morisco translator), 106, 110, 113
Trapiello, Andrés, 166
Tratos de Argel, Los (Life in Algiers), 6, 14, 103
Tres epitafios (R. Halffter), 175
Trials of Persiles and Sigismunda, The. See Trabajos de Persiles y Sigismunda, Los
Trifaldi, Countess, 34–35, 113, 122, 132, 135
Trilling, Lionel, 95–96, 167
Trinitarian Convent, 17
Trinitarians, 4
tropelía, 106
troupe of actors, 31, 144–45
True and Outstanding Adventures of the Hunt Sisters, The (E. Robinson), 165–66
true history device, 111–12, 155
Turgenev, Ivan, 164
Turkish army and navy, 3, 56
Turkish empire, 54
Twain, Mark (Samuel L. Clemens), 84, 138, 162, 168–69
Two Damsels, The. See Dos doncellas, Las
two stylistic lines, 81
Tyler, Royall, 172

Ulysses, 107
Unamuno, Miguel de, 166, 169, 171, 193, 195
Una tal Dulcinea (A. Paso), 172
Urbina, Eduardo, 186
Urdemalas, Pedro de, 15
Urrabieta Vierge, Daniel, 180
ut pictura poesis, 106

Valdés, Alfonso de, 61, 73
Valdés, Juan de, 61, 73
Valencia, 5, 84
Valiant Spaniard, The. See Gallardo español, El
Valla, Lorenzo, 73
Valladolid, 2, 9–11, 13, 42, 93
Valois, Isabel de, Queen of Spain, 2
Vanderbank, John, 45, 157, 180
Van Doren, Mark, 200–201
Vangel Griffin (H. Lobsenz), 165
Vázquez, Mateo, 5
Vega, Bernardo de la, 43

Vega, Lope de, 7, 66, 77–78, 81, 89, 102, 105
Velasco, Don Bernadino de, 102
Velázquez, Diego de, 74–75
Venus, 88, 181
Verdier, Gilbert Saulnier du, 154
verisimilitude, 105, 107
Viaje del Parnaso, El (*Voyage to Parnassus*), 9, 14, 77–78, 88, 106
Viaje infinito de Sancho Panza, El (A. Sastre), 173
Vicente, Gil, 138
Vicente de la Rosa, 29
Vida del Buscón (F. de Quevedo), 43, 84
Vida es sueño, La (P. Calderón de la Barca), 78
Vidal, César, 189
Viejo celoso, El (*The Jealous Old Man*), 16
Vigilant Guard, The. See *Guarda cuidadosa, La*
Vilanova, Antonio, 2
Villafranca, Ana de (Franca de Rojas, Ana), 7, 10
villano. See peasants
Virgil, 88, 98, 107
Virgin Mary, 57, 64; figure of, 29
Visigoths (Goths), 59
visual media, 169–70, 179
Vivaldo, 23, 101
Vives, Luis, 73
Vizcaíno fingido, El (*The Man who Pretended to be from Biscay*), 15
Voltaire, 158
Voyage to Parnassus. See Viaje del Parnaso, El
vulgo. See peasant

Wardropper, Bruce W., 111, 197
Wasserman, Dale, 173, 175, 178, 201
Waverley (W. Scott), 161, 168
Wayne, John, 181
wedding of Camacho, 32, 122, 131. *See also* Camacho the Rich
Weiger, John G., 65, 142, 201
Welles, Orson, 177–78
Welsh, Alexander, 201
Welty, Eudora, 165, 168
Wezel, Johann Karl, 160

Whinnom, Keith, 80
Widowed Pimp Named Trampagos, The. See *Rufián viudo llamado Trampagos, El*
Wieland, Christoph Martin, 159–60, 168
wife of Juan Palomeque, 24, 140
Wife of the Great Sultan, Doña Catalina de Oviedo, The. See *Gran Sultana doña Catalina de Oviedo, La*
Wikipedia, 192
Wilhelm Meister's Apprenticeship (J. W. von Goethe), 160, 168
Williams, Robin, 166
Williamsen, Amy R., 17
Williamson, Edwin, 91, 201
Wilson, Diana de Armas, 17, 47, 200, 203
windmills, 23, 95, 141–43, 179, 181. *See also* tilting at windmills
witchcraft, 60–61
Wizard of Oz, 181
women characters in *Don Quixote*, 92, 204. *See also* characters in *Don Quixote*
women, concept of honor of, 68–69
Wonderful Travels of Prince Fan-Férédin, The (G. H. Bourgeant), 158
Woolf, Virginia, 164, 168
Wordsworth, William, 171

Yáñez, Agustín, 166
Yates, Peter, 177

Zancas, Sancho, 110, 139
Zaragoza, 30, 37, 111, 114
zarzuelas, 175
Zeus, 181
Ziolkowski, Eric J., 202
Zola, Emile, 163
Zoraida, 27–28, 131–32, 197. *See also* captive's tale
Zuleika Dobson (M. Beerbohm), 164
Zulema, 154
Zuloaga, Ignacio, 180
Zurbarán, Francisco, 74

About the Author

HOWARD MANCING is Professor of Spanish at Purdue University. His previous books include *The Cervantes Encyclopedia* (Greenwood, 2003).